THE TEACHER'S SURVIVAL GUIDE

REAL CLASSROOM DILEMMAS AND PRACTICAL SOLUTIONS

Marc R. Major

Rowman & Littlefield Education
Lanham, Maryland • Toronto • Plymouth, UK
2008

Published in the United States of America
by Rowman & Littlefield Education
A Division of Rowman & Littlefield Publishers, Inc.
A wholly owned subsidiary of
The Rowman & Littlefield Publishing Group, Inc.
4501 Forbes Boulevard, Suite 200, Lanham, Maryland 20706
www.rowmaneducation.com

Estover Road
Plymouth PL6 7PY
United Kingdom

British Library Cataloguing in Publication Information Available

Library of Congress Cataloging-in-Publication Data

Major, Marc R.
  The teacher's survival guide : real classroom dilemmas and practical
solutions / Marc R. Major.
    p. cm.
  Includes bibliographical references.
  ISBN-13: 978-1-57886-815-5 (hardcover : alk. paper)
  ISBN-13: 978-1-57886-816-2 (pbk. : alk. paper)
  ISBN-10: 1-57886-815-7 (hardcover : alk. paper)
  ISBN-10: 1-57886-816-5 (pbk. : alk. paper)
  ISBN-13: 978-1-57886-888-9 (electronic)
  ISBN-10: 1-57886-888-2 (electronic)
  1. Teaching—Handbooks, manuals, etc. I. Title.
  LB1025.3.M3364 2008
  371.1—dc22   2008007503

⊗™ The paper used in this publication meets the minimum requirements of
American National Standard for Information Sciences—Permanence of Paper
for Printed Library Materials, ANSI/NISO Z39.48-1992.
Manufactured in the United States of America.

CONTENTS

AUTHOR'S NOTE

This book was originally intended to be a collaboration between me and my father, Robert L. Major, a longtime professor of education at Minnesota State University. Various factors conspired against that ambition, however. The first impediment was of my own making: the longer-than-anticipated organic development process of writing and editing the book. The second was a more profound and intractable challenge: my father's 3-year struggle with cancer. He lost this battle in November 2007, and he will be greatly missed by his family, his friends, his colleagues, and his many students.

Despite this, my father did make several noteworthy contributions to this book. First, he offered early research support, to help find both the right supporting content and a good publisher. Second, one of his previous works, *Discipline: The Most Important Subject We Teach*, is the source of a few of the teaching dilemmas (though not the suggested solutions) included in this work. Third, his wisdom and support were never far from my ear as I wrote.

Because of this original coauthorship intent, and because my father's inspiration pervaded so much of this book's creation, throughout the text I have preserved the use of the plural first person pronoun (we) instead of substituting the singular (I). Though he did not commit the words in this book to paper, much of my father's spirit is present here; therefore, this felt like the right choice.

INTRODUCTION

Whether you're a new teacher wondering what you're getting yourself into or a veteran seeking to improve your craft, this guidebook is designed to lighten your load. Our hope is that the ideas, case studies, and forms herein will save you many hours of work and frustration, and free up your time and energy to devote to your real purpose: teaching students.

Note, however, that a *guidebook* is not a *rulebook*; we do not purport to present a perfect system that guarantees flawless teaching. Given the varied and often unpredictable nature of young people, teaching is a less straightforward endeavor than, say, accounting or water skiing. Demonstrated psychological principles and pedagogical strategies certainly apply, but education is as much an art as a science. As esteemed educator Madeline Hunter points out: "There are no 'rules' in teaching. There are [only] principles which, when applied . . . at the right time to the right student, . . . can dramatically increase the probability [of success]" (Hunter, 1990, p. 10).

To help you excel, this volume embodies decades of accumulated wisdom on teaching, with an emphasis on classroom management. To augment our own experience, we have gathered ideas from hundreds of written works and websites and combined these with the collective insight of countless teachers—both new and experienced—whom we have known and observed. We hope the resulting distillation proves both useful and inspiring.

Note: In many places throughout this book, we invite you to visit our website (www.classroomadvisor.com) for additional resources that, for one reason or another, couldn't be included here. The website also allows you to e-mail your questions, classroom management ideas, and suggestions for future editions of this book.

1

CULTIVATING A CLASSROOM CULTURE

Every group has a culture: beliefs, values, and customs that guide the thinking and behavior of its members. Each school and classroom also has its own culture: a psychological atmosphere that nurtures and shapes students' attitudes about their own identity, classes, school, and learning in general.

Your classroom culture will help shape students' collective personality and spirit. It will sustain particular habits of thinking and working, and undermine others. It will, in fact, color everything in its presence. Think of your classroom culture as the river current that channels the group's behavior in a specific direction. What this direction will be is up to you.

At best, your classroom culture can promote

- a sense of belonging
- mutual respect, healthy conflict
- a common purpose
- inspiration to inquire and achieve

At worst, it can promote

- alienation
- disrespect, fighting

- aimlessness, chaos
- indifference, laziness

What makes the difference? Your conscious effort. A classroom culture will emerge whether you plan it or not—and if you don't proactively shape it, your students will. Take the time to cultivate an engaging and motivating classroom culture in the first few weeks, when the effort counts. Otherwise you will not only squander an immense opportunity but may also find yourself swimming all year against a tide born of your own neglect.

DEFINING YOUR VISION

How can you promote a positive culture in your classroom? First, define your vision of maximum success. If through hard work and a few miracles you meet all your goals by the end of the term, what will that look like? What will have changed about the way students understand and inhabit the world after spending a year with you? Write a short paragraph describing your vision for this ideal end state. Here are a few prompts we find useful for this exercise:

- At the end of this year, students will have changed for the better in the following ways . . .
- At the end of this year, I will have changed for the better in the following ways . . .
- I will know this is true because I will see . . . I will hear . . . I will feel . . .
- Students will know this is true because they will be able to . . . They will feel . . .
- Other stakeholders (parents, administrators, etc.) will take note and respond by . . .

If you get stuck, consider what drew you to teaching in the first place. Was it the opportunity to share your joy of learning? The pleasure of helping people reach challenging goals? The charming and life-affirming nature of children (including, sometimes, even teenagers)? Whatever your reason, your pedagogical vision should reflect it.

Once you have defined your vision, consider how it will translate into a *mission statement*. Many successful organizations attest to the beneficial effects of mission statements to

- clarify purpose
- keep efforts focused over time
- provide guidance for times of uncertainty ("When things get murky, remember the mission!")
- give stakeholders (employees, customers, partners, shareholders, community members, etc.) a common ideal

"Why bother with all this?" you may be asking yourself. "I've never been in a classroom with a mission statement." This may be true. Many ordinary classrooms do not use mission statements, but do you want to be remembered as an ordinary teacher or an extraordinary one?

To create a mission statement, consider your expectations for the class. We believe every classroom culture should encourage three fundamentals: respect, trust, and achievement. In addition, consider what long-term attitudes and skills you want students to develop. Avoid making a list that's too long to remember—choose a handful of key goals. These might include cooperation, curiosity, creativity, critical thinking, perseverance, mutual respect, empathy, emotional awareness, and/or independent thought.

Next, articulate your expectations in a single sentence that expresses the essence of your vision. Make it positive, clear, and concise. A mission statement that's too long, too complex, or uninspiring will soon be forgotten or ignored.

Here's a mission statement we will use as a sample throughout this chapter:

> *We will work together to lift up, draw out, and support what's best in each other so we can all grow every day and succeed to the best of our ability.*

Note how this statement succinctly emphasizes collaboration, inquisitiveness, and individual achievement, while clearly laying out both the mission's rationale and its value.

Here are a few excerpts from some real-world mission statements:

> *To bring inspiration and innovation to every athlete in the world. (If you have a body, you are an athlete.)*
>
> —Nike

> *Protecting the environmental rights of all people, including the right to clean air, clean water, healthy food and flourishing ecosystems. Guided by science, we work to create practical solutions that win lasting economic and social support because they are nonpartisan, cost-effective and fair.*
>
> —Environmental Defense Fund

> *To advocate for education professionals and to unite our members and the nation to fulfill the promise of public education to prepare every student to succeed in a diverse and interdependent world.*
>
> —National Education Association

> *To advocate for the protection of children's rights, to help meet their basic needs and to expand their opportunities to reach their full potential.*
>
> —UNICEF

Of course, a motivating mission statement means little without actions that support it. Whatever your mission, be sure to live it, because nothing will undermine your authority like hypocrisy. Model the attitudes and behaviors you want students to emulate, and don't expect them to do things you wouldn't do yourself. If you follow your own rules without fail, your students will soon absorb them and start behaving to meet your expectations.

To help students along, post your mission statement in a prominent place—ideally, alongside your classroom rules (see Table 1.1). Hammer these home regularly until they become habits.

CREATING CLASS RULES

As we will discuss in chapter 5, "Classroom Management I," classroom rules are critical for establishing boundaries and providing security and stability for your students. We offer four recommendations for rule making:

1. Less is more: Make no more rules than you are willing to enforce consistently.
2. Make your rules clear and visible.
3. Phrase the rules in positive terms.
4. Don't leave out the "why": Always explain your rationale.

Table 1.1.   Example of Mission Statement and Classroom Rules

Our Mission

We will work together to lift up, draw out, and support what's best in each other so we can all grow every day and succeed to the best of our ability.

Class Rules

To succeed in our mission, we agree to . . .

- Respect everyone. Treat others as you would like to be treated, because the only way to earn respect is by showing respect.
- Be prepared. Be ready to work from bell to bell, because our most precious resource is time.
- Persevere. Keep trying even if you don't succeed right away, because effort creates ability.
- Ask questions. If you don't understand, don't be afraid to ask, because nobody knows everything. Thoughtful questions help smart people (including you) get smarter and help human knowledge advance.
- Maintain order. Follow the teacher's instructions immediately, and ask questions at an appropriate time later, because disorder wastes everyone's valuable time.

First, *make no more rules than you are willing to enforce*—not sometimes, not usually, but *always*. The fewer rules you have, the easier they will be to remember and enforce. We have watched first-year teachers issue elaborate lists of class regulations, only to throw them out within a few weeks. Why? Students kept forgetting them, and the teachers themselves found most of them too trivial to merit continuous monitoring and enforcement.

Second, *make your rules clear and visible*. Use simple language and avoid verbosity. Be sure to publicize both the class mission and the class rules, because students need to remember them (and so do you). If necessary, post them on every wall. Stick them on every desk. Put them around your clock. Tape them on your shoes. Mention them every day. Do this until you and the students are sick of hearing them, until you all internalize them. This should take no more than a week, or maybe two.

Third, *phrase the rules in positive terms*. Point out behaviors to pursue rather than those to avoid. Negativity conveys an expectation of misbehavior, which is unhelpful because students tend to rise or sink to expectations, whether stated or implied. Although you should always anticipate the possibility of problem behavior, knowing that misbehavior *could* arise is distinctly different from signaling to students that you expect it. "I know you're going to mess up" is not a particularly motivating message.

Instead, make a show of expecting, highlighting, and acknowledging positive behavior, as we will discuss further in chapter 5, "Classroom Management I." This appreciative approach creates an entirely different emotional dynamic; it builds an aspirational climate that encourages students to race to the top of the class by actively demonstrating desirable behavior, rather than cooperating just enough to avoid negative sanctions.

Fourth, *be sure to explain the rationale behind your rules*. No one likes to be told what to do without having a good reason; this is particularly true of teenagers. Notice that all the sample rules listed in Table 1.1 have the "because" built in.

TEACHING DILEMMA: SHOULD STUDENTS HAVE A SAY IN CREATING CLASSROOM RULES?

I've heard of teachers who start the school year negotiating class rules with their students. I understand they consult their classes about what rules they think would be best for everyone to follow. Would this be a good idea for me to try?

Pro

In theory, student participation in making classroom rules provides two substantial benefits. First, it encourages students to contemplate essential questions of self-government like "Where do my rights end and my neighbor's rights begin?" and "What level of self-regulation and sacrifice is required for learning to advance?" Because schools are microcosms in which students can safely practice the habits required to survive on their own and to perpetuate civilization, the opportunity to engage in this type of adult thinking is valuable.

Second, student participation in rule making encourages compliance; students who have a say in the rules are more likely to buy into, understand, and respect them. Rules that students help create will cease to become "your rules" and instead become "our rules."

This can also trigger a welcome supporting dynamic: Rules dictated by fiat would demand continuous monitoring by you, but rules drafted by social compact tend to get enforced spontaneously by the group that created them. Students will invoke the inimitable power of peer pressure to keep each other in line. And, as we stress elsewhere, substituting students' energy for yours is almost always a good idea, because it creates a windfall of your only truly irreplaceable resource—time.

Con

Many veteran teachers argue that unless the students are very mature and serious about school, student participation in rule making is a time-wasting charade. Students, this logic goes, aren't paid to create classroom rules—teachers are. It is not only the prerogative but also the duty of the teacher to establish sufficient order for every student to learn.

Besides, this argument continues, what if students make a rule that says class attendance, or homework, or class participation, is voluntary—would you really allow such a rule? If not, then students aren't really making the rules, are they? Won't this hypocrisy backfire and make students more cynical rather than cooperative?

SUGGESTED SOLUTION

No matter what kind of students you teach, we *do not* recommend that new teachers invite students to collaborate in making classroom rules. Managing group rule making demands considerable sophistication and finesse, and one misstep can undermine a new teacher's all-important image of confidence and authority.

If you are an established teacher, however, by all means make your own informed decision. With proper framing of the process, students who participate in making the rules can feel respected and empowered, take the task quite seriously, and will almost always come up with the same rules their teachers would anyway. They know from their own experience what behaviors reinforce an effective learning environment, and what behaviors undermine it.

If you opt to give students input into your class rules, here's our recommended procedure to minimize trouble:

1. *Frame the discussion properly.* Make it clear that this is an opportunity for students to take charge of their educations and practice adult responsibility. Present your classroom mis-

sion, and keep this physically in view so it will remain in the forefront of students' minds in the ensuing discussion.

2. *Set clear ground rules for rule making in advance.* For example, any rules made in class should be subordinate to existing laws and school rules. We also advise retaining explicit veto power over any potential rules that you, in your professional judgment, deem ridiculous or untenable.

3. *Open the floor to brainstorming of possible rules.* Write down every suggestion; the winnowing process will follow.

4. *Condense and combine overlapping ideas* to create a short list of potential rules.

5. *Lead a preliminary collective evaluation of the proposed rules,* examining them one by one and measuring them against your stated mission. If students happen to propose ideas that would undercut the class mission or such fundamental human rights as physical safety or human dignity, an explicit discussion may be in order.

Some students may take this opportunity to voice racist, sexist, homophobic, or simply insensitive sentiments, but no matter how outrageous or offensive some of their suggestions may be, interpret them as a reminder of the eternal teen impulse for mischief and as a valuable teachable moment as well as a useful window into your students' mentalities.

6. *Collect ideas from all your classes,* take them home, and synthesize a short list of rules that will apply to all your classes. This is your opportunity to kill by pocket veto any rude, dangerous, or otherwise unreasonable proposal.

7. *Present to the class your streamlined synthesis* of their proposed rules, alongside your mission statement, and be sure to devote plenty of time to answering any student questions or objections.

8. *Close the subject.* Forever after, any time a student objects to one of the class rules as unfair, you can refer to the inclusive process and the agreement achieved in the very beginning.

BUILDING A CULTURE OF MUTUAL RESPECT

Fatso. Fag. Retard. Loser. Freak. These epithets and others like them echo regularly through schools across the country. Although incidents of overt racism and sexism may be less common than they once were, abuse of those perceived as *different* is still very much in vogue in the 21st century. We have seen students who wouldn't dream of using racist or sexist epithets freely harass peers who do not fit their narrowly defined conception of normalcy, particularly classmates perceived to be overweight, unattractive, learning disabled, emotionally disabled, underprivileged, and/or LGBTQ (lesbian, gay, bisexual, transgender, or questioning their sexuality).

Too many school officials, including teachers, sit idly by as young people launch venomous assaults on those perceived to be different. The National Association of School Psychologists (n.d.) reports that, according to its research, teachers intervene in only a tiny portion of bullying or put-down incidents; consequently, a high percentage of students believe that adult help in bullying situations is "infrequent and ineffective."

Wouldn't intervening earlier make education what it's supposed to be: user-friendly and accessible to everyone? Why are teachers so ineffectual in the face of widespread student-on-student harassment? We have identified three key reasons:

1. Teacher apathy
2. Difficulty of detection
3. Inherent challenge of doing the right thing all the time

Teacher Apathy

"Name-calling is a problem?" you might be wondering. "Isn't teasing just a part of growing up?" After all, in some youth cultures competitive insult-tossing has been a venerable institution for generations. "Besides," we often hear, "don't teachers have enough to do without regulating petty and harmless behavior that we all went through when we were growing up?" Kids will be kids, right?

We urge teachers who think this way to think a little deeper. Of course there are degrees of teasing, not all teasing constitutes harassment, and words are colored heavily by the context, tone, and spirit of their delivery. Sometimes students are, as they claim, just playing.

But just how well do you know these students and their complex relationships? Maybe that off-color comment Josh made to Martina was just a standard bit of their ongoing friendly repartee, but don't presume. Given your necessarily limited insight into student relationships, we urge you to err on the side of caution. If in doubt, apply the techniques recommended later in this chapter to intervene as necessary to protect potential victims until you are certain that one participant is not being hurt by the exchange.

The bottom line is that respect, as we define it, means no putdowns, period. Teachers who allow developing adolescent egos to be subject to continual mockery and taunting are not unlike mothers who smoke and drink during pregnancy. Some lucky children emerge from the experience ostensibly unscathed; others suffer damage that may not manifest itself for years.

Less abstractly, consider that *assault* is legally defined as the creating in the mind of another person the reasonable expectation of physical harm (the phrase *assault and battery* describes both the threat and the enactment of violence). Can someone commit assault merely by waving a gun, knife, or even a fist in another's face? Absolutely. Can verbal harassment by itself constitute assault? Although it is difficult to prove in court, this happens in schools every day. And frequently, particularly among teens, name-calling escalates into physical posturing, which—even in the absence of physical contact—can form grounds for legal action.

Legal concerns aside, consider the ethical and reputational implications of the behavior you allow in your presence—both in and out of the classroom. Do you really want to be known as the teacher who looks the other way while students insult and perhaps even assault one another? For those who think we overstate the problems that student harassment can cause, we have two words: Columbine High.

THE DEEPER IMPACT OF TEASING

Despite their often quiet outward appearances, victims of peer harassment do not always fade softly into the background. On April 20, 1999, two students at Columbine High School in Colorado calmly shot and threw bombs at teachers and students, killing 13 people in 15 minutes, and then committed suicide.

Subsequent investigation of the Columbine shootings revealed that the killers had long been taunted and ridiculed by their peers. They had even produced a class video that portrayed them gunning down the school jocks who had helped to ostracize them for being different.

Even before Columbine, 16-year-old Luke Woodham was pelted with insults regularly at his school in Mississippi. His peers called him "four-eyed fat nerd." His mother told him he was fat, stupid, and lazy. "I am not insane," wrote Woodham in a letter shortly before shooting nine classmates at his school. "I am angry. . . . [P]eople like me are mistreated every day. I did this to show society. Push us and we will push back" (Descant and Gregor, 2001, p. 8).

Were these unusual cases? Probably. Most bullying fortunately does not erupt in random mayhem. Could it happen again? You decide. And while you're at it, keep in mind that a recent U.S. Secret Service study of school shootings and similar violence in the United States over two decades revealed that the perpetrators in about two thirds of the cases had been "victims of long-standing and severe bullying" (Parsons, 2001).

Although such violent responses to school harassment are anomalous, the pain and anger generated by "harmless teasing" are not. Tormented youth who don't harm others could well harm themselves. For example, statistics on teenage suicide regularly confirm that students who are or are perceived to be lesbian, gay, bisexual, or transgender are 2–3 times as likely to commit suicide as the average teenager (Gibson, 1994, p. 18).

As one Arizona newspaper notes, a handful of states "perhaps fearful of another Columbine carried out by bitterly alienated teens . . . have enacted laws requiring schools to implement anti-bullying policies." Whether such laws become necessary nationwide will depend on how conscientiously school officials, including teachers, address the issue in their spheres of influence ("Columbine High School timeline," n.d.).

Difficulty of Detection

The second major reason harassment so often goes unaddressed is that it's frequently not obvious. Perpetrators may be ignorant of many things, but they can be quite clever about avoiding detection. Most verbal and physical assaults occur outside the classroom, typically in places authority figures are unlikely to patrol regularly: locker rooms, isolated hallways, school buses, and the territory surrounding the school.

Additionally, the impact of harassment is often invisible to the casual observer. Many students brave taunting and harassment daily without flinching because their parents, their teachers, their peers, and their culture have all conveyed the message that to show emotion in the face of teasing is to show weakness. And a display of weakness risks inviting more of the same.

Yet, as one veteran teacher points out, enduring ongoing verbal abuse inflicts a heavy toll that no child should have to pay. "Students who get called names wear themselves out fighting the abuse all the time, and they end up either not going to class, or going to class and just zoning out. They don't participate because experience tells them that if they do they're going to be attacked. No one wants to have to defend against uninvited attacks all the time. I don't care what kind of mask they put on to save face—no one enjoys being treated that way" (C. Misa, personal communication).

Inherent Challenge of Doing the Right Thing All the Time

A third reason teachers sometimes fail to prevent harassment is that doing what's right is not always easy—particularly for new teachers who may not be much older than the students in their care.

As education professor Robert Major points out, "Student cliques can make or break a [new] teacher. The popular ones, the leaders, . . . can laugh at the misfit and make you laugh along, because if you don't they can bring out their deadly stares, their cold shoulders, their vicious rumors, and the game-playing that will quickly let you know who is really boss. It takes courage to stand up for those too weak to defend themselves; it takes courage to forego popularity to do the right and decent thing" (Major, 1990, p. 30).

Pushy, obnoxious students may seem powerful because of their visibility and in many cases their shamelessness. But never forget that these students are not the majority. The majority will almost always be on your side, seeking order, productivity, and fairness. And many of your most vulnerable students may have no one but you to watch out for them.

Beware also of a trap young teachers often fall into—that of underreacting to a problem for fear of "making a big deal out of nothing." This concern is not entirely unwarranted, for the possibility of looking mildly foolish is real. You might dramatically break up an "imminent fight," only to discover that the supposed combatants were in fact just playing. Or students might engineer minor crises—unknown noises, fire or smoke in a corner, false health emergencies, and so forth—designed to steal your composure. If you react strongly to these stimuli, you risk unwittingly becoming the butt of their joke.

Think for a moment and decide, however: Would you rather overreact and feel silly later because a problem turned out to be minor, or minimize a problem that turns out to be significant? The former may lead to momentary reddening of the face that students will quickly forget, particularly if you show a sense of humor about it. The latter could lead to serious trouble and could ultimately cost you and the school a great deal if harassment or physical injury is involved. You could lose your job, or the school district could be sued for negligence.

SEXUAL HARASSMENT

Sexual harassment, among other problems, is often overlooked because many teachers assume that the victim somehow invites and/or deserves the often crass comments and behavior inflicted on her or him. Sexual harassment in any work environment is generally defined as any behavior of a sexual nature that makes the recipient feel embarrassed, intimidated, or otherwise uncomfortable.

Sexual harassment can be verbal (including jokes, comments, or innuendos of a sexual nature) or physical (including violation of personal space, physical contact, or presentation of suggestive material). Either way, if the behavior is sufficiently pervasive or lasting (or sufficiently egregious, in the case of a single offense) as to create a "hostile environment," it could be punishable by law.

Because education in the United States is generally regulated by the states, we urge you to consult your employer and/or your local union to learn about laws in your area. Certain limited federal guidelines do exist, however—notably Title IX of the Education Amendments of 1972, which prohibits discrimination based on sex in federally funded education programs.

The U.S. Supreme Court held in a 1999 case that "school districts may be liable under Title IX if they act with deliberate indifference to instances of student-on-student sexual harassment." This protection extends to both female and male students, and at least two federal courts have heard sexual harassment claims brought against a member of the same sex (Human Rights Watch, 2001, p. 139).

THE COST OF HARASSMENT

When Derek Henkle was 12 years old, he knew he was "different." His story, although extreme, is not unique. The verbal and physical harassment his public school district allowed him to suffer eventually cost that district hundreds of thousands of dollars in damages. Some would argue that the experience cost Henkle a lot more.

Henkle reports deep feelings of alienation as a gay youth: "Your parents aren't like you . . . . Your friends aren't like you. Nothing is like you. So you're going through this big internal process of, 'Wow, I'm just so different from everything in my environment.' And then on top of that, if you're being harassed in school. . . ."

He describes middle school as "horrible. . . . I was terrified every moment that I had to be out of my house . . . around people that were my own age. You never knew what was going to happen . . . if someone was going to hit you, or punch you, or call you a fag. It got to be so common. . . . It was just beat into my head over and over."

In one incident in his middle school hallway, "This kid came up to me and just started hitting me in the face. . . . All I could think was, 'Why is this person doing this to me? I have not done anything to them.' . . . It's such a hard thing to mentally process—that someone would . . . have such a hate for you . . . . And then you're humiliated . . . beaten up in front of a hallway full of your peers, a lot of [whom] are cheering them on . . . . You just feel so small."

Later, in high school, Henkle says he wrote reports of his harassment as a daily ritual. Though it received dozens of written complaints from him, the school administration took no action, giving students de facto permission to harass Henkle at will. And then it got worse.

One day in the parking lot of his school, "a group of [boys] surrounded me. They said, 'Let's string up the fag and tie him to the back of our truck and drag him down the highway.' They took a lasso out and started throwing it around my neck. They got it around my neck three times, and I was able to get it off. All I can remember is being surrounded . . . and how I was scared . . . for my life . . . all I could do was just keep walking. And they were calling me a fag and throwing a rope around my neck, and genuinely wanted to . . . kill me."

Henkle eventually broke free and made it back into the school building, where a teacher admitted him into her classroom and locked the door. Then he called the school administration, which after an hour-and-45-minute delay decided to deal with the problem the following day, and sent him home on the bus with the same students who had attacked him ("Interview with Derek Henkle," n.d.).

The legal organization that subsequently took up Henkle's cause describes the final chapters of the saga: "Instead of dealing appropriately with his attackers and ensuring his safety, school authorities treated Henkle as if he were the problem and transferred him to an alternative school for troubled students. The principal there told Henkle to 'stop acting like a fag.' After a transfer to yet a third school, Henkle was beaten bloody by another student while two school security guards stood by. Unwilling to take measures to create a safe educational environment for Henkle, school officials had him take classes at a local community college to obtain a GED instead of a high school diploma." After more than two years of legal action, Henkle's former school district paid a $451,000 settlement for its egregious negligence and agreed to implement new policies to protect students from discrimination based on sexual orientation (*Henkle v. Gregory*, n.d.).

Unfortunately, Derek's story is not unique. In dozens of documented cases across the country, the nonprofit Human Rights Watch reports, "teachers and administrators turned their backs, refusing to take reports of harassment, refusing to condemn the harassment, and failing to hold accountable students who harass and abuse. Some school officials blame the [victims for] . . . provoking the attacks because they 'flaunt' their identity. Other school officials . . . [argue] that students who 'insist' on being gay must 'get used to it.' And finally, some school officials encourage or participate in the abuse by publicly taunting or condemning the students for not being 'normal'" (Human Rights Watch, 2001, p. 3).

How to Address Peer Harassment

Although much conventional wisdom presumes that respectful behavior is learned at home, in reality many children grow up with limited guidance in these matters and end up emulating dubious ethics modeled in the media and among their peers. If the need arises, we encourage you to address these issues head-on.

You might start with posting a list like the one shown in Table 1.2—adapted from the Josephson Institute's "Character Counts" project—to remind students of the kind of classroom environment you expect.

Ethical Behaviors to Promote in Students

To maintain a culture of mutual respect in the classroom, there is no substitute for vigilance, consistency, and courage. The best response when you overhear hurtful insults in your classroom or elsewhere is to speak up immediately. Your intervention can be as simple as a pointed reminder like "Personal attacks are not allowed here" or "That's not appropriate behavior." Students may respond that the conversation was not directed at you, but if you are within earshot then you—as the adult, role model, and paid keeper of order—have a clear responsibility to intervene.

As teachers are always on stage to some degree, the stance you take in any conflict will draw the attention of many, so your actions will im-

Table 1.2. Character

Trustworthiness	• Be honest. • Don't deceive, cheat, or steal. • Be reliable—do what you say you'll do. • Have the courage to do the right thing. • Build a good reputation. • Be loyal.
Respect	• Treat others as you would want to be treated. • Be tolerant of differences. • Use good manners, not bad language. • Be considerate of the feelings of others. • Don't threaten, hit, or hurt anyone. • Deal peacefully with anger, insults, and disagreements.
Responsibility	• Do what you are supposed to do. • Persevere and always do your best. • Be self-disciplined. • Think and consider the consequences before you act.
Fairness	• Play by the rules. • Take turns and share. • Be open-minded; listen to others. • Don't take advantage of others. • Don't blame others without considering your actions.
Caring	• Be kind. • Show you care. • Express gratitude • Forgive others. • Help people in need.
Citizenship	• Do your share to improve your school and community. • Cooperate. • Be a good neighbor. • Stay informed and vote. • Respect rules and authority. • Learn about and protect the environment.

Note: Adapted from "The Six Pillars of Character" (n.d.).

pact not only the target students but also any onlookers. Decisive and consistent intervention will send a clear message not only to the culprits, but also to potential future perpetrators of harassment and—perhaps most importantly—to those "innocent bystanders" who watch, impotent, as injustice unfolds in their midst.

This last group is key because, as educational psychologist Larry Brendtro observes, "a small percentage of students, perhaps less than 10 percent, are active bullies, and a similar number are perpetual victims. But when bullying is studied in greater detail, it becomes clear that the most powerful role in the drama is played by the audience. Some become the cheering section for bullies, while a silent majority of bystanders enable bullying by their silence" (Brendtro, 2001, p. 5).

One veteran teacher defines the broad scope of insults she works to prevent. "Everybody's treated equally in my classroom. There's no discrimination, there's no name-calling. There's no talking about a person's different abilities or intelligence levels in my classroom. None of that goes. And they know it's not okay, because I call them to task right away" (L. Thlick-Katchadourian, personal communication).

Teachers who don't intervene firmly and consistently, argues another teacher, offer students a de facto license to abuse each other without consequence. "If the teacher doesn't care, the kids are going to keep saying it. Teachers claim they don't see it or they just say, 'Don't do that anymore.' That's a slap on the wrist. What's needed is a definitive statement like, 'Hate language has no place in this classroom'" (C. Misa, personal communication).

Persistence is required. As another veteran says, "I make clear that name-calling is absolutely unacceptable in my classroom. If they try to laugh it off, I ask how they would feel to be insulted like that. If they tell me they weren't talking to me I tell them, 'It's just not acceptable. If I hear an insult, I take it personally even if it's not directed at me.' Sometimes I have to take them aside and have a little heart-to-heart talk about it. I'll quote Martin Luther King, who said 'Injustice anywhere is a threat to justice everywhere.' That usually gets them thinking" (A. Smithee, personal communication).

BUILDING A CULTURE OF TRUST

To create a culture of trust and mutual respect, David Maister and colleagues Charles Green and Robert Galford offer advice from the world of business that's also applicable in the classroom. Maister et al. (2000) identify a "trust equation" that governs many professional relationships. They assert that trustworthiness (T) is a function of four factors: credibility (C), reliability (R), intimacy (I), and self-orientation (S). We have adapted their concept here, substituting the term *emotional accessibility* (EA) for the authors' original *intimacy* (I) because of concerns that the latter term could be misconstrued in an educational context.

Specifically, they argue, the relationship among the four factors can be depicted as follows:

$$T = \frac{C + R + EA}{S}$$

In other words, the trust your students will have for you is determined by how credible, reliable, and emotionally accessible you appear to be. An increase in any of these factors will increase their trust and thereby improve your relationships and your effectiveness. The factor on the bottom of the equation can reduce both your students' trust of you and your effectiveness: how self-oriented (self-centered, self-aggrandizing, or simply self-interested) you appear to be.

Many people who gravitate to teaching can probably intuit this relationship, but we emphasize it here because many well-intentioned teachers excel in some elements of this "trust equation" but get tripped up by weak performance in the others. Let's break this down in an educational context.

Credibility is the belief in students' minds that you know what you're talking about, say what you mean, and mean what you say. Credible teachers are trusted because they're competent, confident, and truthful. If students believe that you're not authoritative (either in your knowledge of your subject matter or in your personal or professional actions) or that you stretch the truth or you renege on promises, they will not trust you because you will not be credible.

We have seen classrooms full of history students roll their eyes regularly while being regaled with historical tales, because their teacher had been caught fudging certain facts both to avoid appearing ignorant and to maintain the flow of his elaborate oral histories. The moral is, resist the urge to embellish. And never, ever lie. When students uncover the truth—as they eventually will—your reputation may never recover.

You don't have to know every detail of your subject matter. When confronted with a question that stumps you, a sincere "I don't know" followed by a "How would you suggest we find out the answer?" can be remarkably refreshing to students of any age. Even if a student asks an inappropriate question—by, for example, launching an inquiry into your private life—you don't have to lie. Just tell the student it's inappropriate, and move on.

Reliability is the belief in students' minds that you will follow through on commitments. Reliable people are trusted because they behave predictably and fulfill their promises. You may be bright, charismatic, and energetic, but if students believe you are too lazy or forgetful or disorganized to meet their needs in a consistent and timely way, they will not trust you because they will find you unreliable.

We have seen many creative, adventurous teachers underestimate the importance of reliability in maintaining a stable and productive class. If your desk, home, and car are always a mess, if you habitually have trouble deciding what to order for dinner, if you value "spontaneity above all" and hear frequent complaints that you fear commitment, we're talking to you.

We are not recommending flat and repetitive classroom activities; rather, we are pointing out the importance of predictable teacher behavior. Like most creatures, students find comfort in a stable, consistent environment. Occasional surprises can energize them; however, a continuous backdrop of unpredictability merely agitates them. Students should be able to predict easily how you will respond to various actions on their part; this helps them choose the right behaviors.

Of course, reliability also includes competence in the basic clerical duties of teaching. We knew a brilliant high school science teacher whose authority was undermined by this weakness. "She claims I didn't turn in that assignment last week," one top student complained to another. "But I see her walking down the hall with all our papers blowing up out of that box she carries. I'm sure she loses some of them. That's what happened to my assignment—I know it."

Emotional accessibility is the belief in students' minds that you are an open and approachable person who cares about their welfare—physical and psychological, as well as intellectual. We detail these student needs in chapter 2, "Who Are Your Students?" Teachers who can create rapport with others are trusted because they demonstrate compassion, sensitivity, and authenticity.

Of course, being a teacher imposes certain legal and ethical restrictions on your relationships; numerous career-wrecking hazards lurk in emotional proximity to students. At particular risk are the many young teachers who try to become (or act like) a friend to their students. We encourage all teachers to err on the side of caution in this area. Maintain appropriate professional distance and loosen up only after you have established your authority and drawn clear boundaries between yourself and your students. We discuss this further in chapter 5, "Classroom Management I."

On the other hand, if students believe that you're aloof and don't care whether they succeed or fail—in class or in life—they will not trust you. We once knew a language teacher who was so disconnected from his students that he didn't even know many of their names, let alone their skills, interests, passions, or fears. He had a difficult time motivating them in class, because it was clear that he didn't particularly care about his students as people, and they reciprocated the indifference.

This teacher ended up with only a handful of successful students—those who cared intrinsically about the subject—and a lot of failing students. Administrators and parents, struck by the large number of low grades, rightly wondered whether the students had failed to engage in the course, or whether the teacher had failed to engage his students.

Self-orientation is the belief in students' minds that you are focused more on your own satisfaction or aggrandizement than on their needs. Note that this factor is on the bottom of the trust equation, indicating that greater self-orientation *reduces* overall trust—and the inverse is also true. Teachers with low self-orientation tend to be trusted because they are perceived to be highly *service-oriented*—eager to promote their students' best interests at all times, without ulterior motives or hidden agendas. If students believe you care less about them and supporting their learning than you do about looking smart or being comfortable or telling stories about yourself or protecting yourself, they will not trust you.

We knew a mathematics teacher so domineering and uncompromising that students often fled her room, seeking refuge in other classes or the school office to avoid interacting with her. She frequently interrupted and argued with students, colleagues, and supervisors alike, and habitually interpreted legitimate questions from students as incompetence or insubordination.

"You don't know the answer to that?" she would loudly berate students who asked questions. "Everybody knows the answer to that. Don't bring that to me. I'm busy. Go back to your seat and work on it until I'm convinced you've really tried."

Curiously, this teacher took a handful of students under her wing. These lucky few loved her, for she was their tireless and productive champion. However, her extreme self-orientation alienated most of the rest of her school and undermined any support she might otherwise have built through credibility, reliability, and emotional accessibility.

BUILDING A CULTURE OF ACHIEVEMENT

Perhaps the greatest gift you as a teacher can give students, particularly underperforming students, is a positive attitude—a sense that things can go right for them and a belief in their own ability to succeed. Such confidence is rooted in self-esteem, which is typically built on some combination of reassurance and actual success.

Figure 1.1 depicts a virtuous cycle in which students persevere despite setbacks, thereby improving their skills and succeeding in (at

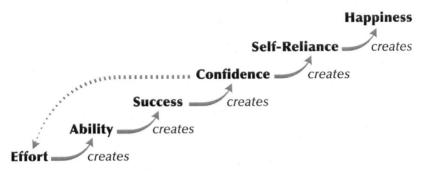

Figure 1.1. Pathway to achievement: A virtuous cycle of success.

least some of) their efforts. This in turn builds their self-confidence, making them not only happier but also willing to try hard at the next task. The more you can engage students in this cycle, the more successful, self-reliant, and ultimately happy your students and your classroom will be.

Note that we do not advocate a warm and fuzzy policy of applauding students for meaningless "achievements" like bringing work materials or meeting basic standards of civility. We do not recommend babying students; our paradigm highlights *effort* as the beginning of all progress.

How can you launch this virtuous cycle of success in your classroom?

1. Make the pathway explicit.
2. Believe your students can succeed.
3. Demystify good habits.
4. Convince students to exert effort.
5. If necessary, start in the middle of the cycle—with success.

First, *make this path to success explicit to students*. Post this diagram if it's helpful. This framework can help you address many student complaints in a compelling and consistent way. For example, if students complain they "can't do the work," refer them to this diagram. Here, it's clear that the source of ability is effort. If students don't succeed, perhaps the work is too difficult—or perhaps they haven't been trying hard enough. If they complain that they "don't like the class," you can point out that lack of engagement may be the cause, not merely the result, of this problem.

Second, *believe your students can succeed.* Some of them won't believe in themselves, but your job is to hold high expectations for them because, as mentioned earlier, students will live up (or down) to your expectations. If you believe it when you say, "You are smart. With work, you can get smarter," your students will believe it, too.

Third, *demystify the good habits of typical successful performers.* This can help all students understand that achievement—in class and in the outside world—does not depend wholly on intrinsic gifts, luck, magic, or some other unattainable factor, but rather is linked closely to hard work.

To facilitate this, try assigning students to collaborate—in work groups, peer tutoring relationships, etc.—so that instead of your *telling* students how to succeed, they *show* each other. Such lessons are typically better received both because they're delivered by peers and because they arise in context, making their utility immediately visible.

Fourth, *convince students to exert effort.* Feed them with your energy. Never stop pushing and giving them reasons to move forward.

As we will discuss further in chapter 4, a crucial element of this equation is regular feedback on students' performance. Assessment should not only tell them what they did wrong in the past, but also keep them abreast of how they're doing now and help them to improve in the future. You probably wouldn't want to wait until the end of each quarter to receive your paycheck; your students are no different. Keep students informed of their progress. Post grades regularly. Return work promptly and discuss how they can improve.

Also, post student work everywhere—not only the perfect papers, but also work representing the greatest effort or improvement—to emphasize the value of striving. Celebrate every success to give students incentive to continue and energy to face a new day. And always emphasize that mistakes do not equal failure; the only failure is not to try.

As we also will discuss in chapter 4, another key to motivating students is framing what you're teaching in a way that engages their existing knowledge, interests, and curiosity. Variety and work at the appropriate level of difficulty will also keep students moving in the right direction. Most of all, the more that students perceive the topic to be relevant, the more successful they'll be. As we will explore in chapter 2, "Who Are Your Students?" there are many valuable skills in life, many kinds of "smart," and many routes to success.

Fifth, for students who don't particularly care about the material but will engage only if they believe their effort will be rewarded, *start in the middle of the cycle—on success.* Help every student taste success by creating assignments that are neither so easy as to be patronizing nor so difficult as to be intimidating. Once students have succeeded at these simple tasks and built some confidence, ladder up to more challenging assignments. We discuss this further in the following Teaching Dilemma and in chapter 2. The ideal is to set *stretch goals* for every student—targets that require students to apply their existing skills and knowledge, plus reach a little bit farther.

TEACHING DILEMMA: STUDENTS CLAIM THEY CAN'T DO THE WORK

In every class I seem to have a couple of kids who tell me they can't do the work. No matter what the lesson is, at least one of them says, "I can't do it." I understand all students are "differently abled," but it's getting ridiculous. Usually most of the kids can do the work, so I don't want to dumb down my lessons for a few who say they can't.

SUGGESTED SOLUTION

Your first response to a situation like this should always be to check whether the student actually *can* perform the task you've assigned. If the student literally cannot complete the work because she doesn't understand the content or hasn't yet mastered the required skills, the problem will require more in-depth attention. This may include a specially focused homework assignment, or perhaps tutoring from you or from a more advanced student.

Students with academic difficulties often feel so incompetent and ashamed that they simply want to give up. But once you can get students like these to talk to you, it's a short step to getting them to work for you. The first step is to demonstrate understanding and support. With discouraged students, try one of the following approaches.

For proud overachievers:

Nobody excels at everything, Sara. I've noticed you do really well in basketball. I'm sure you could teach people a lot about that, right? If someone wanted help learning to play basketball, and she came and asked you for help, how would you feel? Would you think she was stupid? Would you help her?

I remember I needed a little extra help in dividing decimals when I was in school. Everyone else seemed to get it, and I just didn't. And I hated dividing decimals. But you know what? Today I know how to divide decimals. I kept at it and I finally got it. How do you think it felt, having to work that hard? Did I want to give up? Of course. But how do you think it felt finally conquering this thing I hated?

When I look back on it I realize a lot of why I hated it was that deep inside I was really afraid of it—I was afraid of failing. And I did fail at it, the first time . . . and the second time. But I had a teacher who was very patient, and I kept going, and the more I kept going, the less scary it got. And then finally, one day, it clicked.

So it seems to me you have two choices: You can run away from this, because it's not easy. Or you can step up to the challenge as I've seen you do on the basketball court, and I'll be right here to support you.

For more timid students:

Andre, we both know you speak very well. I know you get plenty of practice in my class, at least. But our trouble here is writing. What's your first reaction when you get a writing assignment? What do you think? What do you feel? Let's break it down into manageable pieces, okay? And then we'll tackle it together.

Do you know why I'm willing to take as much time as you need to help you become a better writer? Yes, I'd be remiss in my job if I just ignored your needs, but besides that—writing is a powerful thing.

And in almost any job, you're going to have to do some writing. If you become any kind of supervisor, you'll have to be able to put your thoughts in writing. You'll have to write status reports and purchase requests and employee evaluations. And if you work in any kind of office, that's doubly true.

It's also true, Andre, that you have a lot of good ideas. I'd hate for other people not to benefit from your ideas, or for people to ignore or minimize what you say because you don't communicate it as clearly as you could. You're too bright to let a lack of writing skill hold you back.

If this last portion rings hollow, recall an original contribution the student has made to your class or to the school. In truth, who doesn't deserve to have the best possible reception for his ideas?

Assuming your protester really can perform the work and is just being lazy or generally obstinate, consider one of these approaches:

- *Alter the assignment to make it more meaningful to the student.* Letting students choose a task's content or format can often engage their interests without diluting the assignment's educational value. This does not require spending hours tailoring every assignment to every student; chapter 4, "Communication Essentials," discusses this concept further.

- *Invoke peer pressure to make failure to cooperate more socially costly.* Punishing a group for the misbehavior of an individual is inappropriate, but inconveniencing the class—for example, by making everyone wait until an uncooperative student completes a task— can be highly effective, provided your troublemaker is not someone who thrives on attention or status as an outsider.

- *Withhold a desirable reward until the student complies with your request.* Many mildly recalcitrant students unmotivated by grades can be enticed to work by the promise of some reward—free time, participation in a fun activity, and so forth.

In a few cases, potentially capable students are beaten down by external circumstances or by the system that's supposed to be educating them. You may encounter a few able youth whose failures in school are so frequent and severe that eventually they find it easier to define themselves as incorrigible than to pick themselves up and risk yet another humiliating defeat. We offer suggestions for addressing such escape-seeking behavior in chapter 6.

Occasionally, your whole class may bog down, insisting they simply can't do what you ask, no way, never in a million years, it's just too hard. In such a case, framing can make all the difference. Rather than arguing with them, anticipate this reaction and create a model that shows that they can, in fact, do it.

One high school teacher we know designed an elaborate class project that he feared might intimidate his students. Anticipating complaints that the work required would be far beyond their capability, he pulled aside one of his teacher's assistants and tasked her for 3 weeks with producing a model of the output he wanted the class to produce. With plenty of guidance, she produced a superb product.

He then announced the assignment to students and explained what he expected them to do. They balked. They complained. They wondered if he was kidding. But then he showed them the example—tangible and produced by a student—and said, "This is entirely within your reach. Look at what one of your peers did for this same assignment."

That shifted the energy in the room from self-doubt to wonder and then to inquisitiveness. By the end of that unit, the class had produced work far superior to anything he'd ever anticipated from them. Parents were impressed, and students were proud. All because he insisted they could do it and planned diligently to show them how.

Sample Pep Talk for a Defeatist Class

Once in a while a group of students—perhaps even an entire roomful of them—will try to drag you down with negativity. This happens frequently when low performers feel overwhelmed by a daunting challenge. How should you respond to such mass pessimism? Remember that you create the climate in the classroom and tell it like it is:

> Who here has ever met someone who seems to walk around all day just scowling at everybody? How do you feel being around that person? How many here know someone who always seems to be happy and always has something nice to say? Which person would you rather be around? How do you imagine these two people feel inside? Do you think everything goes right 100% of the time for the positive person? Why do those people always seem so happy?
>
> Now imagine you're about to do something really important; you're about to play in a big game. Do you want to be thinking "I can't do this. They're going to kick the snot out of us out there"? Or would you rather be thinking, "This is going to be tough, but I can

do it"? Which of these attitudes do you think is more likely to lead to success? Why?

Your history does not have to be your future. What's the difference between the past and the future? Which one can be changed? How can that happen—just by magic? Can you remember a time when you failed at something the first time you tried, but then kept at it and succeeded? I'll give you all a minute; I want everyone to think of a time when you overcame an obstacle—big or small, it doesn't matter.

Who's willing to share his or her story? How did it feel when you failed? Why did you persist? Was there ever a time when you weren't sure if you'd make it? How did it feel when you succeeded? What did you learn from that?

What does that imply for your future at this school? Are you destined to fail forever because you've encountered a few setbacks in the past? Now, given all this, should you quit trying? Would I be doing my job if I let you quit trying? Who would lose? And whose fault would that be?

Although this line of reasoning may seem natural and even simplistic to you, to many underperforming students it is an utterly foreign way of thinking.

TEACHING DILEMMA: STUDENTS COMPLAIN THEY'RE "TOO SMART" FOR COURSEWORK

One of my students tells me nearly every day that she's too smart for the work in my class. She says she already knows what I'm teaching or she tells me she shouldn't have to do the work because it's "stupid." Usually she says this loudly and in front of the class. I've talked to her about it after class and I've talked to her parents, but they seem to believe her when she says the work is stupid, and I'm tired of justifying myself to them.

SUGGESTED SOLUTION

There are several possible reasons for this behavior. The first is that the student really does already know whatever skill or content you're teaching, in which case you might consider asking her to assist you or help a slower student for the day, with her credit for the assignment dependent on how she performs that duty. Just ensure that, if you ask her to help another student, she only *guides* her classmate and does not do the work for her. In our experience, this helps reinforce the class material in the mind of the tutor as well as the student needing assistance. Alternately, the student might qualify for a more advanced class; consult her counselor.

Another possibility: Frustrated students often use the word *stupid* to describe work with one or more of the following characteristics:

- poorly framed, leaving students wondering why they're doing it
- poorly presented, leaving students confused about content or procedures
- targeted at the wrong level of difficulty, leaving students thinking it's too hard or too easy

Third, the complainant may not want to do the work because she is repeating the class, or studied something similar in another class. If you are not sure whether the student has mastered the topic, offer a "challenge test" that, if passed, would allow the student to skip the assignment in question and work on something else during the allotted time.

Or try this approach: "It looks like you've had some experience with this before, but I've noticed you're a little fuzzy on some of the details. Since I think it wouldn't hurt to refresh your memory on it, I'm going to ask you to go through with the assignment anyway. But it appears that you have a head start on everybody else, so if you really focus and do a good job, you could be finished in half the time. Then you can have some free time or work on some extra credit."

Fourth, the student could be protesting to conceal an embarrassing deficiency. Often the student who protests most vociferously that she "don't need no help in English" is indeed the student in most dire need. If you suspect this to be the case, take the student aside after class and address the issue, as suggested above.

As for the student's parents, chapter 7 offers suggestions to deal with some common challenges. In this case, we'd recommend the following:

1. *Engage the parents in conversation.* Open dialogue can not only help parents understand your purpose and reasoning, but also demonstrate that you are a competent, helpful, and reasonable person with their child's best interests at heart—in short, someone who deserves their full trust and support.
2. *Prepare compelling support for the lessons that cause concern.* Parents have the right to know what you're teaching, though they don't have the right to bog you down by challenging every move you make. Take this opportunity to explain what you're teaching and why it's important.
3. *Document thoroughly each conversation you have with parents.* Write down their complaints—and quote them when you can—or get their input in writing. Be sure also to write down the things they like about the job you're doing. If they don't offer these, ask. Often, the simple act of thinking through all the things you're doing right will help them (and you) keep perspective.

4. *Seek out a second opinion.* Ask a colleague if you might be overreacting to the situation or failing to communicate or support your case.

If you have made several reasonable efforts to explain yourself but the parents continue to harass you or become belligerent, refer the problem to an administrator or counselor. They're trained and paid to handle such situations.

2

WHO ARE YOUR STUDENTS?

Many teachers start their career with mental images of the classrooms they will lead—typically these are rooms full of eager learners who listen respectfully, contribute appropriately to discussions, cheerfully comply with requests, and take charge of their own education. Although such ideal students do exist, the perfect student is about as rare as the perfect teacher.

Don't get us wrong—some students excel in schools as they are presently constructed. Those students well served by the status quo are not our greatest concern here, however. That's because students who churn out A papers and ace their exams do not ordinarily provide the greatest classroom management challenge. In our view, the true test of a great teacher is how well he can motivate and teach the most reluctant learners.

The purpose of this chapter is to demonstrate that no matter what kind of students you have, you can create the kind of classroom you want if you understand who your students are and what they need.

Much of the rest of this book describes ways you can support a good learning environment. But of course you will not apply these techniques in a vacuum. The classroom is a complex system of relationships among facts and ideas, teaching tools and frameworks, and the energy and ingenuity of the young people in your care. This chapter is designed to help you better understand the last and most important factor in this equation: your students.

MOST STUDENTS ARE NOT LIKE YOU

I wanted to make literature come alive. I wanted to instill a love of the written word. I wanted to discuss F. Scott Fitzgerald's use of metaphor in The Great Gatsby. *They wanted to throw spitballs and whisper dirty words in the back of the room.*

—Marcia Nehemiah, first-year teacher
(cited in Kane, 1991, p. 18)

First, a reality check. You may hear yourself lamenting (as most teachers occasionally do), "Why don't my students care more about school?" If this happens, close your eyes, project yourself back in time, and replay a bit of your own adolescence. Remember those days? The thrills, the drama, the hormones, the trauma?

Now open your eyes and look around. Recognize any recurring themes? Self-doubt, incessant comparison with others, the craving to belong and the continually looming terror of potential rejection—this never-ending soap opera is the world your students inhabit every day. For most, Friday's math quiz pales by comparison.

Remember that your students are *emerging* adults. Do not expect them to think or behave as you do now, or as you did when you were in college. They are much more likely to think and behave like, well, adolescents. Numerous temptations will conspire to divert their attention from school, and some of these temptations will be considerably more alluring than schoolwork. Perhaps what should surprise us, then, is not that students don't give schoolwork 100% of their energy, but that they manage to navigate growth spurts, mood swings, peer pressure, sex, drugs, video games, cars, fashion, music, and so forth, with enough energy remaining to give academics any attention at all.

While researching the landmark study *A Place Called School,* John Goodlad led a team that asked a broad cross section of secondary students to identify the single best thing about their schools. The students ranked "my friends" and "sports activities" as 1 and 2. Tellingly, "classes I'm taking" and "teachers" both ranked near the bottom, outscored even by the choice "nothing," which received 8% of the vote. Goodlad's conclusion? "Clearly, 'school work' is not all of school for adolescents. . . . [Many] may think it quite sufficient to be considered good-looking, popular, and one of the gang" (Goodlad, 1984, p. 77).

This is not to say you should expect the worst from your students. On the contrary, as emphasized previously, students will tend to live up—or down—to your expectations. So apply your passion and ingenuity to make your subject as relevant and engaging as possible, and expect the best response from your students. Just don't be naive about the relative importance students may place on your class versus everything else competing for attention in their lives.

A realistic target: If you do your job well, you will succeed in engaging most students most of the time. (Sorry, but no matter how brilliant a teacher you are, your class will never be *every* student's favorite. This implies nothing about you—it's merely the law of averages at work; given the sheer number of academic disciplines available for study, no single one could realistically be the favorite of every student.)

Should these facts convince you to slip this book quietly back on the shelf and give up teaching to become a cruise director or lumberjack instead? We hope not. Great teachers take the occasionally harsh reality of the classroom not as a cause for despair, but as a call to arms. They marshal their best energy and plunge into the challenge with a strong will to succeed, a ready sense of humor, and more than a little faith in the importance of their cause. It is many of these teachers whose stories you will read in this book. We are proud to call them our colleagues and believe that once you've soaked up their wisdom, you will be proud, too.

ADOLESCENTS ARE MORE THAN COGNITIVE CREATURES

To understand better the complex, competing needs of the individuals in your care, consider each in five dimensions: physical, social, emotional, intellectual, and moral-spiritual (see Figure 2.1).

Adults and children alike must balance needs in each of these spheres. Although elementary teachers typically embrace this holistic reality, their counterparts at upper grade levels tend instead to view young people as academic creatures above all, leading them to conclude that their job as teachers is solely to further students' intellectual development. "All that other fluffy stuff," this line of thinking goes, "should have been sorted out in earlier grades and therefore falls outside the scope of my duties."

In an ideal world, this might be true. In the real world, however, cognitive processing does not occur in isolation from physical, emotional, and social constraints. Overemphasizing the intellectual effectively ignores the numerous other aspects of being that heavily

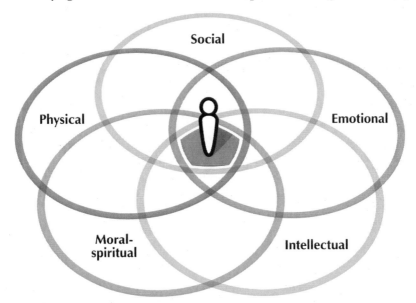

Figure 2.1. The five dimensions of being.

influence school performance, which adolescents themselves often find much more important and engaging.

Consider also psychologist Abraham Maslow's theory that humans share a common hierarchy of needs, from fundamental requirements for physical survival to the compulsion for social acceptance, intellectual engagement, and psychological contentment (see Figure 2.2). Maslow posits that until people satisfy their fundamental needs, preoccupation with these leaves neither the desire nor the freedom to address higher-order concerns.

Viewing students through the lens of Maslow's simple framework can help uncover obstacles to their welfare, happiness, and productivity. If a student is underperforming, ask questions at each level of the hierarchy to guide your preliminary inquiry into possible problems.

For example, does the student get enough food, sleep, and exercise every day? Does the student have a safe, clean, quiet place to sleep and study? Does her home life provide structure and emo-

Figure 2.2. Maslow's hierarchy of human needs.

tional stability? Does the student feel loved and accepted by family, friends, and community? Does he feel competent, appreciated for his or her talents, and encouraged to succeed? Any student who would answer *no* to any of these questions will not be a fully engaged learner. Expect distraction, frustration, and possible misbehavior until these needs are met.

Note to new teachers: Given the numerous pressures inherent in the first year of teaching, the issues presented in this section may seem overwhelming to you. We want to be clear that we do *not* presume that every new teacher will be able to observe and evaluate each student on each of these dimensions; in most cases, this will not be feasible.

Nevertheless, we prefer enlightenment to ignorance. Awareness of these issues can help you understand your students, find ways to engage them, and foster their success. And if you are concerned about a particular student, you may at least be able to refer her to a school counselor or other professional.

THE PHYSICAL DIMENSION

Basic questions from the *physical survival* level of Maslow's hierarchy rarely get asked by secondary teachers. These include questions like:

- Does every student have enough to eat?
- Is every student eating balanced meals?
- Does every student have a fixed and secure place to sleep?
- Is every student sleeping enough?
- Is every student exercising regularly?
- Does any student have trouble with her or his physical, mental, or emotional health (e.g., eyesight, hearing, cognitive processing, emotional stability)?

Deficits in these areas can result in lethargy, hyperactivity, and/or general irritability. Frequently observed physical problems among adolescents include choosing junk food over nutritional food, overeating, not exercising enough or at appropriate times, abusing various substances, and failing to sleep regularly.

Like younger children, teens often need instruction and reminders to practice good habits, yet many will resist such guidance. We caution particularly against lecturing about these issues; most teens will respond by nodding earnestly for the duration of any parent or teacher speech, only to return to their old behavior the moment the preaching stops.

A better tactic is to engage a student in a conversation sprinkled with Socratic questions leading inevitably to a helpful conclusion. Such a conversation might take a path like this:

> How are you feeling today? Is this the first time you've felt this way? Have you noticed any patterns in these feelings? Are these causing you any trouble? Here's what I've noticed . . . . How do you think we might address this, so you can meet all your needs and obligations?

The second level of Maslow's hierarchy, *safety and security*, involves issues such as

- physical safety (protection from crime, natural elements, bullies, parental abuse, etc.)
- adequate physical comfort
- financial stability
- stable health
- psychological stability and security

Students' safety and security is largely contingent upon a stable and consistent home environment. Are parents present, sober, competent, and nurturing? Many parents are overburdened by work or other commitments; they lack time and energy even to oversee their children, let alone to deliver necessary emotional attention and support. Other parents have little education themselves and can merely admonish but not actually assist their children to become good students. A few parents face life pressures or chemical dependencies that render them disinterested in their children's well-being or entirely ineffective. If you suspect that a student suffers from these or similar issues at home, contact a counselor or administrator.

Sometimes your students may be too distracted by outside commitments to have sufficient time to focus on school. Some may be expected to help raise siblings or even have children of their own. Others may find themselves overcommitted to extracurricular activities (sometimes in anticipation of college applications). Still others may be obliged to take part-time jobs to earn spending money or to help pay family bills.

Unfortunately, a few of your students may suffer from outright abuse or neglect by relatives, neighbors, bullies at school, and so forth. However, many parents may not even be aware of potential abuse. In such cases, you may need to intervene.

Other physical issues can also impact teens' self-image, thereby affecting their confidence, effort, and performance both in and beyond the classroom. Questions to ask yourself here fall more directly into the third level of Maslow's hierarchy, affection and acceptance (also discussed in the next section).

- Do your students feel respected by their peers for more than just their physical attributes?
- Are students supported in coping with typical adolescent concerns about
  - physical development
  - body image
  - sexuality
- When students have questions about these issues, do they have access to mature, truthful, confidential answers?

Our website (www.classroomadvisor.com) contains links to useful resources on teen self-image.

Table 2.1. Signs of Possible Child Abuse

	Signs of Possible Physical Abuse / Neglect	Signs of Possible Emotional Abuse / Neglect
The child	• has inexplicable injuries like burns, bruises, black eyes, broken bones—especially in unusual places (i.e., not knees, elbows, etc.) • wears unusually concealing clothing, or refuses to change clothes to participate in physical activities • is gloomy, depressed, overly emotional, and unable to have fun • fights or acts out frequently, toward others or toward objects • seems exhausted, has trouble sleeping or often has nightmares • seems unaffectionate toward and/or afraid of a parent or other adults • spends a lot of time at school and doesn't want to go home afterward, and/or runs away from home • regularly comes to school unwashed, unfed, underclothed, or exhausted • has unmet physical / medical needs • begs regularly for food or money	• has difficulty making friends • avoids interacting with other children • is pushy and hostile, continually nervous, or overly passive • has problems controlling bodily functions (e.g., bed-wetting) • has difficulty learning or focusing • is gloomy, depressed, overly emotional, and unable to have fun • shows sudden changes in behavior, level of engagement • demonstrates self-sabotaging or self-destructive behavior • demonstrates overly mature or overly infantile behavior • abuses alcohol or other drugs
The parent	• offers conflicting or unconvincing explanations for the child's injuries • is excessively secretive and deliberately isolated from other neighborhood parents • inflicts harsh physical discipline, or requests it for the child at school • may have a drinking or drug abuse problem	• describes the child in extremely negative terms—as evil, worthless, nothing but a burden, etc. • appears excessively controlling or unrealistically demanding • acts (or appears to be) indifferent to the child's presence, health, happiness, or performance • demonstrates erratic, unbalanced, or irrational behavior

Note: Adapted from the American Academy of Pediatrics website ("Abuse," n.d.) and the U.S. Department of Health and Human Services Child Welfare website ("Recognizing Child Abuse and Neglect," n.d.).

SIGNS OF POSSIBLE CHILD ABUSE

If you see signs of what you suspect may be child abuse or neglect (see Table 2.1), most jurisdictions require you to report your suspicions, along with any evidence you may have collected, to school and/or local authorities. Failing to do so could cost you your job and could conceivably cost the child in question much more than that. For more information about where and how to file a report, consult your administrator or union representative, or in the United States call the National Child Abuse Hotline (1-800-4-A-CHILD).

The Children's Bureau of the U.S. Department of Health and Human Services (HHS) and the American Academy of Pediatrics have identified common signs that may indicate child abuse or neglect. Note that these are potential (not definitive) indicators of trouble. Although the presence of one or two items from this list does not guarantee that abuse or neglect is occurring, the combination of several of these traits in a single student could signal serious problems.

TEACHING DILEMMA: STUDENT WILL NOT FOCUS

I have a sophomore who does his work some days but seems to spend most of his energy disrupting class and terrorizing his teachers. In my class, he wanders all over the room, talking to everyone and distracting them. When I finally get him to sit down, he stays there for about 3 or 4 minutes, then he's up and wandering around again. I can't figure out why he won't stay focused.

SUGGESTED SOLUTION

Resist the urge to blame the student until you investigate to determine whether he *won't* stay focused or *can't* stay focused. If he's simply unwilling to cooperate, the best solution could be proper intervention—as described in chapters 5 and 6— and a healthy dose of patience. It's also possible, however, that the source of the problem could be largely outside the student's control, in which case you will probably need to engage experts—your school's counselor, psychologist, and administration.

In our experience, the most common causes of this type of extreme behavior are

- a natural chemical imbalance (sometimes linked to poor nutrition)
- emotional anxiety
- stress/trauma at home
- drug abuse
- some form of learning disability (LD)—including, most commonly, Attention Deficit Disorder (ADD) and Attention Deficit Hyperactivity Disorder (ADHD)

When seeking the root of such a problem, start with the easy possibilities. One student we know exhibited behavior similar to that in this example until he and a school administrator analyzed his diet. The problem turned out not to be caused by simple refusal to cooperate, but by actual *inability* to stay focused because of sugar overload—a relatively straightforward problem to fix. In the student's words, "We figured out that the mornings I have two doughnuts and a soda for breakfast are the days when I act out. So I just have less sugar and it's easier to control myself. . . . On days when I eat candy, no teacher can control me" (D. Jackson, personal communication).

Emotional anxiety is another source of many behavior challenges in class. Phrases like "blinded by rage" and "paralyzed with grief" describe the power of certain emotions to short-circuit the brain's normal mode of operation and substitute raw emotion for rational thought. Worry, anger, sadness, and certain other emotions can become so severe as to be cognitively debilitating. Later in this chapter and in chapter 6, "Classroom Management II," we offer recommendations for helping students to monitor and manage their own emotions.

Frequently, troublemaking in the classroom springs from trauma at home. This can include parental arguing or divorce, remarriage, new siblings, illness or death, economic stress, substance abuse, and any form of physical or psychological abuse. Any severe change (or threat of change) can throw students off balance and trigger unpredictable behavior at home and at school.

Although solutions to severe medical, familial, and drug-related challenges are beyond the scope of this book, an administrator or counselor should be able to help you determine whether the student in question suffers from one of these issues. Our website (www.classroomadvisor.com) provides links to useful additional resources.

Regarding learning disabilities in particular, we strongly recommend that every teacher watch Rick Lavoie's brilliant F.A.T. City Workshop video (Lavoie, 1989). In the video, Lavoie leads a roomful of teachers and others through a series of exercises designed to cause Frustration, Anxiety, and Tension, to simulate what children with learning disabilities (and to some degree emotional anxiety) often feel in the regular classroom.

TEACHING DILEMMA: STUDENT FALLS ASLEEP IN CLASS DAILY

One of my favorite students used to be funny, engaging, and on top of his classwork. His positive attitude and great sense of humor made class fun for me every day. Lately, though, he looks bedraggled and can't seem to stay awake all the way through class. When I asked him what was wrong he told me he works the late shift. This keeps him out until 2 or sometimes 3 a.m. He really wants a job so I don't want to spoil it for him, but he's not learning anything in class anymore and if this continues he may not even pass.

SUGGESTED SOLUTION

Students who look groggy in class often earn that appearance by going to bed at ungodly hours, and as this teacher discovered, schoolwork is only one possible reason. Teens are prone to the same diversity of sleep disruptors as adults. Sometimes drugs, particularly stimulants like speed or crystal meth, are to blame. Occasionally, the problem is stress over some kind of relationship conflict (e.g., parents who are always fighting or trouble with a boyfriend or girlfriend). In other cases, youth are not closely supervised by parents and therefore stay up late talking on the phone, watching TV, surfing the web, playing video games, or staying out with friends.

Alternately, we have seen numerous students miss classes, fail to finish homework, and fall asleep in school because they have jobs, which often demand their presence until the early morning hours. Sometimes, they prefer these schedules; other times, they get stuck with whatever shifts are available because they lack seniority, or they tolerate late hours because they are desperate for the money and fear retaliation for protesting.

If you have a student whose school progress is slowing and you suspect one of these factors to be the culprit, we recommend following these steps:

1. First, talk with the student. Is he aware of the problem? Can he suggest a way to solve it? If you can agree on a resolution, try it out for a week. Working it out between the two of you is preferable to bringing in a third party because (a) it's simpler; (b) it gives the student incentive to grow to meet your expectation that he, as an emerging adult, might be able to help solve his own problem; and (c) it demonstrates a level of respect from you that, as we discuss later, will encourage reciprocation. (If you suspect the problem is drugs—particularly a drug like crystal meth—it's likely too deep and intractable to be solved this way; skip this step and jump to Step 3.)

2. If the problem persists, contact the student's parent or guardian to inquire into the issue, solicit suggestions, and devise a solution. Chapter 7, "Communicating With Parents, Administrators, and Others," recommends procedures for this, and especially for dealing with reluctant parents.

3. If conferences with the student and his parents accomplish nothing, call the student's counselor. Many jurisdictions require students to have work permits signed by their schools before they can get after-school jobs. This prevents abuse of employer power, and there's nothing like a letter or call from a concerned school administrator to secure more reasonable work hours—particularly if the employer depends on a regular stream of students from your school as employees.

4. If the problem is the student's after-school job, we do *not* recommend contacting the student's work supervisor directly, for despite your best intentions this could be viewed as meddling in a situation you do not understand. If, for example, the student or his family really needs the

money and your interference causes him to lose his job, that's a terrible consequence that neither you nor your reputation will soon live down. Some students—particularly underprivileged students—only stay in school at all because they have the financial or psychological support of a part-time job. As Maslow's hierarchy implies, survival needs will generally prevail over less urgent needs; if you force the choice between the job and school, the student may drop out of school.

TEACHING DILEMMA: TEACHER SUSPECTS STUDENT OF SUBSTANCE ABUSE BEFORE SCHOOL

I have a student who is very bright but often comes to class late and doesn't always do her work. I'm embarrassed to say I didn't know just what her problem was until one day she came in late and the kids in the back of the room made a big scene about how she smelled like marijuana. I talked with her after class and asked what her mother would think of her coming to school high. She replied, "She's not going to care. I get my weed from her."

SUGGESTED SOLUTION

If you face any student you suspect of substance abuse or addiction, resist the urge to judge, blame, or lecture, as this will probably merely alienate the student. Children of addicts in particular often suffer feelings of shame, uncertainty, and fear; this combined with the allure of easy intoxication can entice them to self-medicate with drugs or alcohol.

You will need to refer such a student to drug abuse specialists and inform a counselor or an administrator; in most jurisdictions, supplying drugs to minors constitutes child abuse. Your best contribution may be to offer a supportive and attentive ear and capture a detailed written record of the student's story. Any written documentation you can produce will help all parties help the child, and will keep you clear of legal trouble, particularly if the problem leads to a child custody hearing and you get summoned to testify in court.

Note that substance abuse among parents is not a minor problem. For example, the HHS estimates that in the United States alone there are 11 million children (under age 18) of alcoholics. Compared to children of nonalcoholics, HHS reports, these children frequently "exhibit [more] symptoms of depression and anxiety, . . . score lower on tests measuring verbal ability, . . . have [greater] difficulties in school [and] are more at risk . . . of physical abuse" (U.S. Department of Health and Human Services, National Clearinghouse for Alcohol and Drug Information, n.d.). Children of drug addicts often display not only these symptoms but also an alarming rate of drug addiction themselves.

Can you unilaterally replace a parent guilty of such clear dereliction of duty? No. Can you help such a parent get help? Yes. Your administration should be able to direct both students and their parents to drug abuse counseling, appropriate medical professionals, and local support groups. As mentioned previously, our website (www.classroomadvisor.com) offers supporting resources for this.

THE SOCIAL DIMENSION

Although to some degree everyone craves *affection and acceptance* (the third level of Maslow's hierarchy) this drive is particularly potent among teens. Sometimes it leads an entire roomful of students to wear identical bizarre outfits; other times it impels packs of youth to commit destructive acts. The quest for belonging can bring out the best and the worst in adolescents, as it has for generations.

To determine how social imperatives might be driving your students' behavior, ask yourself:

- Does every student have real friends who support and accept her, or simply peers she always feels the need to impress?
- Does each student feel connected to a healthy and supportive family or community group, or does she feel isolated and adrift?
- Are the adults in each student's life good role models and competent sources of advice?
- Are these adults available and welcoming, or aloof and inaccessible?

Education consultant Rick Lavoie, creator of the aforementioned *F.A.T. City Workshop*, identifies four levels of social acceptance common among secondary students. In relation to their peers, teens tend to be either popular, controversial, isolated, or rejected (see Figure 2.3).

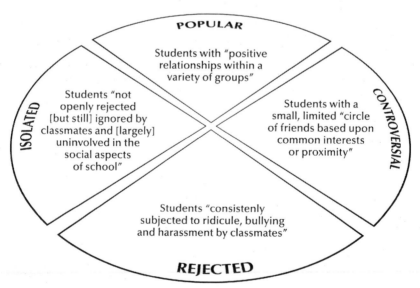

Figure 2.3.   Lavoie's four levels of social acceptance.
Note: Adapted from Lavoie (2002).

So widespread is this segmentation that most teachers immediately recognize these categories. Though restructuring this entrenched system is implausible, teachers can certainly help students improve their social competence, thereby maximizing both their happiness and their chances of migrating within the system (Lavoie, 2002).

Social efficacy, according to researchers Thomas Hatch and Howard Gardner, hinges on the ability to make personal connections with others, understand others' motives and feelings, assert oneself without alienating peers, negotiate solutions to conflicts, and organize and manage groups. Students strong in these skills are often considered charming and charismatic, and frequently gravitate to positions of leadership (Goleman, 1997, p. 118).

Students lacking these skills tend to be nervous and awkward in social situations; many retreat and become loners, and others try to gain attention by other means—often by ridiculing, bullying, or merely annoying their peers.

RELATIONSHIP-BUILDING HABITS

What behaviors tend to make people likable? The list is neither infinite nor mysterious, yet a surprising number of young people (and adults) fail to practice these behaviors and end up, for all practical purposes, socially incompetent. Some have simply never pondered the question. Others don't have a clue how they appear to others, often presuming they're making a great impression when in fact they're alienating, boring, or just confusing everyone around them. (This section is adapted partly from Cottringer, 2002, and Lavoie, 2002.)

There is no need to launch an extended unit on "being charismatic," but we recommend encouraging students— particularly those with low social competence—to practice these basic habits during their regular classroom interactions:

smile	listen
say hello	laugh
be honest	be tactful
be humble	be grateful
extend invitations	share willingly
ask others' opinions	look for common ground
give genuine compliments	treat others as you would like to be treated

Remember that what may seem obvious and elementary to you may be quite foreign to a student with a very different background, home life, and emotional makeup. You will be amazed at the difference that explicit reinforcement of these behaviors can make with those students to whom social graces don't come naturally.

Don't be afraid to post these in your room. We'd bet that even teachers occasionally forget to practice some of these behaviors. Besides, reminding everyone of the keys to civil behavior will make your hours in the classroom much more pleasant and appealing, both for you and for your students.

Introversion Versus Extroversion: Striking the Right Balance

In fast-changing, stimulus-rich, media-saturated cultures, extroverts often appear to enjoy an edge in life over introverts. Bold personalities and behavior tend to get noticed—in the media, at social gatherings, and in the classroom, where outgoing students are often more popular and easier to talk to than their more reserved peers. Extroverts are not inherently more talented or committed or important than their more introverted peers, yet many teachers instinctively treat them as such—interacting with them more often and more positively and evaluating them (whether consciously or not) as more likeable, more ambitious, and more likely to succeed.

On the other hand, academic programs that demand a great deal of quiet thinking—in the form of reading, writing, computation, research, philosophizing, or artistry—can favor introverted students, who often have an easier time focusing for hours at a time on such typically solitary tasks. Through the lens of traditional academic achievement, more introverted students can appear smarter and more successful.

Our recommendation: Avoid viewing either extroversion or introversion as superior; they are simply different ways of processing information and communicating. The world offers ample opportunities for both types of personalities to succeed, albeit in very different types of work.

We urge you to cultivate a balanced classroom environment where both the most outgoing and the most reticent individuals—and the vast majority who lie somewhere between these poles—can thrive. Ideally, over the course of a term every student in every class should feel secure and empowered enough to cultivate the "other" in himself; more extroverted students could practice introspection and traditional academic study, and more introverted students could practice speaking and collaborating with others with greater frequency and effectiveness.

SCIENTIFIC INSIGHTS ON EXTROVERSION AND INTROVERSION

Recent neurological research reveals that introverts have more brain activity overall than extroverts, and that they tend to be "energized by retrieving long-term memories, problem solving, introspection, complex thinking and planning." In contrast, extroverts "have more activity in brain areas involved in processing the sensory information we're bombarded with daily . . . [but] search for more external stimuli to energize them [since they] have less internally generated brain activity" (Magruder, 2005, p. 1).

Neuroscience researcher Marti Olsen Laney observes that the difference between introverts and extroverts "impacts all areas of their lives: how they process information, how they restore their energy, what they enjoy and how they communicate." More specifically, "extroverts gain energy by being out and about," while "being with people takes energy from introverts, and they need to get away to restore that energy." One implication for the classroom: Sensitivity to this difference—and structuring activities to support both types—can help every student succeed (Magruder, 2005, p. 1).

TEACHING DILEMMA: PEER PRESSURE ENDANGERS STUDENT'S PERFORMANCE

One of my kids used to be an above-average student, but recently started hanging around with a group of boys who are clearly a bad influence on him. His class performance has been slipping and a couple of weeks ago I suspect he helped his new friends steal a car. When I discuss this with him, he seems to want to do better but feels a strong need to be "cool" and finds it hard to say no.

SUGGESTED SOLUTION

If additional investigation convinces you that your hunches about this student are correct, don't rush to blame either yourself or the student. The urge to fit in is a natural drive that doesn't begin or end in your classroom. Also, ascribing the problem entirely to peer pressure is simplistic and overlooks an important nuance that can help solve the problem. Peer influence can be either positive or negative, pushing individual behavior toward either end of the spectrum. While some students seem to compete to see who can ditch class most often or take the biggest bong hits, others will compete to excel in academic or extracurricular activities.

Not surprisingly, students most vulnerable to negative peer pressure tend to suffer from one or more of the following:

- low self-confidence (often masquerading as limitless bravado)
- limited social competency
- little parental guidance and support
- stressful and unstable life circumstances

In an extreme case like the one described here, there will likely be no easy solution, but the proverb "It takes a village to raise a child" could hold your best chance for success. To craft an effective intervention, reach out as much as possible for advice and support to all the influencers and community organizations in the student's life. Success in this case will likely require collaboration among relatives, school administrators, counselors and coaches, and any clubs, churches, employers, or other organizations that the student might find potentially appealing.

Within your classroom, first follow the recommendations for engaging and empowering students outlined in chapter 1 and chapter 4. Also consult chapter 6, "Classroom Management II," for additional insight on severe problem behavior.

Second, separate these peers as much as possible so they don't feed each other's problem behavior. If they're in your class together, assign them different seats and work groups. If the problem is severe, you might even request a schedule change for one or all students involved. They may still gravitate toward each other outside your class, but you will send a clear message and time spent apart can encourage them to discover other friends, giving positive peer pressure a chance to lure them in a better direction.

Third, help the student find the center in himself—encourage him to find or practice constructive activities that he both enjoys and performs well. Whether academic or not, anything that gives him self-confidence can eventually help him reject negative influences in his life.

While the next steps may stray considerably from the curriculum you should be teaching, they are very important for certain students, so consider enlisting a counselor to help. One thing that students in such situations need to understand is that many people say *yes* when they want to say *no* because of irrational fears of catastrophic consequences that never occur:

- *Fear of losing or damaging the relationship.* Most relationships are not so fragile; healthy relationships do not require one party to comply continually.
- *Feeling guilty for hurting the other person's feelings.* Other people's happiness does not depend on your agreement; others should take responsibility for their own feelings.
- *Feeling guilty for being selfish or self-centered.* You have the right and responsibility to maintain control of your body and your actions; if you fail to accept this, you could endanger yourself and cause resentment that will surface in other ways.
- *Fear of never being asked by this person to participate in anything again.* This is highly unlikely, but if it happens, the person in question is clearly not a good friend.

There are plenty of others out there who would be willing to respect your limits ("Say no," n.d.).

Another capacity a counselor could help such a student build is effective refusal skills. Many people—young and old alike—feel sucked into bonehead behavior because they see no way to back out gracefully. Share these guidelines with students to help them learn to say no:

1. *Establish clearly in your mind why saying no is important to you.*
2. *Practice putting your thoughts into coherent phrases.* Repeat them in your head, and practice saying them aloud as many times as necessary until they feel natural and comfortable.
3. *When the time comes to assert yourself, say it three ways:* in words, with your vocal tone, and with your body language.
   - *Words:* Use the word *no;* it cannot be mistaken for any other sentiment. If "no" alone feels too harsh or difficult to say, try couching the message in a "good news but bad news" format—for example, "I'm sorry if it means you won't pass this assignment, but *no,* you cannot copy my homework. That wouldn't be right." Or, "I like you too but *no,* I don't want to have sex with you."

      Don't dilute the message with mushy qualifying language like "I don't think so" or "Probably not"— it will not soften the blow, but merely make you look irresolute. An overly aggressive (or hopeful) person could jump on that as a sign that you don't really mean what you're saying.
   - *Vocal tone:* You may not need to sound angry, but don't use an apologetic tone either. Be assertive.

- *Body language*: An erect posture and firm stance will make you look and feel certain, even if you're not.
4. *Repeat as necessary.* Some people like to nag until a *no* becomes yes; don't let yourself be worn down. Just repeat. And repeat. And if necessary, walk away.
5. *If the person won't back down but you can't or don't want to walk away, change the subject or turn the question around* to put the focus on the person making demands, as in: "I've told you no. Why won't you respect that? Why is it so important to you to get me to do this?" (adapted from "Say No," n.d., and "Refusal Skills," n.d.).

TEACHING DILEMMA: FRIENDLESS STUDENT CAUSES TEACHER CONCERN

A lot of my students are a little awkward, but one seems especially troubled. He joined our school in the middle of the year and I know he lives with his grandmother because his mother is troubled, so it hasn't been easy for him. I don't know the exact story because I don't want to pry, but at lunch and between classes this boy just sits alone, usually dressed in black with a lot of dark makeup, listening to his gothic music. Should I worry?

SUGGESTED SOLUTION

First, this student's behavior is not necessarily pathological or permanent. Many young people take time to adjust to new situations, and the middle of the year can be an especially difficult time to enter a new school, both because most other students will likely have established relationships with each other—some stretching back years—and because adolescents can be cliquish and unwelcoming to outsiders. This student may therefore be choosing to keep his head down, to avoid any more attention than what his awkwardly timed arrival has already attracted. Give him time and support and he may well open up.

Second, unusual dress or behavior could indicate any number of things, such as:

- He may be thumbing his nose at authority by rejecting certain social conventions.
- He may feel (or wish to be) different from his peers and want to represent this outwardly. Whether you believe he's really so different is beside the point; what will shape his attitude and his behavior is *his* perception, not yours or anyone else's. If you want to understand this student, the first thing to investigate—respectfully, without judgment—is what he believes (or desires) this difference to be.
- He may simply appreciate and/or identify with the music, style, or message of the subculture in question. Every musical genre includes a variety of sounds and messages. If you really want to learn about the student, listen to the music yourself. If you can't stomach that, at least read up on it; a little research can teach you a lot. (See the sidebar "Seek First to Understand" later in this chapter for a brief analysis of the goth subculture in particular.)

Third, don't make assumptions about any student's background. Find out as much about his home circumstances as you can—from him, from his guardians, from his school counselor, an administrator, or a teacher from a previous year. You can't begin to address his problems if you don't have all the facts.

Fourth, once you understand a bit more about your friend-less student, give him a boost. Model for the class your own acceptance of the student. Notice him, use his name, solicit his views, spotlight his expertise, and be sure to give him plenty of recognition when recognition is due. This, as Rick Lavoie (2002) notes, "conveys the constant message that the child is worthy of attention. . . . [U]se [your] status as a leader to increase the status of the child."

Also, though the precise chemistry of affection is nebulous and students must of course create their own relationships with others, you can cultivate conditions making friendship more likely to bloom. As an observer of hundreds of personalities a day, you should be able to steer students to likely comrades; for example, try creating a class workgroup matching your friend-less student with peers who share some of his interests.

Lastly, keep an eye out for after-school clubs, activities, and so forth, that the student might enjoy. Careful observation and a talk with your school counselor can reveal volumes about this student's emerging identity and unique needs. A little research, explanation, and encouragement on your part can help him find a community to call his own, where he can not only feel comfortable, but also hone skills that will increase his confidence and, in turn, his social efficacy.

Of course, it's always possible that this student is sunk in depression, which has no quick or easy solution. In this case your time, energy, and attention can help lift him up. You might also refer him to the school counselor or psychologist, to identify more detailed interventions.

THE EMOTIONAL DIMENSION

The third and fourth levels of Maslow's hierarchy—*affection and acceptance* and *self-esteem*—highlight the human need to feel confident, respected, and valued as part of a group. These drives loom large in adolescence, and will heavily impact your students. The emotional undertones of these and similar needs will comprise a central element of your classroom.

The best teachers we've seen do not dread the perennial high tide of emotion in the classroom, but embrace it as an opportunity. As discussed earlier, nurturing students' cognitive development is not the sole purpose of teaching; ideally, education should improve as many dimensions of the human experience as it touches.

On the bright side, emotion adds color, vitality, and depth to life, shaping our understanding of ourselves and our world. "There can be no knowledge," writes Arnold Bennett, "without emotion. We may be aware of a truth, yet until we have felt its force, it is not ours. To the cognition of the brain must be added the experience of the soul" ("Arnold Bennett on Emotion," n.d.). Passion also sustains ideals like justice, charity, and altruism that allow communities—including your classroom—to endure and evolve. On a greater scale, Carl Jung alludes to the alchemical power of emotion to promote human progress: "There can be no transforming of darkness into light and of apathy into movement," he argues, "without emotion" ("Jung on Apathy," n.d.).

Emotion can also help students succeed (in school and in life) by generating the willpower to surmount obstacles. Great coaches, mentors, and teachers help students channel their emotions to transcend their innate fight-or-flight insticts and develop an internal drive to excel at whatever they love.

Emotion can more immediately sway mood and performance. As writers, propagandists, and educators know, an injection of passion can bring to life an otherwise flat story, compelling people to care—and take action.

On the dark side, adolescents are notoriously captive to passion. Many teens—and not a few adults—lack sophisticated understanding of their own emotions, and allow raw feelings to interfere, sometimes dangerously, with reason. Your students may occasionally seem possessed—with anxiety, despair, or rage one moment, and with joy, lust, or excitement the next. To outsiders, the only common thread to these mood swings is their utter irrationality, reminding us that Aristotle's *animal soul* exerts a subtle but persistent tug on the adolescent mind.

We have good news, however: you can influence this by optimizing the emotional climate of the classroom. Need to calm a class? Try soothing music and lighting—put on a calming classical CD and dim the lights. Need to build a bit of energy or refocus students' minds? Schedule time to stand up and stretch, do jumping jacks, perform a coordinated chant or cheer, or play a simple physical game.

Pacing is also key. The need to cover a vast curriculum can create strong pressure to blaze ahead continuously. Ironically, however, a class that's *always* charging forward may actually make *less* progress than one that allows for occasional pauses for rest and contemplation.

Why is this true? Because running full-time at full throttle can stress and fatigue both you and your students. Athletes take breaks and change their routines to give themselves time to recover and assimilate the benefits of each workout; a similar logic applies in the classroom. Your quickest students may keep up with a daily sprint, but many others could flounder. Moving too fast can result in either skimming the surface of a great deal of content (which benefits no one in the long term), or backtracking repeatedly to be sure everyone really understands.

We advise creating a class rhythm that emulates a good song or story—alternating bursts of intensity with adequate time for students to regroup and absorb the lessons they're experiencing. Otherwise, the classroom can become a blur in which nothing is learned deeply, and nothing is retained. Chapter 4, "Communication Essentials," offers additional suggestions on pacing, including the essential concept of *wait time*.

One element to manage closely is anxiety. As with athletes on a field or performers on a stage, a touch of stress can boost student performance by releasing adrenaline, raising energy levels, and improving focus. There is a fine line here, however. Too much stress can disrupt performance, creating a screen of emotional interference—an *affective filter*—that prevents clear thinking.

What determines whether anxiety will produce positive or negative results? Research by social psychologist Robert Zajonc and others suggests that pressure—stemming, for example, from having a time limit to perform a task, or from being watched—tends to push performance in the direction of its existing tendency. In other words, good performance gets better and poor performance gets worse. Psychology professor David Myers sums up the research findings: "What you do well, you are likely to do even better in front of an audience; what you normally find difficult may seem impossible when others are watching" (Myers, 1992, p. 563).

For some reason, teachers often make students nervous and then expect them to perform well. Test anxiety and fear of public speaking are two major sources of classroom anguish; the added stress spurs some students to excel, but causes others to crash and burn. These are addressed in the teaching dilemmas at the end of this section.

Beyond these two common situations, everyday activities can generate greater anxiety than you might imagine. For example, teachers frequently ask students to stand in front of the class to solve a problem, recite a poem, draw a diagram, and so forth. To you this may seem like a simple request, and many students may fulfill it with a bit of nervousness but no real difficulty. No matter how easy the task or how competent the student, however, performance will suffer if her affective filter is clouded by

- an overwhelming fear of producing "the wrong answer"
- worries that peers will ridicule her acne, accent, mannerisms, clothing, rear end, and so forth
- a general and chronic shyness

Obviously, some students will be more vulnerable than others to such emotional disruption. And if a teacher compounds a student's anxiety by criticizing her work in front of the class while the student stands there exposed, the student's affective filter may be dense enough to effectively paralyze her—leaving the student barely able to see, hear, or respond coherently. Or the student may lash out, disrupting the class and leaving the teacher, the students, and perhaps herself wondering what's wrong.

Of course, the world outside of school is full of unwelcome stressors, and many college courses—particularly in professional/graduate schools—rely heavily on high-stakes techniques like cold-calling to prepare students for careers in certain fields. But consider whether such an approach is appropriate for all students. Does putting students on the spot really reveal how well they think—or does it reveal only how well they think under sudden, unanticipated, and unrealistic pressure?

The bottom line: We recommend having a clear reason for asking a student to perform *any* task—and particularly those that cause great stress. What objective is served? Will the class learn something uniquely valuable from the experience? Will the student grow in an important way from the experience? If not, consider an alternate strategy. "My teachers always made me do that when I was in school" is an inadequate rationale.

When students feel stressed, help them understand that it's perfectly natural—adrenaline is nature's elixir of self-preservation, fueling the fight-or-flight response that helps creatures survive. Don't be afraid to pull out a story of anxiety from your own experience, if necessary (just be sure it has a happy ending). This can show students that you're human and they're not alone. If a student's problems with stress seem particularly severe, don't hesitate to refer him or her to a counselor or administrator.

Much anxiety is unavoidable, but understanding it is the first step to managing it. The following recommendations can help students cope with stress (the following content is adapted partly from King, n.d.).

1. Learn physical stress-release techniques, for example:
   - quiet meditation
   - deep and regular breathing during the stressful event
   - physical activity immediately before the stressful event
   - physical activity as part of a regular fitness routine, which tends to lower stress generally

2. Maintain physical health to stay strong, resilient, energetic, and self-confident through
   • good nutrition
   • adequate rest
   • regular exercise, which can reduce depression, pain, and stress by activating natural chemicals in the body to generate feelings of well-being and calm
3. Avoid common stress-related activities that exacerbate stress symptoms, such as
   • consuming excess sugar or caffeine
   • getting insufficient sleep
   • exercising infrequently

TEACHING DILEMMA: STUDENTS SUFFER TEST ANXIETY

I have students who do well during most of my class, but when it comes time for a test, they bomb. It's like their brains switch off and they forget all the work we did all term. I know they know the material, but they can't express it on the test. I don't want them to fail, because I know they can perform in other contexts, but I feel like giving them an extra chance or extra credit would be unfair to the other students.

SUGGESTED SOLUTION

First, we invite you to review the section on assessment in chapter 4. Ideally, you will conduct enough small, mid-lesson assessments both to keep students on track to learning what you intend, and also to prevent them (and their parents) from being caught off guard by a nasty shock on the final test.

Second, help students learn to cope with stress, as discussed above.

Third, in chapter 6 we recommend teaching students to map out angry feelings so they can identify and manage them. In a similar vein, Julie King at the University of Oregon identifies four dimensions of anxiety, and recommends that students reflect on recent anxiety and write out in as much detail as possible their experience with all four dimensions.

1. *Cognitive.* Thoughts (often negative) accompanying the "dreaded event," for example, "I have to ace this," "I'm a failure," "Who am I trying to fool?"
2. *Emotional.* Feelings related to the event, for example, embarrassment, disappointment, anger.
3. *Behavioral.* Nervous movements, for example, fidgeting or faster speech, gestures, and so on.
4. *Physiological.* Change in involuntary bodily functions, for example, sweating, dry mouth, digestive changes, pounding heart, throbbing head, chest or throat tightening, and so forth.

King cites a hypothetical student whose journal might read as follows:

Reading for a test—drinking a soda—fidgeting—difficulty concentrating—more fidgeting—thoughts: I don't know who I'm trying to fool, I just don't get this, I am so stupid—go to the test: while taking the test body fidgets, increased perspiration, maybe some difficulties remembering what you know you know—after the test—I hate myself, why didn't I study, I don't deserve to be on this planet, no wonder people don't take me seriously. (King, n.d.)

We urge you to use this exercise to help students

1. Identify and reflect on the feelings and physical reactions caused by anxiety.
2. Isolate the most absurd thoughts. What's the worst that could really happen? Remember that most of what people worry about most of the time never comes to pass. And sometimes, recognizing how outrageously exaggerated our worst fears are can reduce the power they have over us. Stepping back this way to put things in perspective can also give students a good laugh—one of the best ways we know to reduce stress.
3. To address the more realistic fears, practice quiet self-affirmation. Much anecdotal evidence supports the power of positive thinking to help fight severe illnesses; patients with an upbeat mindset and something to live for seem to have better recovery rates than those who have given up hope. We're betting that if cancer survivors can benefit from a good attitude, your students can, too. This can be as simple as the student
   - envisioning what success would look and feel like
   - keeping in mind something he does well to be assured of his own competence
   - applying all his gifts and skills to shift his or her performance on the task at hand in that same positive direction

TEACHING DILEMMA: STUDENTS FEAR PUBLIC SPEAKING

I've heard that a lot of people fear death less than they fear public speaking. This certainly seems true in my classroom. Every year, I have students who beg not to have to give presentations to the class, and there's an unusually high number of absences on days when those activities are scheduled. I don't want to lower the bar in my classes by letting some students out of the requirement, but how can I help them overcome their fears?

SUGGESTED SOLUTION

We agree completely with this teacher's impulse to hold all students to high standards. Keep in mind two critical points here. First, although shying away from uncomfortable situations is a natural urge, your goal should not be to let students avoid growth opportunities. Instead, you should encourage and support them in engaging those opportunities. Great teachers (and mentors of all kinds) help adolescents transcend, rather than indulge, many of their natural urges.

Second, courage is not the absence of fear, but action in spite of fear. Remind students of this frequently, and refer as often as necessary to the "effort creates ability" message in the diagram of the pathway to achievement (see Figure 1.1). Support students as they work through challenges, but don't let them simply avoid activities they find unpleasant.

Releasing students from "requirements" not only ceases to make these requirements, but also denies those students important development opportunities and sets a poor example for everyone else. The moment you start issuing exemptions, you will likely find yourself flooded with petitions for similar treatment. In certain rare cases you may need to adjust an activity (e.g., to accommodate a student with very low skills or a disability), but as a rule we do not recommend excusing students from participation or otherwise lowering the bar.

This is particularly true for public speaking, a skill that surveys routinely identify as one of the most valuable skills for professionals in many fields. At the same time, we recognize that public speaking is one of those rare activities—like staring down from a high dive platform or facing the business end of a loaded gun—that tends to level the playing field. Fear of it can paralyze small children and world leaders alike.

How, then, can you help students work through this common fear? First, help them learn to walk before you expect them to run. Requiring a lengthy presentation from students who have never spoken in public before is unrealistic. Novice speakers are often afraid not only of their peers (not an unenlightened fear in a roomful of teenagers) but also of themselves—they worry they will mess up, or forget their lines, or faint.

To help them build their skills, start small, and gradually ladder up to more challenging tasks. You might start by asking students to stand and report on the findings of one of their work groups. Invite them to prepare a written paragraph explaining a concept or defending a particular position and then read it aloud. Once students master brief, discrete tasks, a longer and more formal presentation will seem less terrifying.

Also teach them some proven speaking techniques. Toastmasters International (n.d.), a nonprofit public speaking club, offers the following 10 tips:

1. *Know the room.* Be familiar with the place in which you will speak. Arrive early, walk around the speaking area, and practice using the microphone and any visual aids.
2. *Know the audience.* Greet some of the audience as they arrive. It's easier to speak to a group of friends than to a group of strangers.
3. *Know your material.* If you're not familiar with your material or are uncomfortable with it, your nervousness will increase. Practice your speech and revise it if necessary.
4. *Relax.* Ease tension by doing exercises [the authors' favorites are wall push-ups, jumping jacks, and long stretches].
5. *Visualize yourself giving your speech.* Imagine yourself speaking, your voice loud, clear, and assured. When you visualize yourself as successful, you will be successful.

6. *Realize that people want you to succeed.* Audiences want you to be interesting, stimulating, informative, and entertaining. They don't want you to fail.

7. *Don't apologize.* If you mention your nervousness or apologize for any problems you think you have with your speech, you may be calling the audience's attention to something they hadn't noticed.

8. *Concentrate on the message, not the medium.* Focus your attention away from your own anxieties, and outwardly toward your message and your audience. Your nervousness will dissipate. [In the authors' experience, giving the audience something other than you to focus on—perhaps a PowerPoint presentation, or some other visual aid—can also help reduce the pressure.]

9. *Turn nervousness into positive energy.* Harness your nervous energy and transform it into vitality and enthusiasm.

10. *Gain experience.* Experience builds confidence, which is the key to effective speaking. (quoted from "10 Tips for Successful Public Speaking," n.d.)

SELF-ESTEEM

For most teens, *self-esteem*—the fourth-level need in Maslow's hierarchy—depends heavily on both a sense of *personal efficacy* and feelings of *affection and acceptance* (discussed previously). Strengths or deficits in any of these areas directly feed or undermine the others.

The implication: Neglecting any of these needs can trigger a vicious cycle, in which a student's feelings of incompetence create a sense of isolation and despair, which deepens the sense of worthlessness, and on and on. Conversely, helping a student fulfill these needs can trigger a *virtuous* cycle: increasing the student's sense of efficacy can buoy self-confidence, making the student more attractive to others while—ideally—improving the student's performance generally and encouraging more of the same.

To gauge students' sense of personal efficacy, consider: Do they value achievement—in academics, athletics, art, music, community activity, or any other worthwhile endeavor? Do they challenge themselves to excel in their various pursuits? Do they feel competent and empowered to succeed? Do they feel appreciated and respected for their accomplishments? Do they feel supported even when they fail? Are they able to keep their setbacks in perspective?

To help students improve their *actual* personal efficacy, follow the recommendations in the rest of this book, starting with the next section on emotional self-mastery.

Promoting Emotional Self-Mastery

Psychologist Daniel Goleman has popularized the term *emotional intelligence* to describe the combination of interpersonal and intrapersonal skills that can enhance—or, by their absence, impair—human performance. Advanced emotional intelligence, he argues, conveys "an advantage in any domain of life, whether romance and intimate relationships or picking up the unspoken rules that govern success in organizational politics" (Goleman, 1997, p. 36).

As we stress later in this chapter in the section on multiple intelligences, there are many kinds of "smart" and many paths to achievement; students who succeed (or fail) in schoolwork will not necessarily succeed (or fail) in life. We have seen many professionals who can barely solve an algebra equation or write a coherent thesis paragraph, but who nevertheless excel in life by virtue of other extraordinary skills including high emotional intelligence.

Goleman defines emotional intelligence as two complementary skill sets: *relationship management* and *emotional self-mastery*. Relationship management is discussed in the previous section and in chapter 6. Among schools that teach students emotional self-mastery, many emphasize

- *identifying and managing feelings*: the capacity to understand, communicate, and control one's own internal emotions

- *goal setting*: the ability to set appropriate "stretch" goals—those that are achievable but not too easy to meet, thereby requiring effort and growth
- *persistence*: the commitment to sustained effort, even amid setbacks
- *impulse control*: the willingness to invest time and effort in projects likely to yield future returns, rather than squandering resources for immediate gratification
- *positive thinking*: maintenance of high self-expectations and belief in the possibility of success, especially when failure seems likely
- *stress management*: presence of perspective to reduce stress at its source, and practice of physical relaxation and other stress-release techniques

Note that we do not expect all teachers, particularly new teachers, to apply this learning systematically in the classroom. Many schools have counseling resources designed to assist students who have severe deficits in the skills identified here. However, understanding these underpinnings of success and engaging students selectively at key opportunities can make your class more productive and satisfying for everyone involved. Here we examine each of the above skillsets in a bit more detail.

Identifying and Managing Feelings

Emotionally competent people can

- accurately identify what they're feeling
- express feelings in a productive way in the appropriate setting
- avoid being swamped by negative emotions (e.g., anger, worry, sadness)
- channel negative feelings to keep them from erupting into negative actions

The relevance of this in the classroom is to watch for emotions that can spiral out of control. As mentioned previously, watch for three emotions in particular that tend to transmute into more dangerous cousins:

$$anger \rightarrow rage$$
$$sadness \rightarrow depression$$
$$worry \rightarrow anxiety$$

Extreme emotions are often difficult to control because they can literally be intoxicating. In certain episodes of fury, terror, or sorrow the human brain can shut down its rational side and switch into an emergency mode in which emotions assume control and make quick decisions—a kind of autopilot driven by instinct, with a simple goal: self-preservation. The fight-or-flight response is a good example of this.

Goleman (1997) calls these events *emotional hijackings*. Are they manageable? Absolutely. Although, as Goleman points out, "we very often have little or no control over *when* we are swept by emotion, nor over *what* emotion it will be, . . . we can have some say in *how long* an emotion will last" (p. 57). Teach students to watch for early signs of its physical signature—an intense burst of adrenaline-fueled energy, followed eventually by exhaustion. Plotted on a graph, this peak-valley pattern looks similar to the climax and resolution cycle of any good drama.

We can also control *how we act* when under the influence of anger. See chapter 6, "Classroom Management II," for specific recommendations on keeping these emotions in check.

The Importance of Goal Setting

As we stress repeatedly in this book, a fundamental purpose of education is to teach students to survive without the teacher. Setting and meeting goals is a crucial life skill that you can help students improve. As with physical fitness training, appropriate goals are usually *stretch goals*, which share several characteristics:

- They are not immediately within the student's grasp, thereby requiring effort to reach.
- The student perceives them as important.

- The student perceives them as achievable (although the precise path to reaching the goal may not be clear, the student should believe that, with proper support and exertion, she can develop the skills to achieve it).

How can you determine whether a goal is set at the wrong level? If a student succeeds the first time at everything she tries, she probably needs a bigger challenge. If, on the other hand, the student repeatedly fails to achieve a particular goal, she may need coaching to take a more creative approach. Or the student may need a few clues, extra practice, or other assistance to help reach the goal. As a last resort, the task may need to be simplified until the student masters the underlying skills needed to meet the original task.

No Success Without Persistence

"Success," Winston Churchill wryly observed, "is the ability to go from one failure to another with no loss of enthusiasm." University of Pennsylvania psychologist Martin Seligman elaborated on this concept: "It is the combination of reasonable talent and the ability to keep going in the face of defeat that leads to success. . . . [F]or a given level of intelligence, your actual achievement is a function not just of talent, but also of the capacity to stand defeat" (cited in Goleman, 1997, pp. 88–89).

Stories abound of accomplished scientists, entrepreneurs, artists, and others who achieved success only after many failures. Consider the game of baseball, in which a player with a .333 batting average—i.e., one who gets a hit in one third of his times at bat—is considered highly successful. Our philosophy is, if you don't fail a few times, you're not aiming high enough.

How can you keep students motivated to keep trying something they've failed at many times? First, keep your message positive. Every great teacher is part motivational coach, skillfully leveraging energy and language to lift students up and draw out high performance. And instead of lingering on the difficulty of the task or using terms like "failure" or "lose," phrase things in terms of progress made, learnings generated, and positive expectations.

Consider how you would feel inside receiving the two types of feedback below:

1. "Don't worry that you failed. It's a tough task, and that's why a lot of people don't succeed. You fell down because you didn't do X, Y, and Z. If you go back and practice some more, maybe you'll do better on the next assignment."
2. "Wow. Looks like you almost did it that time. How close do you think you got? You're about X% of the way there, and with what you learned today, I'm confident you'll do better next time. What do you think? What skills do you want to improve this week?"

Second, remember that the bigger the goals, the easier it can be to get overwhelmed by the detail and complexity of their execution. Remind students of the Chinese saying, "A journey of a thousand miles begins with a single step." Break large projects into smaller, manageable chunks.

Third, apply the same principle you'd use to plan a physical training regimen. Array the challenges to allow students to ease into the project and ratchet up the difficulty over time, as described previously and in our discussion of Bloom's taxonomy in chapter 4, "Communication Essentials."

Fourth, give students tangible reinforcement of both where they're going and the progress they're making by encouraging them to write down their goals and chart their progress. If students balk at this, inform them that star athletes often motivate themselves by keeping journals of how much weight they've lifted or how far they've run. Student portfolios formalize this process. Portfolios are discussed in chapter 3, "Preparing for the First Week of School" and on our website (www.classroomadvisor.com).

Lastly, help students keep the big payoff in sight. Invite them to envision their long-term success in detail. Encourage them to build small steps toward their goals into their daily rituals. Many people stay motivated with the help of a visual reminder: They post a photo of what they want to buy with their savings, the body they want to have after their workouts, or the place they want to go on vacation.

Developing Impulse Control

In the 1960s and 1970s, psychology professor Walter Mischel performed a famous longitudinal study that measured subjects' ability to defer gratification when they were in preschool, and followed up on these same individuals' academic progress more than a decade later.

Mischel's "marshmallow test" worked like this (Mischel, Shoda, & Rodriguez, 1989; "The Marshmallow Test," n.d.): Researchers put a marshmallow in front of each child and explained that the child could either have the one marshmallow at that moment or, if the child could wait a few minutes, he or she could have two marshmallows. Some children grabbed the marshmallow immediately. These more impulsive children were later determined to be

- more often seen by others as stubborn and overreactive
- more prone to jealousy and envy
- more easily upset by frustrating situations
- more troubled with low self-esteem and images of themselves as "bad"

The children who were able to defer gratification and thereby reap bigger rewards were later determined to be

- more socially competent
- more personally effective and self-assertive
- more able to cope with frustration
- more trustworthy and dependable
- more academically successful

Although the ability to control one's impulses and defer gratification may be partly related to brain wiring and chemistry, every student can improve through practice. How can you help?

First, *clearly explain the benefits of deferring gratification.* Repeat as necessary. One example that resonates with many secondary students is saving money for a large purchase (a vehicle, a large trip, college, etc.). Emphasize the magic of compound interest. Show visually the difference between "what you can have now" and "what you could have later." Bring in news stories or guest speakers to testify to the rewards of waiting, despite the inconvenience.

Second, *clearly demonstrate the potential costs of instant gratification.* The world abounds with cases in which the easy route is not necessarily the best route. An extreme example that resonates with many students: Ask about someone they know who barely finished school or dropped out because he could not see it through to completion. In our experience, many such souls end up in low-paying, dead-end jobs or get sucked regularly into get-rich-quick schemes. Others suffer a series of unhappy relationships and/or succumb to a draining compulsion or addiction to drugs, alcohol, gambling, sex, or some form of electronic couch-potatodom.

Third, *teach tactics to help students keep their destructive impulses under control.* These might include the following, each proven successful in the right circumstances:

- Remove the temptation from view. Some of the preschoolers in Mischel's study did this by covering their eyes; successful dieters do it by keeping fattening foods out of the house.
- Engage in a pleasant distraction until negative urges pass. Many of Mischel's preschoolers passed the time during their wait by resting, talking or singing to themselves, and making up simple games. Some video game addicts substitute simple, short games for longer ones, giving them a smaller and less pleasurable buzz that is easier to stop. Similarly, many smokers wean themselves off cigarettes step-by-step, using nicotine gum or patches as temporary crutches to take the edge off their urges until they can control them.
- Take up a healthy habit. Write. Paint. Dance. Play guitar. Join a sports team. Pursue any hobby that keeps you in a state of *flow*—where you're so involved that you lose track of time, and have a product that makes you proud at the end of your hours of practice.

- Keep the big payback in sight, and break large projects into smaller, more manageable tasks, as described above under "No Success Without Persistence."

Harnessing Positive Thinking

Optimistic thinking has numerous cognitive and physical benefits:

- lower anxiety
- potentially enhanced healing, at least as suggested by abundant anecdotal evidence
- enhanced creativity and problem solving ability, possibly due to diminished fear of failure (compared to less optimistic thinkers) and thereby increased willingness to be flexible and think in complex ways
- high achievement, due to high self-expectations and willingness to work to achieve what they perceive to be attainable (less optimistic thinkers tend to ascribe failure to some unchanging personal flaw, and are therefore more likely to give up when facing setbacks or long timelines) (Goleman, 1997, pp. 85, 88)

How can you help students become more optimistic? For a start, help them taste success, as discussed in chapter 1, "Cultivating a Classroom Culture." Remember that more confident students tend to be more successful than others (partly because they tend to be clearer-headed and less deterred by failure) and that the inverse is also true: more successful students tend to be more confident and more positive about their future prospects. From this, it follows that helping students succeed—even at something simple and small—can create the seed from which confidence, a positive attitude, and greater achievement grow.

Martin Seligman also offers insight. First, optimists understand that although they cannot always determine what happens in life, they can determine how they react, and if they are conscious of the emotions they're feeling, they can have some influence over these emotions. This is much like the techniques we recommend for coping with academic anxiety (earlier in this chapter), and for stopping the train of anger (see chapter 6, "Classroom Management II").

"When adversity strikes," Seligman believes, "how you think and what you believe determine how you feel and what you do. . . . When pessimistic people run into obstacles in the workplace, in relationships, or in sports, they give up. When optimistic people encounter obstacles, they try harder. They go the extra mile." And optimism in difficult situations, Seligman observes, often shapes careers. "The people who know how to overcome adversity are the ones who rise to the top of the organization" (Row, n.d.).

Stress Management

In addition to the various tactics offered earlier in this chapter, here are some stress management tips for you and your students (Mayo Clinic, n.d.).

Prevent Stress

First, if there is an activity you hate and you can get through life without it, do so. If a particular colleague or acquaintance causes you stress every time you meet, try avoiding his presence as much as practical and see how that feels. Life's full enough of necessary burdens; why pile on unnecessary ones?

Second, stay organized. This takes a lot of energy, but a great deal of stress originates from this central reality of life: Although many resources are scarce, *time* is the one resource that, once spent, can never be recovered. The less of it you waste, the more you'll accomplish, and the less stress you'll suffer from the weight of unfinished tasks and unfulfilled potential.

Third, learn to prioritize. Consider carefully what's really important, put first things first, and decide which activities are simply not important enough to take on at all. Let someone else do them, or let them go undone. If your world doesn't unravel, maybe they weren't important in the first place.

Fourth, don't take on other people's stress unnecessarily. Practice saying no as often as necessary until your list of commitments is manageable, resolve not to feel guilty about it (some people, refreshingly, explain that they just "don't do guilt") and learn how liberating it feels.

Fifth, stop being a perfectionist. Do you really need that classroom display (or newsletter, or bookshelf, or whatever) to be perfect? If 80% accuracy is fine, let the students do it. If it really doesn't need to be done, let it go.

When Facing Stressful People, Assert Yourself

If someone's behavior bothers you and you must interact with that person, don't try to ignore the problem and hope it will disappear. Submerging feelings is like squeezing a balloon—suppressed emotions usually emerge somewhere; hidden aggression or resentment is, by definition, the root of much passive-aggressive behavior. Make your feelings known—respectfully, honestly, and in private. Don't accuse, use a hostile tone, or start a public confrontation.

Also be aware that certain aspects of your own behavior might be threatening, demeaning, annoying, or otherwise irritating to others; asking about this possibility up front can open a dialogue that may turn a negative relationship around.

Maintain Perspective

When everything seems to be going wrong, stop. Breathe. Take 15 minutes to list as thoroughly as you can everything that's going right. Do you have your health? Do you have people in your life that you love? Do you have a roof over your head? Do you have enough to eat? Do you have reasonable control over your destiny? Do you have a job that you generally enjoy? List all the things, big and small, that you like about your life and your situation.

When you're finished writing, if your *negatives* list is longer than your *positives* list, consider making some serious adjustments to your life. Otherwise, adjust your attitude. To avoid a relapse into self-pity, post your positives list where you can see it when feelings of frustration return. Also try starting a "happy news" file where you can store e-mails, cards, photos, and other mementos that remind you how good life can sometimes be.

Once you realize how bad you *don't* have it, make a simple resolution. It may sound naive or simplistic, but we have had great success with it. The resolution is this: Smile more. If smiling does not come naturally to you or you're just *way* too stressed out to think about it, post above your desk a small mirror next to something that always makes you smile. Or set your computer to autoplay a song you love at particular intervals. Or call a friend to talk, even for just a few minutes—whatever it takes.

Smiling will make you feel better (we promise)—if not because of the positive reactions it evokes in others, then because the longer you keep it up, the sooner someone will ask you why you're smiling and you'll have to think up a good reason.

Doing unrequested, unexpected, unrequited good deeds for others has a similar effect. As an easy start, find a student who probably hasn't heard kind words for a while and offer a sincere compliment. You'll be surprised how quickly it will take your mind off yourself and make you feel better. You might even make a new ally.

Accept Stress That Is Unavoidable, and Move On

When you feel frustrated, don't berate yourself or let negative thoughts overwhelm you. Think back on the last success you enjoyed, and remember the talents that pulled you through. Resolve to learn from your mistakes and to take responsibility in the future for avoiding additional mistakes. Remember: When you lose, don't lose the lesson.

And avoid dwelling on how others have wronged you. Resentment, the saying goes, is like swallowing poison and waiting for the other person to die. If someone crosses you, feel free to get angry but resolve to get over it. This is often easier said than done, but is well worth the trouble to master—if not for the maturity it demonstrates, then for the energy it saves.

When all else fails, remember that "this, too, shall pass." Everything does.

THE INTELLECTUAL DIMENSION

At the top of Maslow's hierarchy of needs sits *self-actualization*, or the reaching of one's fullest potential. This need is felt, to a greater or lesser degree, by nearly everyone. It often includes the drive to be creative and innovative, to solve problems, to understand the world and one's place in it, to discover (or create) purpose in life, and to see how things interconnect. For many, it involves development of a moral and/or spiritual belief system, discussed in the section following this one.

As Joseph Campbell observes, happiness (and often success) flows to those who follow their bliss. The best way to reach your fullest potential, this thinking goes, is to determine what you love and what matters to you, forget your fears and excuses, and dive in.

To reach this goal students need support, and in our view there is no more natural place for this than the classroom. Education professor Howard Gardner concurs: "We should spend less time ranking children and more time helping them to identify their natural competencies and gifts, and cultivate those. There are hundreds . . . of ways to succeed, and many, many different abilities that will help you get there" (cited in Goleman, 1997, p. 37).

It appears that global trends—including the ever-increasing specialization of economies and the ever-broader dispersion of the tools of knowledge, innovation, and communication—are reinforcing this reality. From this vantage point, the professional duty of teachers includes helping each student develop her full potential by finding a place in the economy (and in life) where she fits best. This section recommends ways to begin thinking about that process.

Many Kinds of Smart: What Every Teacher Should Know About Multiple Intelligences

How do you define intelligence? Here's a quick quiz:

1. Who's the smartest person on the list below?
   a. a computer software tycoon

    b. a basketball player

    c. an architect

    d. a nurse

2. Complete this sentence: Intelligence is the ability to . . .

    a. solve math problems faster than anyone else

    b. spell complex words aloud in front of peers

    c. compose and support a coherent thesis in a timed exam

    d. successfully navigate the Amazon River

Answers: All of the above, or none of the above, depending on the situation. Is it possible that a star football player might fall apart if asked to teach a classroom full of kindergarteners? Would a celebrated attorney necessarily be your first choice to perform your mother's appendectomy? How comfortable would a stranded mountaineer be with the Dalai Lama piloting the rescue helicopter?

"Intelligence" is commonly imagined as a single, universal, immutable trait that people either possess or lack in varying degrees. Individuals, this conventional wisdom goes, are born either smart or stupid and each person's natural gifts or deficits in intelligence largely determine her success in life.

We reject this conception for two reasons. First, as stressed previously, we recommend that all teachers embrace the mantra "You are smart. You can get smarter." Refer to Figure 1.1 as a reminder that getting smarter—not unlike getting physically stronger—is largely a function of effort exerted toward that end. Those committed to learning can improve their chances of success in life; this is a fundamental premise of education.

Second, an increasing volume of psychological research is revealing that the characterization of intelligence as a single, monolithic trait is too simplistic. Among education researchers the once-popular concept of IQ has largely been displaced by the idea of *multiple intelligences*—distinct categories of abilities that enable people to understand and solve various life problems. By this definition, intelligence is not uniform, absolute, and unchanging; rather, it is multifaceted, contextual, and continually evolving.

DON'T EXPECT A DUCK TO CLIMB A TREE

I once knew a wise man—a teacher of very young children. Under his supervision, children blossomed. Children who couldn't do math could do math. Youngsters who couldn't play sports could play sports. He was one of those magical people who show you what you can do that you never thought you could do. He used to say that we would never ask a duck to climb a tree—the duck's not equipped to do that with webbed feet. But the duck swims superbly.

This man—this immensely gifted teacher—knew that it was only necessary to help each child to discover the one thing that he or she could do well. And with that as a pivot, with that to give them confidence and a feeling of self-worth, they could do other things—things they never thought they could do. Under his tutelage, children grew in all directions and became happy, busy, eager contributing human beings. (Jameson, 1989, pp. 41–42)

Here, we explore two theoretical models that illuminate the concept of multiple intelligences: Yale psychologist Robert Sternberg's triarchic theory of intelligence, and Harvard professor Howard Gardner's classic theory of multiple intelligences.

Sternberg's triarchic theory argues that every person possesses varying combinations of three types of intelligence: *analytical, creative,* and *practical* (see Table 2.2). Since each confers particular benefits and drawbacks depending on the context, succeeding in life (as opposed to succeeding merely in school) depends not on mastering any single, predetermined type of intelligence, but rather on master-

Table 2.2.   The Three Types of Intelligences

Type	Learns by	Excels At
Analytical mind	Theorizing, analyzing	Explaining, comparing, evaluating
Creative mind	Imagining, experimenting	Envisioning, designing alternatives
Practical mind	Applying theories to real life	Choosing tools, solving problems

Note: Adapted from Sternberg (1994, p. 50).

ing at least one of them and "matching one's pattern of abilities to the demands of a given job" (Sternberg & Spear-Swerling, 1996, p. 21).

To illustrate, Sternberg describes three hypothetical students. The first, blessed with extraordinary analytical intelligence, "did wonderfully on tests and assignments, and was considered brilliant by virtually everyone. For years, she garnered praise—and top grades—by memorizing and analyzing the ideas of others. But that approach didn't work when she had to come up with ideas of her own."

The second student, more creative in nature, managed lackluster academic performance and experienced "myriad rejections and disappointments over the years," but persisted and ultimately "proved to be a veritable fountain of creative ideas. She succeeded despite the way the tests and the schools had assessed her."

The third student earned unimpressive grades in school, "yet when it came to getting, and doing, a job, . . . she had the practical skills that enabled her to figure out what she needed to do to succeed." This student's practical intelligence allowed her to position herself professionally in a way that emphasized her strengths and neutralized her weaknesses (Sternberg, 1989, p. 63).

Note that these three hypothetical students are caricatures; we do not mean to imply that individuals cannot be simultaneously analytical, creative, *and* practical. Indeed, most people share these abilities to some degree, and most students can be taught to improve in all of these dimensions. The main point is that in many students, one proclivity will dominate. And the limited time you spend with each student necessitates wise decisions about what kind of intellectual growth each should pursue.

Analytical intelligence. Analytical thinking is frequently demanded in school; academic environments commonly require such skills as examining, dissecting, comparing, contrasting, explaining, and evaluating. Those who excel at this type of thinking often enjoy school because they fit well into the system, are liked by their teachers, and tend to get good grades and high test scores.

Though typically skilled at following directions, memorizing facts, and picking apart others' ideas, analytical thinkers often generate relatively few ideas of their own and sometimes have trouble applying their knowledge in unfamiliar contexts (Sternberg & Spear-Swerling, 1996, pp. 7–8).

Creative intelligence. Creativity is commonly defined as the ability to generate new ideas, to combine familiar ideas in novel ways, and to find connections where none were evident before. It is often measured in terms of *fluency*—that is, the generation of multiple possibilities—and *flexibility* of thought—that is, the generation of unusual ideas/relationships.

Sternberg and Spear-Swerling (1996) observe that creative thinkers tend to be self-directed "ideas" people who excel at seeing the big picture and imagining alternate possibilities. They naturally excel at creative endeavors but are not infrequently poor to mediocre academic performers who find school confining and don't like to follow directions. Sometimes they end up dropping out of school or attending alternative schools (pp. ix, 7).

Most schools we have visited measure and promote this skill less than they do the others, but you can engage all students' creative intelligence by asking them to create a work of art (in any medium—written, oral, musical, physical, visual) or to conduct an experiment, design a solution to a problem, or imagine alternative "what if" scenarios. Let students know you will judge this kind of work more on content and effort than on "creativity," since there's no objective way to measure that anyway.

Practical intelligence. Practical thinking generally involves applying knowledge and implementing solutions. Students whose practical intelligence eclipses their academic or creative sides often have middling-to-low grades and test scores and frequently fit poorly into school, where the artificiality and abstractness of the setting tends to confuse and bore them.

Such students typically do best in real-world settings, or settings that approximate the real world in a significant way, such as any kind of shop or laboratory setting (auto shop, machine shop, home economics room, computer lab, chemistry lab, etc.). To engage students' practical intelligence in the regular classroom, use models and simulations, or ask them to demonstrate in some way how to apply given knowledge in the real world (Sternberg & Spear-Swerling, 1996, pp. ix, 7, 68).

Overview of Multiple Intelligences Identified by Howard Gardner

Howard Gardner's multiple intelligences (MI) model is similar in spirit to Sternberg's, but more granular in detail. His original framework included seven aptitudes; more recent iterations highlight nine (see Table 2.3). The critical factor for our purposes is not the precise number of intelligences or the way they're broken down in any particular model, but the overarching concept that people can be smart in any number of ways, each valuable in the right milieu.

As even a cursory glance at the list in Table 2.3 reveals, most schools heavily emphasize only a few of these skill areas—typically verbal-linguistic, logical-mathematical, and one or two others. Although debate persists over which of these competencies are valid subjects for study in school, Table 2.4 offers a glimpse of the real-world, vocational applicability of the various aptitudes Gardner (1993) has identified.

Table 2.3. Multiple Intelligences

Type of Intelligence	Common Tasks Requiring this Intelligence
Verbal-linguistic	Reading, writing, listening, speaking
Logical-mathematical	Calculating, forming rational arguments, finding patterns
Visual-spatial	Drawing diagrams, creating art, arranging objects in space
Bodily-kinesthetic	Coordinating physical movement, as in athletics or dance
Musical-rhythmic	Creating, playing, and recognizing music, rhythm, and poetry
Naturalist	Understanding elements, features, and systems of nature
Interpersonal	Empathizing, communicating, and relating to others
Intrapersonal	Comprehending and coping with one's own drives and motives
Existential	Considering questions of life, death, morality, and purpose

Note: From "Howard Gardner's multiple intelligences theory" (n.d.).

Table 2.4. Multiple Intelligences and Occupations

Type of Intelligence	Some Occupations Rewarding this Intelligence
Verbal-linguistic	Teacher, attorney, politician, writer, salesperson
Logical-mathematical	Engineer, accountant, banker, attorney, business consultant
Visual-spatial	Architect, designer, visual artist, pilot, marksman
Bodily-kinesthetic	Athlete, dancer, surgeon, mechanic, typist, factory worker
Musical-rhythmic	Musician, singer, dancer, poet, speechwriter, public speaker
Naturalist	Farmer, doctor, biologist, botanist, meteorologist, chef
Interpersonal	Psychologist, teacher, salesperson, mediator, minister
Intrapersonal	These metaskills—self-understanding and finding a moral
Existential	center and purpose in life—underpin all the others.

Note: From "Howard Gardner's multiple intelligences theory" (n.d.).

The broader definition of *smart* embodied in MI theory can help low performers in particular excel. Students most at risk of failure in school—and most prone to create behavior problems in class—are often those whose greatest gifts lie outside the traditional, narrow, three Rs curriculum. They are the students who, in Gardner's words, "don't shine in the standardized tests, and who, therefore, tend to be written off as not having gifts of any kind" (Gardner, 1993, p. 11). By revealing hidden strengths in underappreciated students, an MI approach can help boost their confidence and therefore their performance across the board (Gardner & Walters, cited in Gardner, 1993, p. 15).

It is not only at-risk students who benefit from this more inclusive teaching approach; however, MI theory makes a compelling argument that recognizing and nurturing a spectrum of talents like teamwork, self-reflection, and visual, musical, and physical artistry benefits all youth.

BENEFITS OF TEACHING TO MULTIPLE INTELLIGENCES

Teaching to multiple intelligences

- makes learning more interesting for everyone
- improves students' strengths by improving various complementary abilities
- highlights alternate routes to success in life
- helps students become more well-rounded, productive, and satisfied adults

First, most students find learning more interesting when it moves beyond the essential but limited skills of reading, writing, and computation. Since most people possess to varying degrees all the intelligences Gardner identifies, a great way to excite students about learning is to incorporate into your classroom activities not only reading, writing, and calculation but also introspection, philosophizing, cooperative learning, music, movement, art, and nature. Teaching to students' multiple intelligences also allows reinforcement of important course material in different modalities. Our website (www.classroomadvisor.com) includes recommendations for MI resources.

Second, because of the interdependence among many of these abilities, failure to develop one can limit the potential of others. Someone who excels at introspection and understanding his moods, for example, may be lost without any skill or practice at developing a life philosophy. A student with excellent strength, agility, and coordination may make a lousy teammate in any sport if he lacks the interpersonal skills to understand others and collaborate with them. And the most brilliant scientist or mathematician could be severely hampered professionally if she lacks the verbal-linguistic skill to articulate her research to the world.

A third way MI-aware instruction benefits all students relates not directly to school, but to life after school. Everyone can benefit from developing numerous life skills; indeed, general education requirements in most high schools and colleges are built around the premise that a well-rounded individual is a happier, wiser, and more productive citizen.

Additionally, many fulfilling careers do not depend solely or even largely on verbal or mathematical ability, despite what narrowly focused college entrance exams suggest. As Gardner argues:

> The single most important contribution education can make to a child's development is to help him toward a field where his talents best suit him, where he will be satisfied and competent. We've completely lost sight of that.

Instead we subject everyone to an education where, if you succeed, you will be best suited to be a college professor. (cited in Goleman, 1997, p. 37)

Since most teachers (by definition) prize schooling, we often misjudge those who do not. Led astray by the accumulation of the simplistic assumptions and raw prejudices we call "conventional wisdom," we conclude that any student who is not thrilled by school must lack intelligence, discipline, or ambition.

In truth, however, formal education is not necessarily appropriate for everyone. Benjamin could bomb all his oral presentations in English but still become a stellar and self-sufficient musician. Although Quinisha might fail to turn in a single geometry homework assignment, she could nonetheless open a successful business after leaving school. Chris may eschew a four-year degree for vocational school, yet through this alternate channel find a career that is both fulfilling and lucrative. Keep in mind that failing to clear the academic hurdles of high school does not equate to failure in life.

THE MORAL-SPIRITUAL DIMENSION

Do your students ever spontaneously generate art? We don't mean strained attempts at painting or poetry churned out merely to satisfy class requirements, but rather artwork (in any form, of any quality) that flows naturally and unbidden from some unseen spring of inspiration—the kind of art students spend hours perfecting, because they view the process not as a task to be checked off a list, but a joyous act of creation.

In our experience, much adolescent artistry is driven by the yearning to *figure it all out*—an instinctive need to understand one's place and purpose in the world and develop a life philosophy. One of the most rewarding aspects of teaching is to help students achieve their full potential, and this is tied closely to what we call the moral-spiritual dimension of human consciousness.

Many students are naturally curious about moral questions, which often touch on issues of far greater interest to them than the content of whatever course you're teaching. And helping students engage ethical questions can potentially prove much more valuable in the long run than knowing the basics of history or chemistry or geometry—it can help them treat people fairly, make important decisions in nebulous circumstances, and develop a life philosophy.

Of course, many people's morality is guided by their particular spiritual tradition, while others lead happy, productive, and ethical lives without any overtly religious creed. The bottom line is that morality—including but not limited to morality rooted in religious beliefs—is an inevitable part of many valuable classroom discussions. Whatever your own belief system, don't let the complexity and political thorniness inherent to ethical questions scare you away from those that arise in your classroom; this would be a disservice to both your students and the society they will eventually lead.

Although some assume that ethical behavior is learned at home or perhaps in a church, temple, mosque, or other community setting, many children grow up with limited guidance in these matters. Students with single parents, or two working parents, or no parents, often model their ethics on representations they see in the mass media and their peer networks. The result: An ethical education that's spotty at best, and counterproductive at worst.

Instead of avoiding ethical questions that arise in the classroom, embrace natural opportunities to help students wrestle with such issues. Although challenging to teach, ethical thinking is central to the personal, familial, and political choices that strengthen communities and perpetuate civilizations. And your students may have few other safe, structured environments in which to engage great ethical questions in a sophisticated and thoughtful way.

To be sure, ethical subjects can be emotionally and politically charged. Most agree that moral education is critical, yet few agree on the ideal mix of family, community, and school influence in young people's moral development. Therefore take care how you address such issues. Teachers should not indoctrinate students or judge their evolving ethical standards, but rather expose students to alternate views and help them practice the critical thinking skills that will eventually allow them to make moral decisions on their own.

TEACHING MORALITY: WHAT THE LAW SAYS

Policies regarding the teaching of morality vary by jurisdiction, but most we have encountered include some variation of the following:

> Each teacher shall endeavor to impress upon the minds of the pupils the principles of morality, truth, justice, patriotism, and a true comprehension of the rights, duties, and dignity of [citizenship] including . . . the humane treatment of living creatures, to teach them to avoid idleness, profanity, and falsehood, and to instruct them in manners and morals and the principles of a free government. (California Department of Education, n.d.)

What about teaching religion? One veteran history teacher who has discussed aspects of the Bible, the Quran, the Sutras, and various other religious texts in his U.S. classroom for many years offers insight on this topic. Whenever these topics arose, one or two students—well aware of the principle of separation of church and state enshrined in the U.S. Constitution—inevitably inquired, "You're not supposed to talk about religion in a public school, are you?"

The teacher's (correct) answer was: "Teaching about religion differs vastly from teaching religion. Our discussions of religion focused on appreciating the history, symbolism, and values in these belief systems, and using them to understand the common roots and divergent behaviors of people in different cultures." As such, this teacher's lessons were entirely appropriate for a government-sponsored school setting. In fact, many explorations of citizenship, world history, art, or literature would be incomplete if the underlying moral and often explicitly religious beliefs were omitted.

The U.S. Supreme Court, in the case *Abington School District v. Schempp* (1963), clarified the advisability (and legality) of teaching about religion in U.S. public schools. Wrote the Court:

> It might well be said that one's education is not complete without a study of comparative religion or the history of religion and its relationship to the advancement of civilization. It certainly may be said that the Bible is worthy of study for its literary and historic qualities . . . [Therefore] study of the Bible or of religion, when presented objectively as part of a secular program of education, may . . . be effected consistently with the First Amendment.

In the same case, however, the Court also held that the U.S. Constitution requires "the Government [to] maintain strict neutrality, neither aiding nor opposing religion. . . . In the relationship between man and religion, the State is firmly committed to a position of neutrality" (FindLaw, n.d.).

Ethical Habits of Mind and Behavior to Encourage in the Classroom

We recommend that every student's education should reinforce the following principles of ethical conduct.

Tell the Truth

Honesty and integrity are basic prerequisites for groups of any size to function. This includes honoring promises, demonstrating loyalty, avoiding secrecy and misrepresentation (except in rare circumstances as described below under "Treat others with fairness and respect"), and generally behaving in a way that encourages mutual trust.

Seek the Truth

A fundamental premise of education is that knowledge is based on the pursuit of truth. Of course, in a world in which much is unknowable, reality must often be approximated. Ethical dilemmas frequently exist in precisely those spaces where there is no definitive, scientific truth. No matter how murky the situation, however, decision making can be improved through critical thinking—including the ability and willingness to uncover facts, weigh evidence, distinguish propaganda from fair-minded discourse, and recognize one's own biases.

It should be noted that recognition of the relativity of truth in certain situations does not imply that thinking in the classroom should be reduced to continual mental meandering in which every conclusion is second-guessed ad nauseam or all suppositions, no matter how absurd, are given equal weight in the discussion of ideas. Diversity of thought is a crucial element of education but, as educational administrator Dennis Gray points out, "the notion that tolerance requires us to affirm all ideas . . . [is] a terrible abuse" of the principle of free expression. "I certainly don't believe that all ideas or opinions are equally cogent, insightful, interesting, or wise, and I don't believe we do children any good by letting them think otherwise" (Gray, 1989, p. 22).

Treat Others With Fairness and Respect

As discussed in chapter 1, "Cultivating a Classroom Culture," respect is a key element of a productive classroom. Respect includes being polite, seeking peaceful resolutions to conflict, and upholding basic human rights such as security of person and property. True respect also extends to include empathy for others as well as appreciation—or at least tolerance—of their opinions and feelings.

To encourage respectful behavior in students, model it unfailingly in both your words and actions. We also encourage you to post the table of ethical behaviors (see chapter 1, under "Building a Culture of Mutual Respect"). Ironically, as mentioned above, respect can sometimes conflict with another rule of ethical conduct: honesty. Certain principles of etiquette make it occasionally acceptable to shade the truth or avoid situations where the truth is unnecessarily harsh, such as, "Yes, you're fat" or "I really don't like you." You will need to find a balance appropriate for your classroom.

Know Your Civic Rights and Responsibilities

As also touched upon in chapter 1, "Cultivating a Classroom Culture," students should expect to uphold certain responsibilities in class. These include the responsibility to consider the consequences of actions before undertaking them, the responsibility to respect and collaborate with classmates, the responsibility to comply with all reasonable requests from authority figures, and the responsibility to work hard on all assignments. Rights students should expect to enjoy include the right to be treated with respect, the right to have their voices heard, and the right to assistance with classwork, as needed.

Every student should also know what rights she and her fellow citizens enjoy under the law—for example, the basic rights in the U.S. Constitution that protect every adult citizen—and the frequent limits to those rights in a school setting. Additionally, every student should honor the responsibilities that accompany those rights—including the responsibility to pay taxes to fund public services, the responsibility to educate oneself about public affairs, the responsibility to learn to distinguish propaganda from reality, and the responsibility to vote and otherwise participate thoughtfully in civic life.

Additionally, to preserve and perpetuate a democracy, all citizens must understand that it is based on the rule of law rather than the arbitrary will of any individual or cabal. Laws are created to stabilize society and provide for the peaceful and fair resolution of disputes. Although legal frameworks vary, in the United States the basic tenets of the rule of law include the following:

- The Constitution is the highest law. Nothing may violate it.
- Everyone must obey the law. No one is exempt—including school personnel, the police, the military, and government leaders.
- The military is always subject to civilian control.
- Government is the only agency in society that may legitimately use (or in rare situations, delegate the power to use) physical force, and then only when following the rules of *due process*.
- Everyone should be treated equally under the law, with the same due process protections.

- The judiciary is independent of those who make and enforce the law, and can overrule their decisions if they violate the Constitution.
- If enough citizens agree that the law should be changed, they can change the law.

Here are a few other suggested strategies to promote students' moral development:

- Study leaders with strong moral credentials—for example, Nobel Peace Prize winners—with an eye toward understanding the challenges they faced, the alternate paths they could have chosen, and the reasons for their actions.
- Practice ethical thinking by pondering and discussing moral dilemmas (see an example and guidelines in the sidebar below).
- Encourage students to join an existing service organization in the community. If they have no ideas, our website (www.classroom advisor.com) offers suggestions.
- Build a service-learning program into your curriculum to encourage students to fulfill academic objectives through community service. We have seen service learning applied in conjunction with all subject areas, to great motivational and instructional effect. For most students, taking action in conjunction with learning makes the subject more concrete and relevant. Our website (www.majorandmajor.com) links to effective service-learning programs.

MORAL DILEMMAS

A moral dilemma is a scenario that centers on questions of ethics, which of course have no right or wrong answers, but which challenge students to consider how they would respond if they faced similar circumstances. Moral dilemmas abound in human history and in good literature. A very simple sample dilemma is included here. Following it, we list tips and a suggested worksheet to help students process it.

SAMPLE MORAL DILEMMA: LYDIA'S DILEMMA

"Bryan, would you like to read next, please?"

"No, Ms. J. I don't want to."

"Bryan? Everyone else has read. We'll wait."

As the teacher stood staring silently at him, Bryan clutched his arms tightly in front of him and tucked his chin into his chest. He said nothing and looked like he wanted to disappear.

Moments passed. Monica sighed loudly. Darius stared out the window.

"Bryan?" Ms. J. prodded gently. "Just one paragraph. That's not so much."

"I told you I don't want to."

The standoff continued, until other students stirred in their seats and audible grumbling began to creep up from the rear of the classroom.

Then Ariel broke the silence. "Come on, Ms. J. He's not going to read. He doesn't know how."

"Shut up!" Bryan's face reddened.

"Go ahead, then," said Ariel.

"Ariel," Ms. J. admonished, "let's not pass judgments. I'm sure if you were in Bryan's shoes you wouldn't like it if—"

"It's true, Ms. J. He can't read," chimed in Ariel's friend Brenda. "Don't even bother. He's only going to get locked up, anyway."

"Yeah," Peter added. "You don't need to know how to read in prison. You just need to know how to fight. And he's already got an A in that."

The class broke into laughter at this. Even the teacher briefly wanted to smile.

It was true that Bryan was frequently in trouble at school. And rumors said he and his buddies spent most of their weekends stealing cars and breaking into houses.

Still, Lydia felt bad. She didn't know Bryan that well, but they were lab partners in science class and he didn't seem like a bad guy. In fact, if he hadn't known how to fix all the equipment in that class, they probably wouldn't have finished any of their assignments on time, and she might be failing science.

Lydia wanted to speak up for Bryan. She wanted to tell everyone the good things she knew about him, but it didn't seem like the right time . . . and Ariel and Brenda and Peter were so popular . . . and what they said was true, at least partly . . . and what if she embarrassed Bryan more by making a bigger deal out of it? . . . and what if she embarrassed herself by jumping into the conversation? After all, Lydia really wasn't the type to start an argument. So in the end, despite her feelings, Lydia kept her mouth shut.

Eventually, the teacher called on someone else to finish the reading, and Lydia looked over at Bryan from time to time and noticed that he kept his head down and looked mad . . . or maybe sad . . . for the rest of the period. When the bell rang, he slipped quietly out of the class and walked down the hall alone.

Moral Dilemma Response Guidelines

Imagine Lydia is your friend, who has approached you and told you she has just been through the situation you read about and didn't know what to do. Think of similar situations you may have experienced. Were you ever the target of public humiliation? Were you ever the perpetrator? Were you ever "just" a bystander? What feelings did you have? Looking back, what responsibility do you think you bore? Now, write down your advice for Lydia. Start by completing the statements below, and add as many of your own ideas as you like.

Dear Lydia,

After much thought, I would say that the best thing you can do right now is . . .
This is important because . . .
This may be difficult because . . .
You can make it easier, though, by . . .
What I think you definitely should not do is . . .
Finally, if something like this happens in class again, I would suggest that you . . .

Your friend, . . .

Tips for Using Moral Dilemmas

Ask All Students to Write Their Responses Silently Before Discussion

Writing their responses gives all students a chance to devote concentrated thought to the issues at hand. This helps prevent students from spouting nonsensical responses off the top of their heads. It also allows everyone to respond without having to make the response public if they prefer to keep it private. We also recommend asking students to take time afterward to write whether and how their opinions were changed by the discussion.

Leave Plenty of Time for Processing

Processing could include discussion, debate, journaling, related readings, or watching relevant videos or guest speakers if an issue is particularly volatile and/or misunderstood. One high school teacher suspended her regular curriculum for a week to focus intensively on teaching tolerance when a spontaneous student discussion revealed deep-seated animosity toward a particular minority group. It was a classic *teachable moment*: "They kept making derogatory comments about 'faggots' and I told them we were going to have to address the issue because I didn't think I could be in class with a bunch of bigots. They said they weren't bigots—most of them were [ethnic] minorities—

but then I explained what bigotry is and they said, 'But what's wrong with that? Everybody says it'" (K. Wolfe, personal communication).

Discuss Students' Responses

Much of the value, and fun, of moral dilemmas lies in the discussions they spark. Invite students to share their responses to the dilemmas, along with the reasoning behind these—individually or by some kind of voting mechanism like a show of hands. Our favorite technique is to draw a line across the classroom representing a spectrum of belief (e.g., from "strongly agree" to "strongly disagree") and ask students to stand at the spot on the spectrum that best represents their opinion about the question at hand. This encourages them to consider the question carefully, for they must literally stand up for their beliefs. Moving around the classroom also diffuses lethargy.

Often, a few students will find themselves outvoted by their peers. This does not mean students should change their positions; rather, it might be a sign that they had not considered all available evidence when making their original choices.

Alternately, if most students come to the same conclusion, you can change the dilemma slightly to encourage a greater diversity of opinion. Ask "what if" questions that raise the cost of following the preferred course of action, or add factors that change the equation for at least some students. This could include altering the setting, introducing extenuating circumstances, or making a particular character more or less sympathetic to certain students—for example, by changing the character's race, gender, personal history, attitude, or behavior.

Help Students Recognize Contradictions and Unintended Consequences

When choosing a course of action, students often fail to consider all the ramifications of their choices. Use Socratic questioning (described in chapter 4, "Communication Essentials") or another method to help students understand unintended consequences of their decisions—including any harmful outcomes their chosen actions would create. This can help students recognize how behavior rooted in fear, convenience, or other self-centered motivations can contradict stated ideals of justice, fairness, tolerance, and so forth.

Don't Take Obnoxious Opinions Personally

Moral dilemmas are powerful tools, but keep in mind that students may sometimes say shocking things. We have personally been caught off guard by profoundly disturbing expressions of violence and intolerance ("I'd end discrimination by killing all the people I don't like and selling off their babies"—that sort of thing). If this happens to you, it's probably no reflection on you and does not necessarily signal the imminent decline of civilization.

Sometimes students will say outrageous things simply for the shock value. Don't get upset; this would play right into their hands. Instead, keep in mind that adolescents are no strangers to posturing and that much of their behavior in the classroom will be targeted not to please you or fulfill the course requirements, but to impress their eternal audience: their peers. Hence, they often give quite different responses in public than they would individually.

Other times, being adults-in-development, students will throw out half-baked ideas that sound dangerously definitive but are actually small steps in a long struggle to form an intelligent worldview. Still other times, their statements will reveal a limited understanding of history or the real-world ramifications of the implementation of their ideas. Such situations mark clear opportunities for development; use them to determine where to focus your teaching energy.

Instead of despairing when a student says something outrageously offensive, use humor to defuse the most absurd statements and capitalize on such *teachable moments* to drive home the values of respect, fairness, and responsibility. Refer as necessary to the section "Ethical Behaviors to Promote in Students" from chapter 1.

Be aware also that much of what students say in such situations is what they have learned at home. In fact, they may often be quoting parents or other relatives. Thus if you work to modify their perceptions, you will be moving them farther from the family hearth. That's a touchy process. Make certain that nothing you say could be taken home and cited as an insult or challenge to parents or their dignity.

CONNECTING WITH STUDENTS

Once you've begun to understand students in their multiple dimensions—including the various internal drives and external pressures that shape their attitudes and behaviors—you can move proactively to bridge the inevitable cultural chasm between you and them.

Strategy 1: Demonstrating Interest in Their "Real Lives"

When invited to describe a favorite teacher, most students we surveyed recalled not how brilliant a scholar or public speaker the teacher was—though the best typically score well in at least one of these categories—but how the teacher listened, offered advice, enjoyed her job (including the part about spending most of the day with students), or generally cared about students not just as students, but also as individuals. "Ms. W. keeps me laughing." "I always know Mr. C. cares about me." "Ms. B. is always willing to listen, even when it's not about school." These are the characteristics students remember, and these are the qualities that differentiate competent teachers from stellar ones.

Giving your students an optional personal interest survey at the start of the year is a great way to learn more about them. The process takes just 15–20 minutes and sends a clear signal that you understand that students have personal lives and that you care about them as more than just academic beings. Our website (www.classroom advisor.com) provides a model survey we have used for this purpose.

Attending student events is one powerful way to show your students you care about them as people, not just as students—a critical distinction to them, particularly those who invest far more in the extracurricular than the academic component of school. Your visible presence will also concretize for parents not only your identity but also your professionalism and your commitment to their children, which will give you indispensable leverage in the event of future conflicts.

At this point you may be thinking, "That sounds great, but where am I going to get that kind of time?" This is a valid point, especially if you're a first-year teacher. Let's say you just finished a long day in which two lessons succeeded, three blew up in your face, lunch was cold and nasty, and students needing extra help sucked up your entire prep period. You're exhausted. As 5 P.M. rolls around, you desperately want to go home and start to unwind. However, the school is putting on a production of *Arsenic and Old Lace* at 7 P.M. and you sort of vaguely committed yourself to attend, but you suspect it's going to be dreadful and would much prefer to be home, doing anything else. What will you do?

Consider the pros and cons. If you go to the school play, you

- will learn more about students by observing them in a non-classroom environment
- will earn respect from students and parents by demonstrating interest in students
- will impress administrators and colleagues by your dedication
- could stay at school and catch up on work until the play starts
- might actually enjoy yourself, because watching kids meet challenges and have fun can be heartwarming

The cons are that you

- will spend several more hours than necessary at school
- will give up a potentially productive or relaxing evening at home or elsewhere
- will possibly be subjected to a really bad play

From here on, it's your call. Of course you won't go to every extracurricular event all year, but set a reasonable target for yourself—perhaps one or two student activities per month. Even if your contract already obligates you to coach the track team or coordinate the junior prom, try to attend other events to meet a variety of students and parents.

Strategy 2: Appreciating Youth Culture

Another crucial question: How can teachers win over youth whose attitudes toward adult authority range from disinterest to defiance?

Our answer: Familiarity with teen culture is the closest thing we've found to a magic spellbook to lower student resistance (that, and a sense of humor, which we find useful in nearly every situation).

It isn't necessary to embrace teen culture, but at least try to understand it because it colors so much of how your students think. Consider it anthropological field research. Every glimpse you get of how adolescents view the world will help you understand their tastes, values, and generally bizarre behavior.

To brush up on youth culture—which we assure you has changed since you were a teen, no matter how young you are or act—try the following:

- Go to a movie theater on a weekend evening to join an adolescent audience for the latest teen comedy, romance, or adventure movie. Consider it a cheap safari to see teens in their natural habitat. Repeat at least a few times each year.
- Rent or borrow the latest hot video game console and waste a few hours playing the most popular video game you can find. Trust us, this will give you plenty to talk about with your students—particularly the boys—in moments of downtime.
- Turn on MTV or another teen-oriented channel at home and leave it on in the background until your ears bleed.
- Ask students about their favorite radio stations. Preset your car radio to one of those stations and listen to it occasionally.
- Ask students what Internet sites they hang out on. No, what sites they *really* hang out on. Social networking websites and any site featuring anything grotesque are good bets. Spend an hour perusing these; you may be shocked and repulsed, but you will certainly be enlightened.
- Pick up a magazine targeted at—or just frequently read by—your students. This might be *Cosmopolitan, Vibe, Latina, Car and Driver, Gaming World*—whatever's on store shelves in your students' neighborhood. This will give you a feel for the language and imagery that connect with teens, and clue you into many issues they face. Teen magazine editors and marketers spend millions trying to get inside children's minds and turn them into rabid

consumers. As a consequence, they know their stuff. Why not piggyback on their well-funded efforts and use some of their communication techniques to enhance your mission?

• Spend a few hours just absorbing the sights and sounds at the most popular mall, basketball court, beach, or skate park in your students' neighborhood (just avoid the public restrooms). If your students see you hanging out there, they'll suddenly realize you're a regular person.

If after these activities you have further questions, great! This marks a two-way teachable moment, which your students will love. Ask them sincerely and nonjudgmentally about some aspect of their culture that has you mystified and watch your most incorrigible students drop their guard and rush to clue you in. This could even make a good writing assignment or a topic for an oral report.

SEEK FIRST TO UNDERSTAND: A SAMPLE YOUTH SUBCULTURE EXAMINED

A funny thing about subcultures: What one group or generation enjoys, another calls "ugly" and even "dangerous"—often more out of ignorance and fear than experience. As one recently retired teacher we know remarked, "Elvis was considered evil by a lot of people when I was growing up. Now he's on a postage stamp."

In a previous teaching dilemma, a teacher expressed concern about a student who "dressed in black with a lot of dark makeup, listening to his gothic music." The goth subculture is one of many that provokes uncertainty, anxiety, and perhaps even fear among outsiders. Of course, at one level this is precisely the point: If everyone understood and was comfortable with the symbols and language involved, it would lose its power to shock and—in theory at least—subvert. These are teens, after all.

But it's not really so inscrutable. Try asking a student what it all means; if this proves inadequate, try the proliferation of Internet sites dedicated to explicating the finest detail of every imaginable taste and fetish. A bit of online research can teach you a lot, and provide a strong base from which to build bridges to otherwise indifferent and inaccessible students.

For example, goth adherent Cory Gross has created a website demystifying that subculture for the layperson. Goth, in his analysis, is "fundamentally a modern Romantic movement couched in . . . pop-culture vocabulary."

Gross cites literary scholar Montague Summers, who describes the Romantics as writers and artists who "created a fresh world, a world which never was and never could have been, a domain which fancy built and fancy ruled. And in this land there will be mystery, because where there is mystery beauty may always lie hid. There will be wonder, because wonder always lurks where there is the unknown. And it is this longing for beauty intermingling with wonder and mystery that will express itself, perhaps exquisitely and passionately in the twilight moods of the romantic poets, perhaps a little crudely and even a little vulgarly in tales of horror and blood" ("Gothic," n.d.).

Lest his readers fret that horror and romance are antithetical concepts, Gross explains the essence that in fact deeply connects them: their rejection of narrow, mundane fears and dreams, and their embrace of the Sublime—that is, "that which inspires infinite awe, dread, horror, ultimate appreciation, and an understanding of our own humble place in the cosmos . . . The Sublime astonishes and shocks us into an awareness of that which is greater than ourselves: Nature and Divinity, Time and Space" ("Gothic," n.d.).

Bet you never thought of goth that way. We didn't. Though your students may not explicitly express these sentiments, in our experience Romanticism describes well the spirit of adolescents generally, goth or not. Keep this lesson in mind the next time you feel like grumbling, "Kids these days! What are they thinking? I'll never understand them." And realize they probably don't understand why you're so grumpy and out of touch either.

MAKING MULTICULTURAL CONNECTIONS

Classrooms in much of the world are growing more multicultural every year. No matter where you teach, you could encounter children from any cultural background and from any region of the globe. You will of course be expected to provide an excellent education for all these students, regardless of how unfamiliar to you their languages, habits of mind, or other cultural characteristics may be.

Although the prospect of intercultural contact excites the adventurous, it can intimidate the unprepared. If you are teaching at a school in which you are a minority, expect to be tested. The community may not value the same aspects of education as you do, and may not respond to you precisely as you would anticipate. Students may seem insolent or withdrawn, and parents may appear pushy or unappreciative, depending on your expectations. You may also encounter resistance or even hostility until you have proven your skill and your motives. Those who approach this challenge with patience, inquisitiveness, and humility, however, can expect to be enlightened and exhilarated.

We set forth here numerous examples of cross-cultural contact in the classroom, to highlight some of the challenges inherent in communicating with individuals of diverse cultural backgrounds. Generalizing about other cultures is a tricky pursuit, however. As ethicist Barbara Koenig points out, "the last thing you want is . . . to start making shopping lists—Koreans do this, Mexicans do that." So beware of overgeneralizing; keep in mind that a variety of perspectives and habits exist within every population (Carey, 2001, p. S6).

With that caveat in mind, a brief exploration of cultural misunderstanding follows. In her book *Multicultural Manners*, Norine Dresser relates fascinating anecdotes of cultures clashing in various contexts, including the classroom. The book illustrates the ways divergent perceptions of time, color, clothing, body language, and male-female relations can lead to profound—and occasionally disastrous—confusion and misinterpretation.

This is particularly true since cultural attitudes often function at the emotional level, where they are largely impervious to alteration through rational discourse. You can argue with students all day about why they should or shouldn't feel a particular way, but since feelings are not typically acquired through intellectual processes, they usually can't be addressed intellectually. Most people can't unthink their feelings or what they believe in their hearts to be true.

Some examples of cultural clashes that are of particular relevance to education follow.

Family Values

A teacher was mystified by one Latina student's apparent lack of concern about missing class. The girl had accumulated enough absences to earn a stern warning, but then missed several more classes almost immediately to "help her family." Among many Latin Americans, Dresser notes, "allegiance to the family is primary," which means family needs like caring for younger siblings, working for the family business, or visiting relatives in their home country frequently trump the short-term demands of any single family member's education (Dresser, 1996, p. 50).

A 1995 study by C. and M. Suarez-Orozco cited by Beverly Daniel Tatum highlights an interesting contrast that often arises between Latinos and whites in this regard. In Tatum's words, achieving at school and at work were considered important by Latino teens [in the study] because success would allow them to take care of family members. Conversely, White American teens considered education and work as a means of gaining independence from their families. (Tatum, 1997, p. 137)

Color Shock

An English teacher corrected papers using red ink, failing to understand the horror that the color engendered in the parents of his many Korean students. For many Koreans and some Chinese, only the names of the dead are written in red. The school administration eventually asked all teachers to use other colors (Dresser, 1996, p. 38).

A Sign of Respect

A fifth-grade teacher was frustrated by one Vietnamese student's refusal to participate in class. The teacher did not understand that many young people from certain cultures are explicitly taught "not [to] ask questions, argue, or challenge the teacher," for this is taken to be presumptuous and disrespectful. In this case, the teacher gradually coaxed the student into becoming more vocal (Dresser, 1996, p. 41).

Modesty Misinterpreted

A counselor urged a Jamaican student to pursue vocational rather than college-preparatory coursework because he perceived the student to be too indigent and too reserved to excel in college. In fact, the student was not poor but dressed conservatively because she considered wearing flashy, trendy clothing at school inappropriate. And she did not speak up in class because she did not want to appear "uncouth." The student went on to college despite the counselor's misguided assumptions (Dresser, 1996, p. 45).

Similar situations in our personal experience include the following:

Backtalk

A nonblack teacher grew annoyed and offended by a handful of African-American students who talked and laughed loudly during every video she showed—most disturbingly during a Holocaust film. Through consultation with colleagues she came to understand that, far from ignoring the movie, these youth were engaging in a common ethnically specific practice of appreciation by maintaining a running commentary that interpreted and punctuated the action onscreen. Eventually, the teacher came to an accord with these students whereby she accommodated their responses and they agreed to comment less raucously.

Conscientious Objector

A nonreligious teacher was surprised by families of fundamentalist faith who prevented their children from participating in particular educational activities. In one case, parents excused their daughter from comprehensive health education, tolerance education, and education about other religions. This teacher had few options—he could not override the parents' wishes. Even so, some of the information likely found its way (albeit in a distorted form) to the excluded student through her classmates.

Mr. Manners

A white teacher of small-town upbringing was frustrated by the refusal of many urban students (of all ethnicities) to use the word *please* when requesting something from him. The teacher interpreted student statements like, "Let me have some paper" as commands, which he resisted. Politeness also failed these same students when pushing to move past each other; instead of a simple "Excuse me" they barked profane orders like "Move, m——f——!" which led more than once to physical altercations.

Upon asking his students why they omitted what he viewed as basic elements of civil discourse, this teacher learned that adolescent pride and street survival habits convinced many students that niceties like "please," "excuse me," and "I'm sorry" made them look weak. As one student explained, "I ain't gonna say no 'please.' That's like begging. You'll either give me what I want or not. I ain't begging for it." That particular student ended up incarcerated (though not for the way he spoke to his teachers). The teacher eventually adjusted to a different level of politesse in his classes, and remembered that his own modeling of good manners would have some effect on his students.

Breaking the Ice

A white teacher reported a cultural disconnect similar to those experienced by many white North Americans and Europeans doing business in parts of Latin America and Asia:

> I learned that I am very Anglo-Saxon compared to my Latino students. Courtesy demands of them that they greet everyone warmly, ask how they are, engage in some pleasantries—in other words, make some personal contact every day before anything else happens. I was all business and got class started as soon as the bell rang. They experienced that as coldness. (B. Burket, personal communication)

Judge Not

A Latina student reported a non-Latino teacher castigating her upon learning of her pregnancy. "How could you get pregnant? You shouldn't be having sex at all!" the frustrated teacher railed. "How are you going to take care of a child? You're practically a child yourself!" Although probably well-intentioned, such personal judgments usually only alienate students. This particular student shot back that her personal life was none of the teacher's business, right before storming out of his room. Whether she attributed his comments to his cultural background is unclear; what is plain is that this kind of crass judgment is inappropriate to make about any student.

Fighting Words

An Asian-American student volunteered to read aloud in class and reported that his non-Asian-American teacher—perhaps disheartened by one too many poor readers in her class, or too fatigued to realize what she was saying, or simply under the spell of her own misguided sense of humor—told him not to bother. "Not today," she said, "I don't like the way you read." Whether the teacher was referring to the student's pace or accent or some other factor, the student responded by hurling a book that narrowly missed the teacher's head; the student was expelled from that school.

Cultural Drivers of Student Attitudes and Behavior

Rosa Hernandez Sheets, writing with Geneva Gay, also reports interesting findings on cross-cultural communication at the secondary school level in the United States. Though the study Sheets conducted was relatively small, many of her observations ring true with teachers experienced in multicultural settings.

Few teachers would be surprised to learn that "males of all groups were disciplined more frequently, publicly, and severely than females," a phenomenon in which hormones and gender-role expectations undoubtedly play prominent parts. What might raise eyebrows, or at least stir curiosity, however, is the rank order by ethnicity of the frequency with which students were disciplined. In the classrooms Sheets observed for her study, African-Americans were disciplined most often, followed by Latinos, Asian-Americans, and finally whites (Sheets & Gay, 1996, p. 85).

What cultural differences might explain this disparity? Sheets' interviews with students revealed that white students tended to blame behavior problems largely on "unclear rules, and bad student attitudes," while minority students—particularly African-Americans—frequently "feel they are not given a fair chance to tell their side of the story in a confrontation, or that their viewpoints are not taken seriously or treated with integrity" (Sheets & Gay, 1996, pp. 87–88).

Sheets and Gay also found that Latino and Asian-American students often consciously avoided conflict "because getting into trouble brings embarrassment and shame to their families," while African-American students tended to be "less likely than other ethnic groups to concede to teachers' authority and directives when they feel unjustly accused or have not been given ample opportunity to state their case." The researchers found that, compared to members of other ethnic groups, the African-American students they observed were "driven more by their personal standards of rightness and loyalty to friends" and were more willing to "come to the defense of a friend even [at the cost of] creating trouble for themselves" (Sheets & Gay, 1996, pp. 88, 89).

Our own experience suggests that a long history of racial tension also factors significantly into this dynamic. We have worked with many students of color—particularly African-Americans—who have been implicitly (and sometimes explicitly) instructed by their parents and various cultural figures to stop the generational cycle of inequality and disrespect by resisting abuse (or perceived abuse) from those in power, particularly those from different ethnic groups. Since many adolescents already tend to magnify in their minds any perceived slight against them, resistance to authority given this historical experience is not difficult to understand.

Students of varying ethnic backgrounds also frequently disagree on what makes a teacher likeable and worthy of respect. "Caucasian students," Sheets and Gay note, tend to deemphasize teachers' personal qualities in favor of "teaching abilities and classroom management skills [and view] teachers who are not personable or who evoke the power of their position [as merely exercising] the prerogatives of the role" (Sheets & Gay, 1996, p. 87).

Many students of color, on the other hand,

> tend to place more emphasis on . . . caring, respect, concern, dignity, and connectedness with teachers. [Like most students of any color] they have little tolerance for teachers who "dis" them—i.e., embarrass, insult, or demean them publicly to show their intellectual or positional superiority. . . . This lack of respect generates distrust and compromises the teacher's credibility with the students, who reciprocate by being noncooperative." (Sheets & Gay, 1996, p. 87)

Any student can probably recall teachers whose insensitivity and self-absorption led to misunderstanding and sometimes outright conflict. Though not always explicitly cross-cultural, such episodes are often tainted with overtones of cultural condescension.

RACIAL BIAS

Any discussion of intercultural communication would be incomplete, of course, without some mention of a widespread and often unintentional phenomenon all teachers should understand: racial bias. This is an issue around the world that members of the ethnic majority often overlook, but which members of minority groups typically cannot escape. In this brief discussion, we seek not to provoke guilt, anger, or resentment, but to inspire self-reflection and thoughtful consideration of the issues.

In the present context, we apply psychology professor Beverly Daniel Tatum's definition of *racism* in the United States not as individual feelings or acts of intentional meanness or injustice, but as "a system of advantage that structurally benefits Whites and disadvantages people of color on the basis of group membership." The reality, Tatum points out, is that "all White people, intentionally or unintentionally . . . benefit from [this system]. Despite . . . rhetoric about affirmative action and 'reverse racism,' every social indicator, from salary to life expectancy, reveals the advantages of being White" in the United States (Tatum, 1997, pp. 8, 11, 103).

In her remarkable essay "Unpacking the Invisible Knapsack," Peggy McIntosh has identified numerous kinds of privilege that members of the American ethnic majority (herself included) enjoy. She writes:

> I have come to see white privilege as an invisible package of unearned assets that I can count on cashing in each day, but about which I was "meant" to remain oblivious. . . . I think whites are carefully taught not to recognize white privilege, as males are taught not to recognize male privilege." (McIntosh, 1989, p. 10)

White teachers—which is to say the vast majority of teachers in U.S. schools today—would do well to recognize and consider McIntosh's observations. White people, for example, are never asked to explain why "all white people" do this or that. Accomplished white people are never thought of as a "credit to the white race." And white people can feel free to be angry or rude, dress poorly, and have loud parties without these behaviors being blamed on their race.

Among McIntosh's other observations about white privilege are the following:

- "I can turn on the television or open to the front page of the paper and see people of my race widely represented."
- "I can be sure that my children will be given curricular materials that testify to the existence of their race."
- "When I am told about our national heritage or about 'civilization,' I am shown that people of my color made it what it is."
- "I can arrange to protect my children most of the time from people who might not like them."
- "I can be pretty sure that my neighbors [wherever I choose to live] will be neutral or pleasant to me."
- "I can go shopping alone, pretty well assured that I will not be followed or harassed."
- "If a traffic cop pulls me over, I can be sure I haven't been singled out because of my race."
- "I can be pretty sure that if I ask to talk to the 'person in charge' I will be facing a person of my race."
- "I can be pretty sure of having my voice heard in a group in which I am the only member of my race."
- "If my day, week, or year is going badly, I need not ask of each negative episode or situation whether it has racial overtones."

Again, the point of such observations is not to induce guilt but to highlight certain frequently overlooked but quite destructive aspects of the social system in which we all live and operate. In the United States, for example, those who are white, male, of above-average income, young, able-bodied, heterosexual, attractive, Christian—or several or all of the above—enjoy unearned privileges so pervasive and comfortable that they often seem not to exist at all, like the air.

If you are in the ethnic majority (in your geographic region or just your classroom), be aware that many of your students may have a view of the world, and particularly of authority, very different from your own—a view heavily colored by prior experiences over which you have no control. The best way we have found to cope is to demonstrate through your deeds that you are someone to be trusted and respected. Seek always to understand. Try not to judge. Work to educate, not alienate. And don't lose faith. Be patient. Eventually your students will learn to judge you not by the color of your skin but by the content of your character.

WHAT DO THESE INSIGHTS IMPLY FOR TEACHERS?

First, think carefully about how you interact with students generally. No one—not even someone with teaching credentials—has the right to be rude. We have seen teachers say and do things to students that would be unequivocally unacceptable if the target were an adult. Of course, sometimes students do very uncivilized things—but as we stress at various points in this book, you are morally and professionally obligated to model acceptable behavior.

Second, anticipate that your actions may elicit different reactions from different segments of your class. Some students are willing to right a perceived injustice by pushing back. Other students, out of fear, embarrassment, or some other form of discomfort, simply withdraw. They comply reluctantly but remain silent and may eventually stop coming to school. In chapters 5 and 6 we present various strategies for coping with classroom conflict in a way that doesn't alienate the population you're charged with educating.

Third, watch how you react to behavior of students from different backgrounds. It's easy to misinterpret behavior that's unfamiliar. Your and your students' perspectives may diverge more than you imagine. At what point does "discussing" become "arguing," for example? How loud is "too loud"? What kinds of comments or actions constitute "disrespect"? Are teachers "always right"? How much submissiveness should teachers expect from students? At what age and in what circumstances should children be treated like adults? Divergent value systems generate divergent answers to these questions, which can cause massive conflict if unaddressed.

Fourth, beware of overreacting. Both students and teachers interviewed in Sheets' study believed teachers could do more to solve problems within their classrooms rather than sending students out for disciplinary action by the administration. An escalating cycle of ever-harsher punishments is clearly ineffective if it fails to change behavior. Many students of color in particular

> already believe they will not be treated fairly under the best of circumstances and they expect the worst kind of treatment. When schools "get tough" with these students, their expectations are affirmed but their problematic actions may not be reduced at all. (Sheets & Gay, 1996, p. 91)

Finally, promote activities that will expand students' understanding and absorption of the prevalent culture, while taking proactive steps to understand and affirm the diversity in your classroom. Reach out to students' families to understand more about their cultural and familial traditions, which in turn can give you insight into their values and help you communicate with them on their terms. Also encourage students to understand and take pride in their backgrounds, whether through assignments that invite them to research or express some aspect of their cultures, or through extracurricular activities. Additionally, help students find accomplished adults or older kids from the same or similar backgrounds—at school or in the community—to serve as role models.

3

PREPARING FOR
THE FIRST WEEK
OF SCHOOL

PLANT THE SEEDS OF YOUR REPUTATION

Like it or not, you will be scrutinized continuously in the opening weeks of school. The first impressions you make among students, colleagues, and administrators will reverberate for months to come, so take care to cultivate an image you want to live with. In which of these columns would you want to be placed?

Are you . . .	Or are you . . .
A confident and well-prepared manager?	A timid and disorganized novice?
An incisive, articulate thinker?	A confused and mumbling mess?
A humble, inquisitive learner?	A self-absorbed, obdurate know-it-all?
A passionate, animated coach?	A bland, lifeless functionary?
A respectful and patient nurturer?	A pushy or frigid egomaniac?

Students will quickly judge what kind of classroom leader you are and will expect to follow the patterns you establish in the first week of school. Following the suggestions in this chapter will establish you as an organized professional who knows where the class is going and exactly how to get there. Whether this is 100% true at the outset is unimportant. What matters is that students believe it, because this will give you the confidence to forge ahead, even if—as many first-year teachers do—you find yourself staying barely one step ahead of the students for most of the journey.

FIND A MENTOR

New teachers often complain of feeling isolated from their peers and clueless about how to gauge and improve their own effectiveness in the classroom. This is ironic considering that they are typically surrounded by teaching experts. Your colleagues will likely have decades of collective experience addressing precisely the problems that will plague you; don't ignore this vital resource. One of the first things you should do, then, is find a seasoned colleague willing to serve as your informal mentor.

Unless you are hired the day before school begins, you have no excuse not to meet your fellow teachers in advance. And don't just limit your contacts to colleagues from your department, or even from your grade level. The more diverse feedback you get, the better; nearly every teacher can teach you something useful.

Most colleagues you approach will be more than willing to help— they are teachers for a reason, after all; they may be very busy, but usually you'll only need to ask. Just be sure to do your due diligence (see Table 3.1).

Your district may have a *mentor teacher* or *peer assistance* program, which may pay a veteran to come observe you in action or pay a substitute to cover your classes while you observe other teachers. Even if the district won't cover it, you can probably persuade a colleague to come in and watch you; sometimes, a visit as brief as 15 minutes can yield a deluge of insights.

Your teacher's union, which may call itself a *professional association*, will likely have resources to support you throughout your teaching career. While not all unions are created equal, many provide valuable services including malpractice insurance, legal fee payment in the event that you face a legal charge stemming from your practice as a teacher, and representation in the event of a serious conflict with your school district. Contact your local union representative or look up your state union online for more information.

Table 3.1. Doing Your Due Diligence

Which Teachers to Seek Out	What Questions to Ask
• What are different teachers known for? • Who's well-respected? • Who's well-organized? • Who's especially innovative? • Who's got great rapport with the students? • Whose style seems most like yours? • What pitfalls can this person help you avoid? • Whose style differs most starkly from yours? What might you learn from this?	• What are their most- and least-successful classroom tactics? • What insights can they offer about your school's particular population of students? • What advice can they give you on handling your troublemakers? • What tips do they have for navigating the bureaucracy and politics of your school? • If they were in your shoes, what would they most want to know?

ORGANIZE YOURSELF

Dress the Part

As in a job interview, seemingly superficial traits can send profound messages. "You'd be amazed," says one elementary classroom veteran. "Even little kids treat you differently when you're dressed up than when you're wearing jeans" (N. Arroyo, personal communication).

For young teachers of secondary students, the stakes are even higher. "I can't overemphasize the importance of a professional appearance," one high school administrator stresses. "Especially for new teachers—if you're anywhere near the age of the kids you're teaching, you need to establish some professional distance. Don't try to look or act like their buddy. Dress like a professional" (R. Cornner, personal communication).

Although many brilliant teachers rarely don anything more formal than *business casual* attire, others swear the way they look really can affect how they feel, and how they perform. One veteran attests, "Wearing a tie reminds me that I'm teaching. It's important for me to have a little cue to assume my teaching persona every morning. It's a reminder to take the job seriously" (D. Griffin, personal communication).

Create a Filing System You Will Actually Use

With all the tasks you will face as a first-year teacher, filing may seem to be a trivial nuisance, but you will lose valuable hours looking for misplaced paperwork—or recreating lost materials—if you don't create a smart storage and retrieval system at the outset. And efficient record keeping is critical. Certain records will be required by your school; others will enhance instruction, save time in the future, and/or give you backup during parent conferences.

Table 3.2. Ten Useful Organizational Tools

1	Seating chart and attendance procedure	Diagram of seating arrangement with seat assignments determined by particular student characteristics
2	Student skill file	Records of students' abilities and disabilities as determined in previous grade levels, provided by counselors, the administration, or your department chair
3	Student portfolio	A place for students to store and catalog their completed work and track their own academic and personal growth
4	Student behavior file	Your private notes on students' (mis)behavior and your responses—congratulations and remediation
5	Grade book	A day-by-day record of what you plan to teach and what you actually taught, to help you plan for future years
6	Lesson plan book	Your tool to track students' attendance and academic progress in your class
7	Teacher's lesson file	The centralized collection of all the lessons you've taught, including complete instructions and all supporting materials
8	Lesson clipboard	A simple list of what lesson occurred on what day, for quick reference by students returning from an absence
9	Past month's lesson file	A revolving collection of handouts and materials for all lessons presented in the past month, for self-service access by students returning from an absence
10	Students' work-in-progress file	A cabinet, box, or other container in which students can keep work until they finish it

Ten Useful Organizational Tools for Every Teacher

1. Seating Chart and Attendance Procedure

As detailed later in this chapter under "Organize Your Space," your students' productivity will depend largely on how you arrange them within the classroom. A seating chart is a critical part of this.

Some high school teachers—typically those with small and/or advanced classes—allow students to choose their own seats. Although this may work for experienced teachers, new teachers who follow this model often come to regret it. Teenagers are not rational adults; their self-selected seating patterns are typically the exact inverse of the optimum. Students who choose their own seats tend to cluster by friendship groups, and often end up too busy socializing to focus on work. Additionally, who normally gravitates to the front of the room? Eager learners and teachers' pets. And in the back? Mostly timid kids and troublemakers. This is not a blueprint for maximum productivity.

Wary of appearing capricious, many teachers seat students alphabetically. This helps them learn names and leaves no room for students to plead for a better deal. Others, realizing that adolescents generally travel (and cause trouble) in single-gender packs, alternate random males and females. Still other teachers let students choose where to sit on the first day, observe their behavior for a brief period, and then shuffle the seating arrangement.

Compiling your seating chart before students ever set foot in the room will move the first day along faster and leave little opportunity for argument. And publicizing your plans will save you future headaches. Tell students on the first day, "Your seat in this class *will* be changed, guaranteed." This can help ameliorate the territorial tantrums that erupt whenever adolescents are asked to change seats.

To assist in the tedious task of creating seating charts, consider investing in simple, affordable computer software that can help you configure and rearrange student seating endlessly. Fifteen minutes spent learning how to use the program can save you hours of drawing boxes and writing names. And when you need to reshuffle students, you can rearrange them either manually or automatically (alphabetically, numerically, or randomly) with a mouse click.

Some software even integrates this function with the cumbersome process of taking attendance—just click on students' names on the onscreen diagram to register their presence or absence, and print the results or send them electronically to your attendance office. Our website (www.classroomadvisor.com) offers links to some recommended software packages.

2. Student Skill File

A student skill file is a secure place—perhaps half a drawer in a filing cabinet—where you keep records of student abilities and disabilities as determined in previous grade levels. If this information is not given to you by the administration, request it—particularly for students who are showing signs of academic, behavioral, or other trouble. Knowing each student's reading level and any perceptual or processing limitations will help you anticipate problems and personalize instruction.

We recommend creating a simple system of codes to denote various student needs—you might create one code for "reading difficulty," another for "hearing trouble," another for "ADHD," and so on. Codes are easy to list on your seating chart, grade book, attendance cards, or wherever else you could use a reminder, while camouflaging from students' prying eyes the sensitive information they represent.

Keep in mind the inherent limitations of this information, however. Although sometimes based on firsthand observation of a student—as when a parent or school official reports a physical or emotional problem—much information in such files is generated by standardized tests, which can be inaccurate for any number of reasons. Test results can be skewed by many factors—including student fatigue, anxiety, misunderstanding of instructions or lack of interest or investment.

In addition, students' abilities and interests evolve over time, so what was true yesterday may not be true tomorrow. A third-grade test or teacher's notation indicating that "Tyesha seems weak in math" may no longer be true when Tyesha reaches high school.

Also be aware that negative expectations can prove self-fulfilling. Students viewed as "slow," for example, may not only resent being so categorized but may also begin—deliberately or subconsciously—to ratchet down their performance to meet this low expectation.

3. Student Portfolios

Portfolios are assessment instruments that, instead of comparing students to each other, compare students to themselves over time. They are collections of student work selected by the students themselves, typically in collaboration with the teacher or with each other. The idea is for students to reflect on their long-term progress and invite selected others to do the same. Like people who gain or lose weight over time but don't notice because they live with themselves every day, students are often unaware of the progress they've made without material like this to demonstrate it to them.

We strongly recommend creating portfolios in your classes if your school or department does not already require them. They are among the most comprehensive assessment tools available, and the pride students take in maintaining and updating them testifies to their motivational and educational power.

Portfolios also allow all stakeholders (students, teachers, parents, and administrators) to view, question, and critique both student work and the assignments leading to its creation. As such, they are valuable for everyone in the classroom. Teachers can even apply the feedback to improve their own craft.

Many resources exist for creating classroom portfolios. Our website (www.classroomadvisor.com) offers links to some of these.

4. Student Behavior File

Designate a three-ring binder or box of 5 x 7 cards—one page or card per student—as your behavior file, in which you can document behavior problems and improvement. This will help you quickly spot patterns among your students. Guard it as you would your attendance records, however, as it may become the target of theft or vandalism attempts, particularly when you are absent.

Note that vague scribblings like "James was disruptive" are unhelpful. Take two minutes while the offense is fresh in your memory to record the date, time, and a specific description of the student's behavior and your response. For example:

- 11/7, period 4: Britney threw wads of paper at Clayton and refused to stop after several requests from me, so I sent her to Mr. Zamora's classroom for the rest of the period.
- 11/10, period 4: Britney repeatedly interrupted other students' presentations with remarks like "That's so stupid," and "Why don't you sit down if you don't know what you're talking about?" Sulked but completed behavior citation when moved to time-out seat.
- 11/23, period 4: Britney refused to sit down when instructed to do so, and loudly called Marlene a b—-h. Severity clause—sent her to office and left message for her mother at her work.

This sort of documentation will assist you in the event of a parent conference—particularly with parents who insist their children could never be anything but angelic. In fact, many administrators will refuse to take disciplinary action against a student unless you prove the problem has repeated itself and can show what remedial measures you have attempted.

Even if a student's misbehavior isn't severe enough to warrant immediate sanctions, make note of it. Some students are adept at flying just under the teacher's radar. These clever manipulators know exactly how much they can get away with and will push you right . . . up . . . to . . . your . . . breaking point—but not beyond. These are the students who are loud, but never quite the loudest. They are often "innocently caught" in the middle of "someone else's" trouble. They are stealthy instigators who enjoy stirring up problems and watching others get blamed. Their game succeeds because they can turn antagonism to cooperation in an instant when the spotlight is on them; indeed, some of them may be your highest academic performers. Documenting their behavior will help you—and them—spot and stop destructive patterns.

Another reason for keeping these records is that your memory will likely be imperfect. You may see James misbehaving and think, "Not again! I've had it up to here with that kid." But when you look at his card, you may see that in fact he hasn't committed any offenses in three weeks. "Hmm. . . . Maybe it was Harvey who made me so mad." Perhaps it's time to remind James how good his behavior was recently and invite him to return to that pattern.

But why just respond to trouble? What about preventive maintenance? Documenting good works, particularly on the part of students who are not ordinarily well-behaved, is not unlike changing the oil in your car to keep it out of the mechanic's shop. We hope you do it regularly. Congratulating and thanking students for good behavior tends to produce more of the same.

Many schools have dusty stacks of sadly underused "commendation reports"; they work much like a positive version of discipline referral forms, but many teachers don't even know they exist. Whether or not your school provides a form for the purpose, sending home a note of appreciation is one of the best ways to win over students on the edge, as well as the often-frustrated parents of these students. And once the word gets around, and it will, this can also build general class morale.

5. Grade Book

Your grade book can take any number of forms, which an administrator or fellow teacher can show you. We recommend a computerized grade book, which will let you calculate students' grades instantly and let them know where they stand in your class at any given moment. As discussed in chapter 1, "Cultivating a Classroom Culture," and chapter 4, "Communication Essentials," such regular feedback is critical.

An electronic grade book is also easy to duplicate, which eliminates the danger of losing your only copy. Many computer grading programs also link automatically to student attendance records, making it easy to factor students' attendance directly into their grades if you choose (and are allowed by your district) to do so.

Our website (www.classroomadvisor.com) offers some suggestions for and links to popular grading programs.

TEXTBOOK RECORDS

If your school checks out textbooks to students, spare yourself a giant headache by maintaining strict records of who checks out which book and keeping this information in a place where you are certain not to misplace it—like next to each student's name in your grade book. Or keep it on a separate clipboard and make a big show of requiring students to sign out and sign back in their assigned textbooks.

Do not take this duty lightly. Why? Students frequently lose textbooks, and their sizeable replacement cost gives even the most scrupulous youth incentive to try to con you—as in, "Oh, yeah. I returned that three weeks ago. Don't you remember?" If you fail to keep a watchful eye on your textbooks, they'll disappear almost as fast as your pencils but cost 1,000 times as much to replace.

6. Lesson Plan Book

Whether or not your school requires it, maintain a lesson plan book religiously. For this purpose, feel free to reproduce the lesson planning form described in chapter 4, "Communication Essentials" (a blank version of the form is downloadable from our website, www.classroom advisor.com). Use the form before and after each lesson. Before each lesson, record what you plan to teach each day. After each lesson, note what you actually taught as well as suggestions for improvement the next time through.

This process is to classroom instruction what reliable accounting is to business: ugly to contemplate and tedious to perform, but indispensable for retracing your steps if anyone—including you—wants to look back someday and figure out exactly what you did with your time and resources.

If you are a first-year teacher who remains unconvinced, think of your second year on the job. In the very likely event that you teach some of the same classes, why reinvent unnecessarily? A day-by-day account of the previous year's activities will give you a base from which to work, which you can then adjust as necessary. As any writer will tell you, editing existing content is usually a lot easier than facing a blank page. Even a sloppily maintained lesson plan book will spare you from reliving much of the first-year pressure, and free your energy for more creative endeavors.

7. Teacher's Lesson File

The best lessons ever devised are useless unless you can access them at the moment you need them. Some teachers keep all their lesson plans in a single binder; others create a hundred different "lessons in a box," keeping each lesson plan in its own file folder along with any student handouts or materials necessary to deliver that lesson.

The lesson-in-a-box method, although more time- and space-intensive to establish, saves you the trouble of gathering materials anew every time you want to deliver the lesson. It also provides a simple and (virtually) foolproof prepackaged lesson for a substitute teacher—"Just add instructor." Just be sure to compile a master index—ideally on computer—so you can recall and coordinate what you have.

8. Lesson Clipboard

Students returning to school after an absence can consume a great deal of your time with legitimate inquiries like "What did I miss? How can I make up the assignment? What materials do I need?" Every such administrative question you do not have to answer directly is a precious minute conserved.

The lesson clipboard is an automated mechanism designed to help students figure out for themselves what happened in class when they were absent. With this simple system, students take responsibility for reviewing the missed assignments and collecting necessary materials before approaching you with questions; this increases their self-reliance and reduces the burden on you.

The lesson clipboard is a list of which lesson occurred on what day, and exactly which materials were used to complete the assignment. It is in fact the "table of contents" for the past month's lesson file (tool 9). See Table 3.3 for a short sample.

Although updating the lesson clipboard is simple enough to make part of your lesson planning/documentation routine, it does take time. Enlisting a teacher's assistant (TA) or trusted student to update the clipboard for you each day can further reduce your burden. With correct guidance, students can not only enjoy this but actually do an excellent job; sometimes, explanations from a student's-eye-view are the easiest for other students to grasp.

If you are computer-savvy or have a computer-literate TA, you can create an electronic version of your lesson clipboard, accessible on an in-class computer terminal or on your homework website. Our website (www.classroomadvisor.com) provides links to real-world examples.

Table 3.3. Sample of Lesson Clipboard

Date	Lesson Title	Handouts and Other Required Materials
March 3	World Cruise: intro	3 handouts: • "You won a world cruise!" • distance calculation worksheet • blank port description table
March 4	World Cruise: skill building	Above 3 worksheets, plus • globes • string • rulers • calculators • travel guidebooks • Internet
March 5	World Cruise: resources	Above materials, plus • National Geographic magazines and CD-ROMs • list of suggested websites

9. Past Month's Lesson File

The past month's lesson file, which the lesson clipboard (tool 8) is designed to index, is a revolving collection of materials for the previous month's lessons, for self-service access by students returning from an absence. In practice, it's a tickler file—similar to the kind of box (with numbered slots, one for each day of the month) that many people maintain to keep their personal bills up to date—created to handle documents not for the coming month, but for the month just elapsed.

As illustrated in Figure 3.1, the simplest form of the past month's lesson file is a box of folders that houses all handouts and supporting materials for every lesson presented in the past month, and updates them on a rolling basis. This is how it works: Organize your lesson folders by date in a file storage box using numerical sorting dividers, widely available in office supply stores. Then at the end of each day or week, rotate in the most recent lesson folders and rotate out the oldest batch, so the most recent month of lessons is always accessible to students.

A word of warning: Be sure nothing in this file is the *only* copy you have, because at least some of the contents of each folder will likely get "misplaced." This is a fact of life with virtually any system that allows student access. We recommend assigning a TA to review each lesson folder and make photocopies as necessary to restore it to completeness before you move it back to permanent storage. This will leave you prepared for the next time you need to teach that lesson.

Usage example. At the end of the day on March 17, place that day's lesson in slot 17 of the past month's lesson file box. If slot 17 is already occupied with another lesson folder (which it should be—namely, the lesson for February 17, unless that date fell on a weekend), make room for the new (March 17) lesson folder by bumping the old (February 17) lesson folder back to its permanent home in your file cabinet (see Figure 3.1).

Contents of each lesson folder.

1. Overview sheet: step-by-step lesson instructions, from the student's point of view. If you have a TA in a given period, you could assign him or her the job of "process assistant" for the first 10 minutes

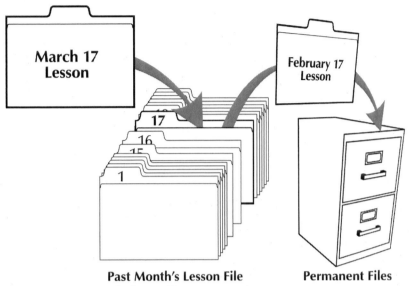

Figure 3.1. Past month's lesson file usage example.

of every new lesson—taking notes not on the content of the lesson but on the steps the class goes through for each assignment. Ideally that student could type these steps into a word-processing program, for editing by you and permanent storage.

2. Any necessary reading materials
3. Any necessary handouts
4. Directions for finding other needed materials

10. Students' Work-in-Progress File

The students' work-in-progress file is usually a box, shelf, or collection of cubbyholes in which students can keep half-finished class projects and work materials. Art classes typically have dedicated spaces for this. In other classes, this may simply be a collection of folders in which students keep their papers. This reduces the likelihood of loss or damage, and is especially sensible for oversize or fragile works. Such a space is essential in schools without lockers, or with students who tend to lose whatever they take home.

ORGANIZE YOUR SPACE

Particularly if you are a new teacher, you cannot afford to be anything less than the firmly established master of your space. If you have your own classroom, take charge of every corner. Your organization—or lack thereof—will send an unmistakable message not only to your students, but also to any parents or administrators who happen by.

And don't neglect to make your classroom pleasing to the eye. Why spend every day in bleak and uninviting surroundings? Follow the model of elementary teachers, who excel at creating classrooms filled with colors and shapes that pique students' curiosity while maximizing organizational efficiency and informational impact. Elementary teachers also display student work everywhere, giving students a sense of pride and ownership of the classroom, as well as models to guide future learning.

If you lack either the time or the inspiration to create such an environment, enlist students to help. You will inevitably find some with an artistic eye who would love to assist. Besides, enrolling students in such jobs increases their sense of proprietorship over the space. It can also help prevent vandalism; in many communities an unwritten honor code prevents one crew of taggers from tarnishing another's graffiti on the street; this respect sometimes carries over to the classroom as well.

If you need inspiration or ideas, connect to several examples of well-organized classrooms through our website (www.classroomadvisor .com).

Create a Self-Service Classroom

Fast food restaurants put thousands of competitors out of business by automating production and redesigning their processes to force patrons to serve themselves. The result: More customers served by the same personnel, in the same space, at lower cost.

Although we certainly do not advocate a one-size-fits-all education delivered on identical plastic trays by identical plastic clowns wearing identical plastic smiles, a certain amount of automation and

HOW TO MASTER YOUR SPACE: LESSON FROM A LION TAMER

Never allow students in your room without your presence. This is common sense for theft and legal liability reasons. But being the first person in your room and the last to leave also conveys visually and viscerally that the classroom is your domain and students should behave accordingly.

Veteran teacher Michael Kelley offers an interesting analogy: A lion tamer in a circus, he observes, "is always the first in and the last out [of the lion cage]. . . . Because he's the first entity in the cage, he's establishing that it's his territory—it belongs to him. When the lions are allowed in later, they enter with the implicit understanding that the tamer is king of the cage, and they're merely guests invited at his whim. If the lions were to enter first, they'd recognize the empty space as theirs and might attack to defend their territory" (Kelley, 2003, pp. 80–81).

self-service can free you from trivial tasks like distributing materials, announcing assignments, and cleaning the room. The time and energy thus conserved can be applied toward tasks that actually require your expertise, like enticing students to think.

The classrooms displayed here make frequently used items easily accessible and require students to find their own work materials and clean up after themselves. Some teachers even train TAs to monitor the system and enforce the rules (see "Work Smarter, Not Harder: Never Do Anything the Students Could Do").

Art teacher C. Yoshida maintains order even in an inherently messy discipline (see Figure 3.2). As in any workshop, organization facilitates productivity. A sure recipe for disaster is

Lack of organization + Teenagers = Chaos

Figure 3.2.   Mr. Y.'s art classroom.

Structure Your Space to Minimize Conflict

As discussed in chapter 2, "Who Are Your Students?" adolescents are largely physical creatures. They can be awkward, hyperactive, and territorial. If your classroom layout does not accommodate this, you're asking for trouble.

TEACHING DILEMMA: STUDENTS WON'T STOP DISTRACTING EACH OTHER

One of my classes seems to be full of kids who won't stop touching each other. I don't know if they're in love with each other, or detest each other, or what. Some days it seems like both. But their behavior definitely disrupts their work.

SUGGESTED SOLUTION

Misconduct by easily distractible students tends to escalate in direct proportion to their distance from the teacher. Therefore, seat troublemakers as close to you and as far from their friends as possible. If their behavior still distracts others, try seating them to one side of the room and surrounding them with quiet members of the opposite sex.

If you see productivity of the class as a whole degenerating over a period of days and suspect your seating arrangement might be partly to blame, take a few minutes to draw up a new seating chart but don't spring it on the students until the last 5 minutes of class. "As I'm sure many of you noticed," you might announce, "the quality of our work slipped today. I tried several times to keep you on task, but now I think it's time to change things around. So pay close attention as I go around the room and point to the place where I have assigned each of you to sit, starting tomorrow."

This tactic makes your reasoning transparent, places responsibility for the change squarely on the students where it belongs, and best of all leaves little time for student complaints. Just be prepared the following day for the vast number of students who will have "forgotten" where they are supposed to sit. Don't let this get under your skin; adults would do the same thing.

Sample Classroom Layouts

The layout of your room will impact student traffic patterns and interaction, so put some thought into exactly what behavior and movement you'll want from students, and arrange your classroom accordingly. We discuss desks here, but tables or some combination of the two can generate similar outcomes. If your classroom is so packed with students that there is minimal space for innovative seating arrangements, much of this will not apply to you, but we hope you find some of the key principles useful in any case.

First, where you place yourself in relation to the students is critical. As we discuss under "Classroom Management," many great teachers are rarely in their seats. Instead, they are continually moving about the classroom to ask and answer individual questions, motivate students, and keep them on task. There will be quiet moments, however, in which case your desk's location will influence student productivity.

Some teachers prefer to position their desks in the back of the room (as in Ms. B.'s classroom, Figure 3.3), reasoning that when you're not in front of the class, being behind students lets you keep a better eye on them, because they never know when you're watching.

> Sometimes you can see from the way a kid is sitting that he's doing something he ought not to do, so you can sneak up on him and scare the snot out of him. If I'm sitting in the back, students can also come back and get help with their work without worrying about other kids watching them and making fun of them. Then there are kids who would rather watch mold grow than do their work; moving the teacher's antics out of their view eliminates a potential distraction. (B. Burket, personal communication)

Other teachers put their desks front and center:

> I like to have eye contact when I'm sitting at my desk, because eye contact means control. If a student is writing on a desk or whatever, I can just glance up and it's got to stop, because he knows I'm watching. I find the constant threat of being caught is a good deterrent. I put the desk in the center so I'm an equal distance from both sides of the room. Otherwise, kids can get away with murder in whatever corner's farthest from me. (C. Hipkins, personal communication)

Although lighting and telecommunications connections will probably limit your choices for your desk's location, consider also these

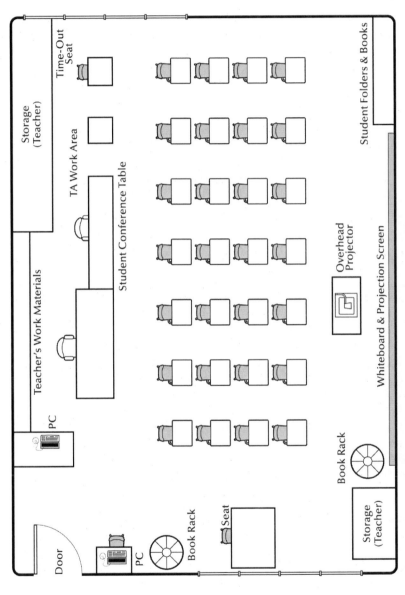

Figure 3.3. Ms. B.'s classroom.

factors: First, placing your desk near the main door helps control the flow of students into and out of the classroom. A few teachers prefer the opposite, however, because they fear "students can just snatch something from your desk and disappear before you realize what's happening." We assume that a teacher who wouldn't notice students sneaking in or out of the room would have bigger problems than theft, but tempting weak spirits invites trouble.

Second, the configuration of your work area will determine your level of privacy and security. Many first-year teachers—particularly those who try to be extra-friendly with their charges—find students do not share their concept of "professional distance." We have watched students wandering behind and rummaging through teachers' desks even while the teachers were sitting at them. Allowing students to swarm unfettered, particularly in your space, can cause you stress and signal to students that they, not you, are in control. One veteran reports:

> I found in my first year that I needed to show students very concretely where appropriate limits are. Once I arranged my desk to . . . cordon off my territory, the students stopped invading it. They had no trouble seeing what was their space and what was my space." (R. Cornner, personal communication)

Third, the arrangement of your desk, phone, computer, and any other frequently used equipment will impact your ability to monitor student activity in the classroom. Beware of creating blind spots in the room that students can vandalize with impunity. Figure 3.4 shows Mr. M.'s room arrangement during his first year teaching. What areas do you imagine were plagued by vandalism and garbage? Figure 3.5 shows the same room layout with dashed lines to represent Mr. M.'s line of sight when he sat at his desk. Shaded areas indicate problem spots he could not directly monitor from a distance. Note that student work folders and textbooks were also far from his watchful eye.

Mr. M. had envisioned the compartmentalized rear corner as a quiet study area for students working on independent projects or for

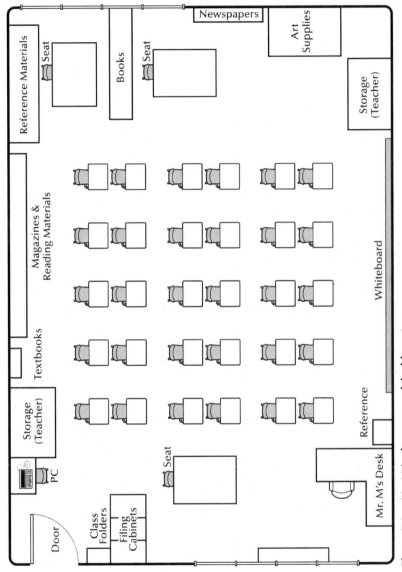

Figure 3.4. Mr. M.'s classroom, original layout.

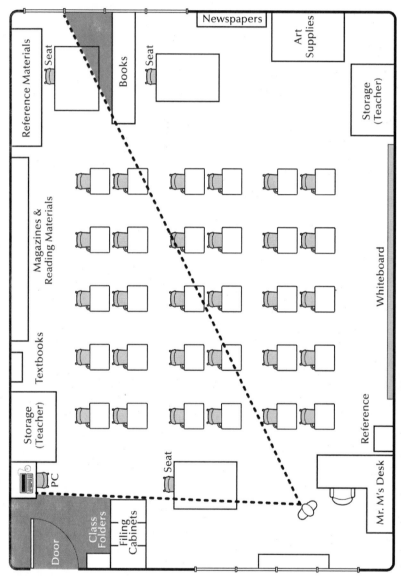

Figure 3.5. Mr. M.'s classroom, problem areas.

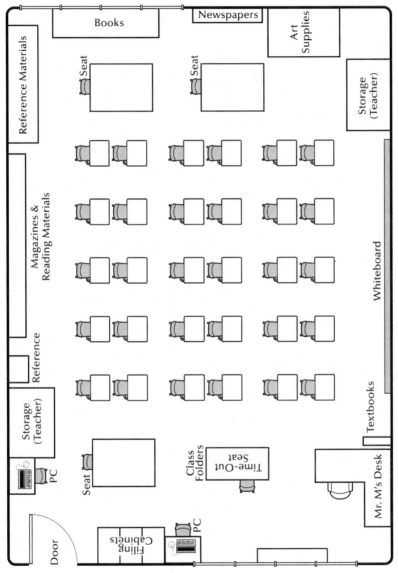

Figure 3.6. Mr. M.'s classroom, reconfigured.

those who needed temporary isolation from the group. As teens often do, however, his students took advantage of the corner's relative privacy to vandalize and trash the area. Students scribbled graffiti in books and deposited gum and other refuse in those remote locations.

The subtle but powerful changes reflected in Figure 3.6 simplified and opened up the room. His new classroom layout also established a time-out space next to his desk, where troublesome students could be closely monitored.

Mr. M.'s room depicts a traditional all-seats-forward desk array. This layout is designed to focus students on a single point in the classroom and limit their interaction. Mr. M. chose a mix of desks and tables, to allow individual and group work when necessary. He also arranged the students' desks not in long rows from front to back but clustered in pairs, each pair separated from the rest by vertical and horizontal aisles. This, in the words of one middle-school teacher, "makes it ridiculously easy to get from any point to any other point of the room immediately"—useful indeed in a room full of teens (P. Gin, personal communication).

Note also in Figure 3.6 that Mr. M. positioned furniture around his desk to clearly demarcate the end of "student territory" and the beginning of "teacher territory." The only students allowed in his territory are those invited to be there (assistants) or those ordered to be there (detainees, in the time-out seat). He has also placed class folders, textbooks, art supplies, and reference materials where students can reach them easily, but not all in one location. This creates a self-service classroom while avoiding congestion. He has placed student textbooks near his desk so he can easily keep track of them and has left no corners of the room outside his view. Even the student computer is positioned so student activity on it is public knowledge.

Figure 3.7 shows another all-seats-forward configuration for a very large computer room. Note the aisle down the center that allows the teacher easy access to every student. Note also that the position of the monitors, with all students facing away from (and therefore all screens facing) the teacher's desk, allows the teacher to view every student's onscreen activity from her seat at the rear of the class. Be aware, however, that without computers to absorb their attention,

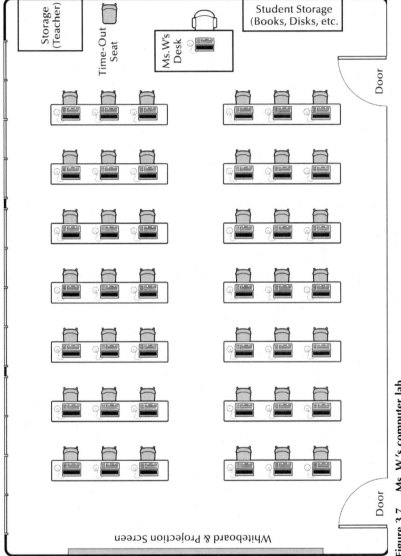

Figure 3.7.   Ms. W.'s computer lab.

students placed this close to one another would be likely to talk to, touch, and otherwise disturb each other.

Ms. B. has cordoned off her space using her desk and a student conference table as barricades (see Figure 3.3). This configuration allows students to approach her with questions in relative privacy, because both her desk and the conference table are positioned behind students' backs. As in Mr. M.'s room, she keeps a time-out seat in a remote corner, has the sole student computer screen visible to the room, and has student materials and reading books easily accessible to students and distributed in several areas to avoid traffic pileups.

One special education teacher we counseled had arranged his room as in Figure 3.8 and wondered why his students were so talkative and unfocused. He had crammed the students' desks together in the middle of the room and set up a table for joint student work in the rear that—purely because of its distance from the teacher—generated trouble.

Part of the problem was that his desk and the dead space next to it consumed an outsized chunk of the room. Because their desks were confined to an unnecessarily tight space, students regularly invaded his "teacher territory," hovering at his desk and even wandering behind it to play with the computer when he was distracted. Adding to this trouble, the sole whiteboard in the room was not only too small but also located inexplicably in the corner, far from every student's view.

When he changed his room to the layout represented in Figure 3.9, his problems diminished. This layout simultaneously separated the students from each other—reducing the touching and hitting that invariably prove a major distraction among teenagers—and brought them all closer to him. Note that the shifting of his computer also effectively cordoned off a personal "teacher's area," which students were less likely to enter. The addition of a second, central whiteboard and the positioning of student desks nearer to it increased the attentiveness of all his students.

The week following these changes, Mr. P. reported his students were happier with the new arrangement because they could all see the board and no longer felt like they were on top of each other. One

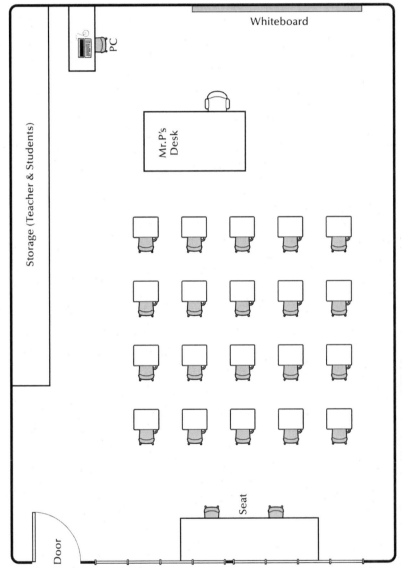

Figure 3.8. Mr. P.'s classroom, original layout.

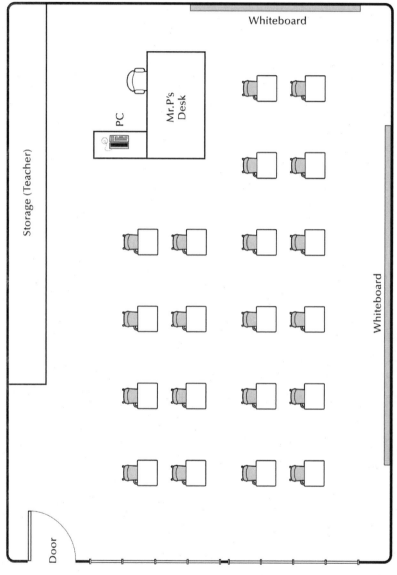

Figure 3.9. Mr. P.'s classroom, reconfigured.

question naturally arises here: If the students were uncomfortable before, why didn't they speak up about it? Perhaps they didn't realize the source of their discomfort—or even that they were uncomfortable. As discussed in chapter 2, "Who Are Your Students?" the responsibility for spotting symptoms of trouble and finding solutions falls to the professional trained and paid for that task—you.

Seating Configurations to Achieve Particular Effects

To encourage students to interact with each other, try clustering desks so that small groups of students face each other, as in Figure 3.10. Desk clusters function as group tables, which by nature encourage collaboration (and lots of talking), with the additional advantage that they can be quickly reconfigured and resized as necessary for different activities.

If you want students to interact as a whole class, try arranging the desks in a circle or horseshoe. If the teacher's seat is a part of the configuration, sitting at the same level as the students, this sends a powerful message of equality and cooperation. If removed from the circle, the teacher tends to interfere less with the students' discussion. In either case, the circle offers the advantage of teacher-student proximity.

A horseshoe shape (Figure 3.11) tends to limit interaction slightly more than a circle, because there's a definite "front" where students know to focus. This focal point can be occupied by any number of activities, from demonstrations to guest lectures to student presentations. The opening also allows the teacher to move among students as necessary to squelch trouble quickly.

Some teachers prefer facing rows or clusters, as shown in Figure 3.12. The arena effect puts all students close to the action and within easy reach of the teacher in the event of a discipline problem. Placing the teacher's desk and the demonstration area at opposite ends of the central corridor forces teacher movement, which we highly recommend for both instructional and classroom management reasons.

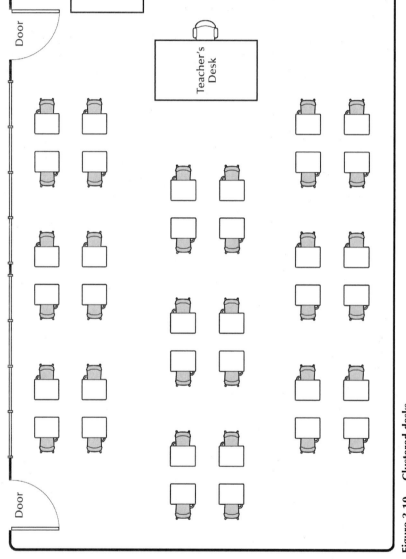

Figure 3.10. Clustered desks.

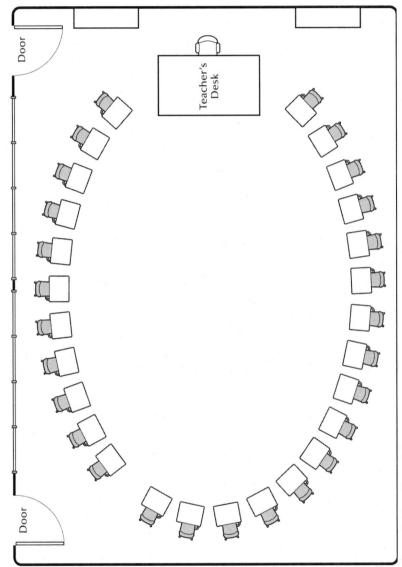

Figure 3.11.   Horseshoe.

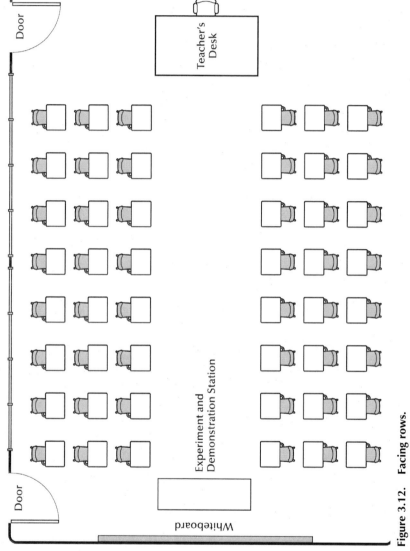

Figure 3.12. Facing rows.

ORGANIZE YOUR STUDENTS: ESTABLISH CLEAR RULES AND ROUTINES

In chapter 1, "Cultivating a Classroom Culture," we discussed the importance of rules and recommended procedures for creating them. As a reminder, here are the basic tenets of rule creation:

1. Less is more: Make no more rules than you are willing to enforce consistently.
2. Make your rules clear and visible.
3. Phrase rules in positive, not negative, terms.
4. Don't leave out the "why": Always explain your rationale.

The Importance of Routines

Imagine a firefighter who waits until the fire alarm rings before rooting through his closet for his uniform . . . who then has to search through the clutter on his desk for the keys to the fire truck . . . who on the way to the blaze makes several wrong turns because he doesn't know his way around town . . . and who, when he finally arrives at the scene, has to locate and attach the proper hoses, crossing his fingers in the hope that he didn't leave behind any necessary connectors.

Ridiculous? Let's look inside two classrooms on the first day of a large group project, and see if we spot any similarities (and differences):

CLASS A

Students enter the classroom. Nothing is written on the board. The teacher hands out a fat packet of instructions and some of the materials and then starts explaining the project. The students sit silently during the explanation, asking no questions before choosing partners and breaking into small groups to begin working. It quickly becomes evident that no one was really paying attention to the directions, so the teacher explains to each group separately what to do. Many students have trouble understanding the lengthy written description of the project. Someone wants to use the bathroom and interrupts the teacher to ask for a pass. Since no one seems to know where certain necessary supplies are, several students wander around the room searching, and distract their classmates in the process. Only the teacher has scissors. The colored pencils are not where they're supposed to be. Students wonder what kind of paper they should use. Several students sit idle for half the period until the teacher, frazzled by the experience, notices them doing nothing and demands an explanation. By this point, tempers are flaring and little has been accomplished. The period ends with the classroom in a mess, the teacher stressed out, and the students feeling like they wasted an hour. For the next two weeks, the teacher herds reluctant students through a project few fully understand, and swears by the end never to do extended group projects again.

CLASS B

The teacher has instructions on the board and a completed model project on display when the students enter the classroom. As students enter, each is given a color-coded sticker to wear. All needed materials are clearly displayed and easily accessible to students. Students are given only the materials they need for each stage of the project and touch nothing else until the teacher finishes explaining the activity and answering questions. Students who need to sharpen pencils or use the restroom do so unobtrusively, and otherwise everyone remains seated. The teacher then leads the class through a sample version of the project. Finally, the teacher directs students to find their fellow group members by finding all classmates with matching colored stickers, and points to signs on the walls indicating where in the room each group should meet. For the next two weeks, students follow the model and the teacher practices MBWA (management by walking around), wandering from table to table helping, encouraging, and troubleshooting for groups of students. By the end, the projects range from acceptable to brilliant, and the teacher has enjoyed performing the role of coach/mentor rather than nag/tyrant.

In teaching as in firefighting, routines make processes more efficient. It may sound silly or beneath you to map out what to do when a student wants to use the restroom or fails to bring a pencil to class, but if 5 minutes spent planning for a task saves you one minute *every time* you have to perform that task—well, you do the math. For a task you'll perform numerous times every day (e.g., taking attendance, checking students' grades, writing hall passes, etc.) routines will save you countless hours by year's end, which you can devote to more of what you're supposed to be doing—teaching.

In researching *A Place Called School*, John Goodlad and his team discovered that organizational matters consumed an average of 20% of class time in American secondary classrooms (Goodlad, 1984, pp. 98–99). Imagine trying to cram all of your assigned curriculum into 180 school days, and then imagine losing one fifth of that time—a full 36 days—to mindless tasks like taking attendance, passing out papers, allowing student movement around the room, and so forth.

The good news is that the best classrooms Goodlad studied required less than 10% of class time for organizational matters. You can bet that these classrooms did not get so efficient by accident. We believe 10% should be every teacher's target, and the procedures in this section can help you get there.

How can you measure your efficiency with class time? Invite a colleague, counselor, or other staff person to observe an average class, time your processes, and offer feedback. How much time did you use to take attendance? get the class quieted down? make announcements? focus the group on the day's lesson? answer non-curricular questions? address off-task behavior? What procedures might you use to improve?

Alternatively—and we recommend this exercise for *every* teacher— record a day of your teaching on video and review it yourself. Time- stamped footage can help you analyze and tighten each segment of your classes.

Better yet, watching yourself can give you nuggets of insight un- available from any other source. How's your posture? Do you screech when you're under stress? Is your voice monotonous enough to lull even you to sleep? Do you gesticulate like a windmill in a hur- ricane? Is there disengagement or off-task student behavior that you don't notice because you're so engaged in delivering your lesson? Do you focus more on one side of the room than another? The camera does not lie. If you can handle harsh truths, the exercise will make you a much better teacher.

Class routines can also help preserve your sanity by their sooth- ing influence. Part of the value of ritual is its capacity to calm agi- tated minds and bodies. And, since few minds or bodies need calm- ing like those of adolescents, certain principles of ritual may be usefully adapted to the school setting. Although leading tai chi, yoga, or meditation sessions in your classroom would perhaps not be practical, deliberate pacing and planned patterns of movement can nonetheless deliver a similar benefit.

HOW TO TEACH ROUTINES

Imagine instituting silent reading time for the first 15 minutes of a particular period every day. After a week or so of consistent guidance from you, students will accli- mate to the pattern—they will learn to find books, seat themselves, and begin reading on their own. The rou- tine for silent reading time will become automatic.

Exactly how does this work? Not by magic. You must explicitly teach students how to follow the routines. As

Madeline Hunter asserts, "children . . . can't be expected to do something well just because they've been told they should, any more than a first-grader can be expected to know how to read because his teacher told him he should" (Hunter, 1976, p. 26).

For the example above, try telling students:

Today we're going to begin SSR—Sustained Silent Reading. The whole school participates, so you're not going to be able to get out of it by transferring out of this class. But I don't think you'll hate it. In years past, students have enjoyed the opportunity to read something of their choosing, rather than what's been assigned to them. And studies have shown that this program can improve students' reading ability. I love it, and I'll be reading, too.

We're going to follow the same pattern every day. When the class bell rings, I'll set this timer and you'll have 60 seconds to find a book or magazine and get to your seat. That's not a lot of time, so try to remember where you put what you were reading the day before. If you need more time, get to class early, because when this timer rings, everyone should be in a seat and all talking will stop. That means I don't want to hear you telling your friend how your team did yesterday or how cute some boyband is, even if that's what you're reading about, got it? No talking means no talking. Read about it quietly and talk about it after.

Everyone, myself included, will read silently until this CD player starts. It will play for 3 minutes. That's when I'll take attendance, and you should put your reading material away back where you found it, not underneath your chair, and get the materials you'll need for the day—they'll be listed on the board. Any questions before we run through it once for practice?

Are Routines for Everyone?

Every year, many young teachers reject class routines. Presuming they will liberate youth from the oppressive constraints of "the establishment," they unleash hormones more powerful than they imagined and quickly find their classes sliding toward chaos. These neophytes discover too late that audacity and ingenuity are no substitute for systematic planning and consistent reinforcement of good habits. The wise teacher seeks order first, creativity second.

On the other hand, too much repetition quickly becomes tedious. Form is different from content, however. Productive behavioral habits are not the end but the means to education. They constitute merely the foundation—the necessary but not sufficient precondition—for meaningful learning.

As later chapters detail, good teachers offer a varied learning experience within an orderly framework. They promote innovative thinking without blurring lines of authority, and then continually modulate their lessons' pacing, variety, and level of difficulty to keep students engaged in learning.

Top 10 Suggested Routines

Here we discuss some of the biggest time-wasting activities that occur every day; these are obvious candidates for standardization. Be sure students know what to do when

1. The bell rings, signaling the start of class.
2. They want to ask a question.
3. They need to use the restroom or feel ill.
4. They did not bring their work materials.
5. They finish work early.
6. They do not finish work on time.
7. They want to turn in or retrieve work.
8. They want to know their grades.

9. They return to school after an absence.
10. The bell rings, signaling the end of class.

Let's examine each of these situations individually.

1. The bell rings, signaling the start of class.

A disorganized classroom: Students straggle into class late and then wander around the room talking to friends, disturbing class-mates, rummaging through materials, and so forth. This typically wastes at least 5 minutes of each period. The teacher takes attendance by reading students' names aloud, then announces what will happen that day. Several students who weren't listening waste more time by asking the teacher to repeat and finally, 10 minutes into the period, the class slowly grinds into gear.

An efficient alternative: Condition students to be seated the moment the bell rings, and either get them started on work right away or use a sponge (question, problem, or puzzle) to lure students into "study mode" immediately upon entering the class, giving you 3–5 minutes of quiet time to take attendance, make adjustments to a seating chart, welcome a newcomer, or complete other *administrivia*.

Sponges can be pulled from the course textbook, from the daily newspaper, from the Internet, or virtually any other source. What effective sponges have in common is the level of interest and focus they inspire in students. Here are a few sample generic sponges (you can find additional examples on our website, www.classroomadvisor.com).

- Respond to this quote (or news item, or political cartoon, or image) in your journal.
- List in your journal five things about _____ that you like and five things that you don't like. For each, write a sentence explaining why you feel the way you do.
- Where do you think the photograph on the board was taken? Why?
- Try to solve this math problem (or brain teaser).
- Find the spelling or grammatical errors in these five sentences.
- What's wrong with this picture (or argument)?

In addition to having a ready sponge activity, post an agenda on the board or overhead that outlines your plan for that class period (see sidebar). Students have the right to know where they are going, and they tend to cooperate and comprehend more when told in advance what will be demanded of them. Additionally, creating an agenda forces you to plan precisely and helps keep you on track during the period.

2. *Students want to ask a question.*

A disorganized classroom: During class discussions, students interrupt each other and the teacher with a barrage of questions, comments, and irrelevancies, often yelling to be heard over the

---

SAMPLE AGENDA FROM A SECONDARY MATH CLASSROOM

Math B—November 15
You will need:

- Book
- Your homework from yesterday

Procedure:

1. Warm-up
2. 6.2 HW solutions
3. 6.3 Distributive Property
4. Practice 6.3 Reteach
5. One-minute paper

Homework:

- Section 6.3: Problems 13–35, odd
- Study for Quiz 3 (6.1–6.3) on Tuesday

---

general turmoil. Much of the students' energy is dissipated, and much of the teacher's energy is expended trying to control the noise level.

An efficient alternative: Some kids become adults without ever realizing that decorum requires different behavior in different situations. They have only one voice—loud and constant. Anyone who has ridden with teenagers on a public bus or subway will instantly understand what the classroom can devolve into with no conversation-management procedure.

To cope with this, classroom veteran George Watson recommends a system of color-coded "permissible talking levels" (Watson, 1986, p. 12). Our preferred system is a slight variation on Watson's suggestion: Affix a red, yellow or green dot to the board to signal how much talking you will allow in class for a given activity (see Table 3.4). For example, for silent reading or writing, post the red dot indicating no talking allowed. For orderly discussion, the yellow dot reminds students to raise their hands before speaking. The green dot, allowing free nondisruptive conversation—within certain volume and content limits—might be appropriate for group work, artwork, and so forth.

Table 3.4. Permissible Talking Levels

Level	Definition	Examples
Red	No conversation, period	Funerals, live theater
Yellow	Polite conversation; raise hand before speaking	Dinner with your grandparents, boss, or probation officer
Green	Free, nondisruptive conversation	Restaurants, stores, museums, and other public places

Note: Concept based on Watson, 1986.

3. Students need to use the restroom or feel ill.

A disorganized classroom: Students interrupt the teacher at any time, during any activity, with requests for hall passes. Each time, the teacher must stop, hunt for a hall pass form, fill it out, and sign it. The entire process can take 1–2 minutes, including the time required to get the class back on task after the interruption.

An efficient alternative: Hang a clipboard with a sign-out sheet next to a permanent hall pass so students can simply "ask, sign, grab, and go." Requiring students to sign their names—including the times they left and returned—will help you spot patterns of abuse. The time component can reveal who routinely takes 20 minutes in the "restroom," who was out of the room at the same time that Building 15 exploded, and so forth. Students may try to game the system by listing false times, but wandering by the clipboard a few times—in full view of the students—to verify their timekeeping should keep potential duplicity in check.

Having a single permanent hall pass that students must take with them will ensure that only one student leaves the room at a time. The "We all need to go to the bathroom at the same time, really!" maneuver is a perennial student favorite, and naively unleashing herds of rowdy adolescents into an otherwise calm environment is not the way to win points with your colleagues or your supervisors.

Whatever object you use as a permanent hall pass should be

- unique, so students can't re-create it and sneak out *en masse*
- marked with your name so any "lost" students can be shepherded back to your room
- durable, to withstand use by many wet-handed teenagers and a regular thorough cleaning
- not alluring as a toy or weapon

Because even the most innocuous item can be converted to dark purposes by the wily teenage mind, eliminating all risk of horseplay with your hall pass is impossible. Nevertheless, try to avoid certain obvious attractive nuisances. For example, one teacher we know was asked by colleagues to stop using a frisbee as a hall pass because of the raucous hallway behavior it encouraged. Another teacher had to give up using a heavy wrench as a pass when a student threatened to use it to bludgeon a schoolmate.

4. Students need work materials.

A disorganized classroom: Students must ask the teacher for materials necessary to complete an assignment. The teacher must search through drawers and cabinets to locate the requested items. Repeated for different students, this process can consume half a class period.

An efficient alternative: Organize your room to make it as self-service as possible, as described previously. For activities requiring special materials or equipment, arrange—or better yet, ask your TA to arrange—all necessary items before the class starts. If you have several different classes working on different group projects on the same day, provide a separate box or tote tray to keep each group's belongings together and accessible.

Order will be further enhanced if you prohibit students from leaving their seats without explicit permission from you, except for certain predetermined purposes (e.g., to sharpen a pencil, use a tissue, etc.).

5. Some students finish work early.

A disorganized classroom: Students who complete their work ahead of schedule sit idle, carving their names into furniture or distracting their classmates. In either case, they siphon the teacher's attention from students who are trying to finish the assignment and might need help.

An efficient alternative: Make it clear that students who finish work early should either

- tutor a peer in need,
- finish work for another class, or
- choose and complete an activity from a list of extra-credit possibilities. To inject the element of surprise and encourage students to practice diverse skills, you might write each activity on a separate card and let the student draw an activity randomly from a bag or box.

6. Students do not finish work on time.

A disorganized classroom: Confusion reigns for the last 2 minutes of class as students realize they're out of time and scramble to figure out what to do with unfinished work. Everyone asks where to store the day's work, whether it should be finished as homework, whether being half-finished will earn them partial credit, and so on.

The teacher yells instructions heard by less than half the herd of students stampeding toward the exit.

An efficient alternative: Monitor students' progress, and watch the clock or set a timer so you can stop the class several minutes before its scheduled ending time to announce and post instructions regarding unfinished assignments. Should students take them home and bring them back completed the next day? What if they already have a homework assignment scheduled for that night? Should students keep their work in the classroom for completion in class the following day? Whatever you decide, make it explicit.

7. Students want to hand in finished work or retrieve graded work.

A disorganized classroom: Students must ask where to put their finished assignments, and how to get back their graded work. Sloppy piles of papers—some graded, some not—clutter the room and no one is immediately sure which pile is which. Students sometimes claim the teacher loses their work, and the teacher claims students simply don't hand it in.

An efficient alternative: Set up "in" and "out" boxes where students can deposit completed work and retrieve it later. Also take time to discuss key assignments—individually or collectively, as needed—when you return them to students. Review the criteria against which the assignments were graded, discuss common errors and success strategies, and suggest specifically how students can improve their future performance.

8. Students want to know their grades.

A disorganized classroom: Students harass the teacher every day, asking about their grades, what assignments they're missing, what work they can perform for extra credit, and so forth. Students who lack the time, energy, or inclination to nag the teacher are simply in perpetual darkness about their standing. This may result in unpleasant end-of-term surprises and legitimately angry parents who argue, "You can't give my son a D! He told me he was doing fine in your class. Why didn't I know about this earlier?" This is dangerous territory; antagonize key stakeholders—students, parents, and administrators alike—at your own risk.

An efficient alternative: Post grades regularly (we've found bi-weekly notification to be ideal—it's frequent enough to give students time to take corrective action, yet not so frequent as to make you feel like all you do is post grades). Be sure to mask students' names for posting purposes—most computer grading programs will let you substitute ID numbers for student names and print scores in any order.

9. Students return to school after an absence.

A disorganized classroom: Students returning to school after an absence ask the teacher for missed work, consuming valuable teacher time to reconstruct, explain, and provide materials for the missed lessons.

An efficient alternative: Maintain the lesson clipboard and past month's lesson file discussed earlier. These allow students to figure out what they missed and gather materials on their own, halving the time you'll need to explain things to them. Additionally, if your school maintains a telephone "homework hotline" or school website allowing students and their parents to monitor homework assignments, keep your class information updated.

10. The bell rings, signaling the end of class.

A disorganized classroom: Students cluster raucously at the door in anticipation of their release, storming out the moment the bell sounds and leaving swirls of litter in their wake. Graffiti gradually accumulates in the door area, and nearby teachers complain about the noise.

An efficient alternative: Five minutes before the end of class, give students a warning so they can either be in their seats prepared for a wrap-up of the day's learning or—if you're in the middle of a messy multiday activity—they can finish what they're doing and prepare for cleanup. In the latter case, three minutes before the class ends, announce cleanup time and patrol the room to assist and monitor the process. Have students return to their seats once cleanup is finished, and remain there until the bell rings.

Some teachers ask "all students" to help clean up, which frequently results in only a few conscientious students pitching in voluntarily while the rest weasel out of it. A better alternative is to pre-assign each task to a specific student, as on the room responsibility

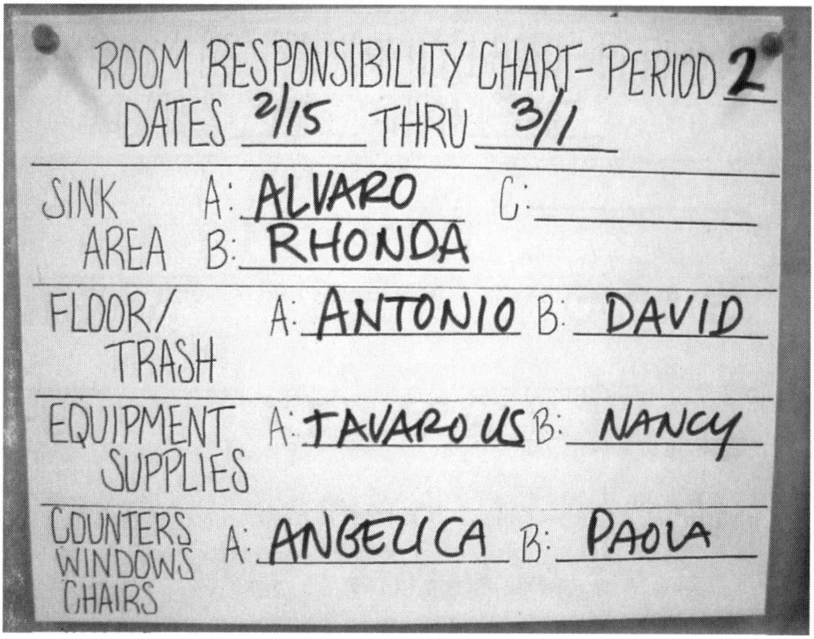

Figure 3.13. **Room responsibility chart.**

chart (Figure 3.13). Rotate cleanup assignments and assign multiple students to each task in case one is absent. In addition, posting the assignments reminds everyone of students' duties, and visually reinforces the concept that all students share the responsibility for maintaining a habitable workspace.

SAMPLE CLEANUP ROLES AND DUTIES

- Timekeeper: to remind you when to initiate "cleanup time"
- Floor patrol: to move all books, trash, and so forth, from the floor to their proper locations
- Desk patrol: to clear all desks and move items found to their proper locations

- Textbook organizer: to help collect and place in numerical order all textbooks
- Supplies organizer: to return any equipment and supplies used to their proper places

WORK SMARTER, NOT HARDER: NEVER DO ANYTHING THE STUDENTS COULD DO

"How are you so productive? What's your secret?" aspiring managers ask seasoned executives. The typical reply? "Surround yourself with good people and support them as they do their jobs." Oh, and find an outstanding assistant.

Alas, you probably won't have a personal secretary or executive assistant. But you will have a roomful of young people eager to contribute to your collective enterprise, especially if it means they can get out of class for 5 minutes to, say, deliver a note to the office, or pick up the school's recycling from each classroom, or handle any other *administrivia* that floats your way and doesn't distract significantly from their learning.

We encourage you to spread the wealth here—many students will enjoy helping you, will learn organizational skills, and will become more engaged in school because you asked them to help and trusted them with responsibility.

Be aware, however, that a few students might view doing your "chores" as some kind of undeserved punishment, which they will perform badly if you force the issue. A few other students might beg to run your errands regularly because they prefer this to schoolwork. Guard against both extremes; after all, you're running a classroom, not a work camp or a courier service.

For more complex tasks, your school can probably provide you with a student eager to work as a teacher's assistant (TA). Typically, students earn generic elective credits for working one period per day as a TA, and the youth who seek these positions are generally not the ones hostile to you or your mission. A well-trained TA can save you countless hours of filing, organizing, record-keeping, decorating, errand-running, and other essential but mind-numbing drudgery. A great TA can go further, performing tasks like research, word processing, graphic design, database management, mass mailing preparation, and other functions typical of an executive assistant.

We recommend maintaining a clipboard specifically as a TA "to do" list—someplace to jot down unfinished tasks as they pop randomly into your head. Otherwise, your TA may finish organizing all your bookshelves and then sit idle.

Keep in mind that how much you ask students to do will depend partly on how competently you want the job done. If you're too much of a perfectionist, you'll end up doing a lot of grunt work yourself. On the other hand, prioritizing and lowering your standards just a little on the less important tasks can leave you a lot more time for the things that really need you.

Imagine, for example, that you have accumulated a to do list that looks like the one in Table 3.5. Note that all of these tasks can be delegated, which in this sample would save you more than six hours and keep your TA busy for a week.

Table 3.5.   TA to Do List

Task	Time
Assemble photocopied handouts for upcoming unit	20 min.
Collect second floor's recycling	30 min.
Find and print out online info on student poetry contest	30 min.
Sort through magazine pile for articles on biotechnology	90 min.
Change current events bulletin board	45 min.
Reorganize encyclopedia shelves	30 min.
Clean off overhead transparencies	20 min.
Check with other teachers about participation in student dinner	60 min.
Clean writing off back tables	20 min.
Sort through art cupboard; recycle or discard unusables	45 min.

Beware, however: Asking a student to complete a task without providing adequate supervision can easily create more work than you had before. Even an activity as seemingly simple as collating and stapling will need to be redone if your well-intentioned but inattentive TA inverts pages or inserts staples so far from the corner as to obscure the content. At least one of your students could probably find a way to mess up even the most apparently straightforward task. So treat it like any other lesson:

1. Give careful instructions, verbally and in writing.
2. Model the task and invite questions.
3. Watch and offer input as the student practices the task.
4. Check back periodically to monitor the student's performance.

THE FIRST WEEK OF SCHOOL

Table 3.6 is our suggested plan for your first week in the classroom. Several features contribute to this model's effectiveness:

- It forces everyone in the class to get acquainted and learn each others' names.
- It exposes students immediately and repeatedly to class rules and procedures.
- It eases students back into school while giving your administration a two-day buffer to process latecomers and adjust student schedules before you launch the actual curriculum.
- It establishes expectations of academic rigor via regular homework assignments.

Frequently Asked Questions About the First Week

Q. Why bother having students and parents sign the rules document, especially since it isn't contractually binding?

A. Many classroom veterans find that the act of signing something puts kids a little more in awe of the document. Additionally, a signed document is a helpful rebuttal to students who plead ignorance of rules when found in violation of them. If your students or their parents complain that they've already signed a rules agreement for the school, insist that they sign yours as well. That will convince them that you're serious, and reinforce those of your rules that may be more strict than school rules.

Table 3.6. First Week of School

Day 1	Day 2	Day 3	Day 4	Day 5
• Set up attendance cards or sheets. • Collect student home & parental data. • Conduct "getting to know you" activity and name game. • Introduce class rules. • Use every student's name at least once.	• Review Day 1 icebreakers & student names. • Establish seating chart. • Introduce and practice class routines. • Send class rules home for students and parents to sign. • Use every student's name at least once.	• Adjust records & seating chart. • Review student names. • Review & practice rules and routines. • Begin first lesson, discuss evaluation procedures, and assign homework to be finished by the next day. • Use every student's name at least once.	• Review homework & complete or recap the first lesson, from the previous day. • Explain the format of any notebooks, portfolios, etc., you will be using and assign homework involving them. • Use every student's name at least once.	• Review homework. • Collect rules agreements, signed by parents. • Begin next lesson, with a different format (for variety)—and don't forget to assign homework. • Use every student's name at least once.

Q. Why should I waste valuable class time on kindergarten activities? My students are old enough to ask each other's names if they want to know; I'd rather get to work and save the touchy-feely stuff for someone else's class. Isn't it a waste to spend the first day on games and "busywork"?

A. No, for three reasons.

First, on the opening day the school administration will probably still be ironing out schedules, and you will need time in class to complete student identification forms, assign books and seats, and lead students through your classroom management procedures. Classroom management specialists Harry and Rosemary Wong explain it well: "The ineffective teacher spends the first day of school attempting to teach a subject and spends the rest of the year running after the students. The effective teacher spends most of the first week teaching the students how to follow classroom procedures" (Wong & Wong, 1998, p. 191).

Second, nobody wants to be back in school on the first day—not you, not your colleagues, and certainly not your students. The only people in the world who are happy when school starts are merchants hawking back-to-school supplies and the parents of school-age children. Students will want to catch up with each other, and need to release their pent-up back-to-school energy. You can channel this energy in a positive direction by engaging students in some very valuable (and yes, fun) "getting to know you" activities.

Third, it's true that your students could ask each other's names. But they won't. We've observed classes at the end of a school year in which students didn't know the names of classmates across the aisle. That forms a poor basis for classroom cooperation. Consider how you might feel if a colleague didn't know your name, even after you had worked together for several months. In addition, getting some sense of students' identities and interests can help you connect the class material to students' "real" lives outside school.

If that's not immediately practical enough: Knowing students' names is one of the most effective disciplinary tools you'll have, particularly in the first few weeks of school. We observed one teacher who didn't know students' names several weeks into class, and the disregard this implied was reciprocated in spades. His students incited chaos at every opportunity and then hid behind their anonymity.

Since he didn't know students' names, the only responses this hapless teacher could offer were weak admonitions like "Young lady, please listen" and "Young man, please sit down." Meanwhile, his students loved the spectacle of their teacher as a plaything. As they pressed his buttons, he howled and spun his wheels until his veins seemed ready to pop.

Using a student's name sends the message that (a) the student is important enough to you to merit the time it takes to learn his name, and (b) the student's behavior and progress in class are being closely monitored. People in a crowd do things individuals would never contemplate because they believe anonymity shields them from responsibility. If you know students' names, you can sling these across the room to stop misbehavior before it starts. This technique might sound like this:

Teacher:	Who can remind us what we learned about noble gases at the end of the period yesterday? Bryan!
Bryan:	Huh?
Teacher:	I'm sure whatever you did this weekend makes a gripping story, Bryan, but right now you need to turn around and stay focused, please. What can you tell us about the noble gases?
Bryan:	Um, there are six of them?
Teacher:	Okay. Who can add to Bryan's description? Sherisse?
Sherisse:	They're stable.
Teacher:	All right. Vanessa, it's easier to focus if your eyes are here and not on Javier's paper. Who can add something else? Lisa, are you with us? You have that look like, "I have a question." No? We're going to move pretty fast today, but stop us if there's something you don't understand. Who can add to what Bryan and Sherisse have given us?

And so on. The experienced teacher—even in lecture/discussion mode as in the above dialogue—uses students' names continuously to monitor understanding, keep everyone engaged, and remind all students of their membership in a group with a shared mission.

Q. What activities can help my students get acquainted?

A. Here are a few common icebreaker activities:

Memory Challenge: Students sit in a circle, and the first volunteer reveals her name and something she likes that begins with the same letter. For example, "I'm Joanna and I like jellybeans." The next person then recites the previous name and introduces himself or herself, as in, "This is Joanna and she likes jellybeans. I'm Mike and I like music." After the last person in the circle recalls everyone's name, the teacher should give it a try and then invite volunteers to do the same. Some teachers find that some form of recognition or token prize increases student engagement.

Personal Coat of Arms: Each student creates a large shield or flag that visually depicts four elements of her or his past, values, hopes, passions, and so forth (see Figure 3.14). Pairs of students can use the completed coats of arms as prompts when introducing each other to the class. In our experience, students of all ages enjoy making the personal coat of arms and post them with pride on permanent folders or binders they use to store their classwork.

Common Ground Bingo: Students circulate and try to find classmates who meet criteria listed in the boxes on their game cards—for example, "Find someone who has lived out of the country," "Find someone who can whistle," or "Find someone whose favorite subject is math." The winner is the first person to complete the card with signatures of people who meet the criteria described in the boxes.

Our website (www.classroomadvisor.com) provides a blank personal coat of arms template and sample bingo forms, as well as links to additional examples of icebreaker activities.

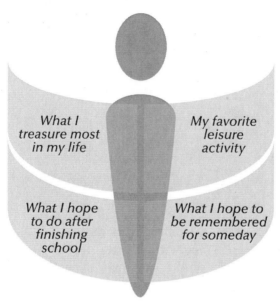

Figure 3.14.   Personal coat of arms.

Q. What activities can I use to teach listening skills?

A. In chapter 4, "Communication Essentials," we recommend a
few proactive (and fun) activities to reinforce listening skills.
These exercises can not only spark lively discussions about
communication problems and the value of listening, but also
provide memorable case studies to reference if challenges arise
during the year. Our website (www.classroomadvisor.com) offers additional recommendations.

If Your First Day Is Disastrous

If your first attempt is a belly flop, should you give up? Think of it
this way: Even if you make an absolute fool of yourself in your first
go-round, students will usually forgive you. For one thing, they have
short memories. Any teacher who has tried to elicit a summary of
the previous day's lesson from a group of teenagers at 8 A.M. can verify this. Besides, it's not like things always go perfectly in their other
classes either.

Also, unless you gave an opening-day lecture with your fly unzipped, whatever you thought was disastrous was probably much less significant to your students. In reality, your house could burn down and the average student would be less concerned about it than about the untimely zit that he fears could ruin his upcoming date with Suzie Whiteshoes. This is nothing against you; it's just that teenagers have enough to worry about just, well, being teenagers.

If your best-laid plans start spiraling toward disaster, talk to someone who's been there (preferably a fellow teacher, *not* an administrator—why draw attention to yourself as a whiner or incompetent in your boss's eyes if you can avoid it?). Find a kind colleague and describe—or, ideally, ask your confidant to come and observe—your problem class, and solicit all the suggestions you can.

If you made it through your first day with no major mishaps and you're still standing, congratulations! You're on the way to succeeding at one of the most challenging, important, and deeply rewarding jobs in the world.

4

COMMUNICATION ESSENTIALS

Engaging students in learning is your fundamental duty as a teacher. Conveniently, it's also the surest way to please the various stakeholders—students, parents, and administrators alike—on whose satisfaction your job rightly depends. And it's a great proactive classroom management tool because, as emphasized repeatedly in this book, students who are absorbed in learning are also much less likely to make trouble.

Effective communication is key to engaging and motivating students. As entire libraries have been written on this topic, this short chapter is not intended to be comprehensive; instead we seek to highlight how communication techniques can either support or undermine effective classroom management.

LAYING THE GROUNDWORK

How can you structure content delivery to maximize student interest, understanding, and retention? We recommend building your lessons around a uniform lesson-planning template like the one we present here (modified slightly from Madeline Hunter's classic model). Table 4.1 describes the components of an effective lesson.

Table 4.1. Components of an Effective Lesson

Timing	Lesson Component	Description
Pre-lesson	Curriculum standards	District curriculum goals addressed by the lesson
	Learning objectives	Specific actions successful learners will be able to perform by the end of the lesson
	Assessment (pre-lesson)	Survey or other tool to determine what students know about the topic and their attitude toward it
Lesson	Assessment (mid-lesson)	Teacher actions throughout the lesson to ensure that students are on track and truly understanding • Informal checks (continuous) • Quizzes, other standardized devices (periodic)
	Framing	Preemptive answering of the questions "Why are we studying this? Why now? How does this connect to everything else?"
	Hook	Engaging riddle, question, anecdote, etc., at the start of the lesson to capture students' attention and draw them in (usually ties to previous lessons; ideally kept in view all period)
	Input	Presentation of new content and/or skills to be learned (via reading, observation, lecture, discussion, discovery, etc.)
	Modeling	Demonstration for students of skilled application of the new skills and/or information
	Guided practice	Student practice under guidance of the teacher (with supervision and assistance)
	Independent practice	Student practice without the teacher, in class or at home
	Closure	Summary of lesson and link to following lesson
	Homework	Follow-up assignment to reinforce past learning and/or to prepare for a coming lesson
Post-lesson	Assessment (post-lesson)	Test, essay, performance, or other assessment to determine whether students met the intended learning objectives

Curriculum Standards

Every jurisdiction requires students to master certain skills and content in each subject and grade level. Refer to your district curriculum standards to help you plan lessons that help students meet these required learning goals.

Learning Objectives

Determine specifically what students will be able to do by the lesson's end. Post these for everyone's review at the start of the lesson; this will inform students where they're going and help hold everyone accountable.

A simple, common format for lesson objectives is TLW (The Learner Will), describing what the learner will be able to do to prove competence at the end of the lesson. For example:

By the end of this lesson, the learner will be able to

- solve a quadratic equation
- create a coherent argument to support a chosen political platform
- coach a peer to improve the ease of use of her website
- analyze the use of metaphor in two poems
- generate and test a hypothesis about cell growth in different chemical environments

Note that these objectives are all specific to the lesson at hand and observable. Vague phrasing like "Students will *understand* X or Y" creates objectives that are inherently unprovable. You cannot know students have understood unless you can observe some performance flowing from this understanding.

Assessment

Assessment in general is the process of determining where students stand in relation to the material they're supposed to be learning. Here we focus on three categories of assessments (see Table 4.2 and Figure 4.1).

Table 4.2.   The Three Types of Assessment

Type	Purpose
A. Pre-lesson assessment	Determine what students already know about the topic and their attitude toward it
B. Mid-lesson assessment	Determine whether students are on track to success, *while there's still time to course-correct and reach the intended goals,* through • Informal checks for understanding (continuous) • Quizzes and other standardized devices (periodic)
C. Post-lesson assessment	Determine whether students succeeded in learning what was intended (and whether the teacher succeeded in teaching it)

Assessment Type A: Pre-lesson Assessment

Before the lesson begins, conduct a short test, survey, or other pre-lesson assessment to understand students' *current reality* in relation to the material to be learned. This could be as simple as asking students to take a short quiz, write answers to a few questions, or perform an abbreviated version of whatever post-lesson assessment you plan to use to evaluate student learning at the end of the lesson. Stress that students' scores on the quiz will not be part of their grades. You can't hold students accountable for knowing something you haven't yet taught them.

As many of your lessons will build explicitly on previous lessons, a pre-lesson assessment will likely not be necessary for every lesson. We advise using one whenever the chain of learning continuity is broken (e.g., at the start of each term, each new unit, or whenever the concepts to be presented seem particularly challenging).

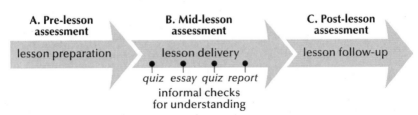

Figure 4.1.   The three types of assessment in relationship to a generic lesson.

Assessment Type B: Mid-lesson Assessment

Imagine being captain of a ship. Would you point your vessel in the right direction, give your crew instructions once, then close your eyes and hope to reach the proper destination unscathed? We hope not. Students, like a ship's crew, require continuous monitoring, coaching, and course correction. And given teens' notoriously limited attention spans, most require regular direction and prompting to stay focused.

Rare indeed is the student courageous enough to stop the class and ask for clarification the moment she doesn't understand something. Most adolescents, already terrified of wearing an out-of-style haircut or the wrong shoes, cannot imagine publicly asking questions that might make them look "stupid." The onus therefore falls upon you to be sure your students are getting it. While the lesson is in progress, apply two types of assessment to be sure students are on track to learning what you intend.

First, continually check for understanding in an informal way. Listen for uncertainty in students' tone of voice, watch for lost looks, and keep an eye open for what Madeline Hunter calls "bright eyes"—visible signs that what you've been talking about all period has finally clicked. Ask questions and demand answers (just be sure to give students sufficient time to think through what you're asking). Also invite students to explain ideas in their own words to determine the depth and quality of their comprehension.

One of our favorite techniques for checking for understanding is "doing the Columbo" (named for the fictional television detective who solved crimes partly by playing dumb). The goal: Pretend to be curious but ignorant about a topic to lure students into demonstrating their understanding of it.

One high school psychologist demonstrates "doing the Columbo"—she cocks her head, places a finger on her chin, and wears a puzzled expression to accompany the earnest-sounding claim, "I'm not sure I understand. Can you explain exactly how . . . ?" (M. Hironaka, personal communication). Most students jump at such a chance to display their knowledge and, in the event that a student makes a statement of questionable validity, others almost invariably step in to offer elaboration or correction.

The second type of mid-lesson assessment consists of more formal and periodic checks for understanding. These commonly take the form of brief quizzes, journal entries, short oral reports, and other minor assessments that can be conducted frequently and easily. The purpose is twofold: first, to acknowledge and occasionally reward student progress, and second, to ensure that students are on track before they prove they're not by failing a test or other major assessment.

If you discover through your mid-lesson assessments that students didn't learn what you tried to teach them, don't just issue a bunch of Fs and move on. Try again. Educators Neil Postman and Charles Weingartner remark on the absurdity of many teachers' explanations of high failure rates:

> It is not uncommon . . . to hear "teachers" make statements like, "Oh I taught them that, but they didn't learn it." There is no utterance made in the Teacher's Room more extraordinary than this. . . . [I]t is on the same level as a salesman's remarking, "I sold it to him, but he didn't buy it"—which is to say, it makes no sense. (Postman & Weingartner, 1969, p. 50)

Our view is that repeatedly issuing failing grades to students who perform unsatisfactory work benefits no one. In the part-time jobs many students hold in the "real world," they do not mop only part of the floor or serve only half of the customers and then walk away thinking, "Oh well, I guess I failed that." If a work task is sloppily completed, the logical consequence is that the task must be redone until the outcome is satisfactory. Teachers should accept no less from students.

The teacher who frequently "fails" students does indeed fail them; in our experience, such teachers frequently do not use all available techniques to reach all students. If a task you've assigned proves too difficult for many students, don't simply watch them flail and then give Fs to students who didn't succeed. This may sound laughable, but we have seen many teachers whose "sink or swim" mentality effectively does just that.

Instead, modify challenging tasks as necessary, or ask questions that help nudge students in the right direction, along with coaching and encouragement to help them reach the goal. Much of the rest of this book offers additional suggestions to support student success.

Of course, it's always useful to point out that some people failed because they simply did not do the homework, or because they had unnecessary absences. Without embarrassing individuals, this can help them understand the cause-effect relationship. Many adolescents are locked into a kind of magical thinking and don't see how they contribute to their own problems.

Assessment Type C: Post-lesson Assessment

This type of assessment is what most people think of when they think of *assessment*—it is the test, performance, or other mechanism conducted at the end of a lesson (or unit, or term) to determine whether students have mastered the skills and knowledge set forth in the initial objectives.

Many students find post-lesson assessments stressful because they're uncertain about how they will perform, but if you conduct regular mid-lesson assessments and course-correct as necessary during the lesson, the outcome of the post-lesson assessment should surprise no one.

As described in chapter 2, "Who Are Your Students?" and later in this chapter, incorporating appropriate variety into lessons and assessments can better engage students, improve their learning, and give you a more complete picture of their performance. Our website (www.classroomadvisor.com) provides several sources of innovative assessments to help expand your repertoire.

STRUCTURE OF EFFECTIVE LESSONS

Framing

To greatly increase comprehension and retention of new concepts, help students organize and integrate these into their existing understandings of the world. The act of *framing* creates a sort of mental scaffold by making explicit what is to come and tying the current lesson to what students know already. Pre-lesson assessments can yield insights useful for this purpose.

Framing also preemptively answers questions like "Why are we doing this? Why are we studying this now? How does this relate to what we've studied in the past?" Students may not ask these questions aloud, but they will be wondering. If they're still wondering when the lesson is over, you'll need to do a better job framing future lessons.

If you are a natural storyteller, beware: Lessons should not unfold like tales of suspense, which deliberately leave the audience hanging with no idea when or how the next plot point will unfold. This may make an entertaining narrative, but it neglects opportunities to reinforce concepts and can thereby reduce student retention.

One young teacher relates a personal story that illustrates our point:

> I grew up in a family of great storytellers, and it rubbed off on me. It's an art that comes in handy in all kinds of situations, especially the classroom. The problem is, a lot of stories rely on subtlety and surprise; [the audience has] to listen carefully and wait for a punch line. This can work great with some audiences, but isn't always ideal for the classroom. You can enthrall them with a lot of great stories, but in the end they may have trouble sorting it out and figuring out what's really important. (A. Smithee, personal communication)

Of course, if you can keep students paying attention by keeping them on the edge of their seats, this is a good thing. But don't feel obligated to be a master storyteller. Instead, err on the side of repetition. This may seem dull to you, but *hammering the important* will improve student learning. As a veteran teacher describes:

> The first time I tell students something, it goes here [with his finger, he traces the imaginary arc of an idea flying over students' heads]. The second time, it goes here [he shows an idea bouncing off students' foreheads]. The third time, it comes out here [he shows an idea coming out of students' mouths]." (R. Meester, personal communication)

Hook

Like the hook in a news story, the *hook* of a lesson comes at the beginning and focuses students' attention while enticing them to care about the upcoming content. Create a good hook by telling a compelling story, posing an intriguing riddle, or asking a challenging question that will be answered by the lesson to follow.

Input

This is the phase of lesson delivery that many people think of first when they think of teaching: Give students the information they'll need to build the knowledge and skills targeted in the lesson objectives. This may be delivered through any communication medium—lecture, reading, observation, discussion, discovery, and so forth. As discussed in chapter 2, "Who Are Your Students?" different individuals have different strengths, so reaching all students (and reinforcing the content for every student) may require multiple modes of information delivery. More visual learners may need to see the information, kinesthetic learners may need to touch it, interpersonal learners may need to discuss it with someone, and so on. You will likely need to repeat the input in several formats.

Modeling

Following the input stage, demonstrate for students what they will be expected to do and learn during the lesson by applying the new material. *Modeling* normally includes explanations, examples (perhaps including samples of other students' work), analogies, demonstrations, and so forth. These can be performed by you, a student, an outside expert, or anyone else with a high degree of competence in the task at hand. Be sure to help mediate the material and make your reasoning transparent by talking through the thinking underlying each step as you model it.

Guided Practice

After modeling what you expect of students, instruct them to work through an exercise while you circulate through the room to monitor and assist them. Education researcher Eric Jensen offers these guidelines for giving students feedback: "The more often the better. The more immediate the better. The greater the specificity, the better. The more appropriately dramatic, the better. The longer feedback is delayed, the less useful" (Jensen, 1996, p. 285).

Madeline Hunter recommends recognizing hardworking students by telling them exactly what they did right and reiterating the principles they employed to get there (Hunter, 1976, pp. 19–21). For example, you might observe aloud that a student's work is excellent, adding, "It looks like you're using the right ratio to convert those figures. At this rate, hopefully you can get started plotting the path on your map before the end of the hour."

Note that this type of commentary not only fulfills the specificity requirement, but also prompts the student to continue working. Without this additional prodding, approval messages sometimes backfire, particularly with low performers who may reason, "Oh, she likes what I'm doing. I guess I've done enough for today."

Independent Practice

Reinforce learning by assigning additional exercises for students to work through on their own. This often starts in the classroom and continues at home.

Closure

Review the lesson's main points with students to help clarify, reinforce, tie together, and anchor key learnings in their minds. Also underscore how the lesson connects to the rest of the course material—i.e., repeat the framing you set out at the start of the lesson, and preview the framing you will offer for the lesson to follow.

Our website (www.classroomadvisor.com) provides a repro-
ducible blank form we encourage you to use in planning your own
lessons, and a completed sample for your reference.

KEY ELEMENTS OF EFFECTIVE LESSONS: RELEVANCE, VARIETY, AND LEVEL OF DIFFICULTY

On your best days, diligent planning and passionate execution of
your lessons will awaken students' intellectual curiosity and trigger
flashes of student insight—those elusive *Aha!* moments—to remind
you why you embarked on your career.

Don't expect to be routinely dazzled by student engagement and
inquisitiveness, however. As mentioned previously, a large portion
of your class may frequently sit blankly and ask—or, if they're more
polite, quietly wonder—"So what?" As intimated earlier under
"Framing," your job is to make the material not only intelligible but
also enticing. The bottom line: Our job as teachers is to show students *why they should care.*

How? This section explores three elements of outstanding teaching: relevance of the material to students, variety of lessons, and appropriate level of difficulty.

Relevance

As Einstein observed, "It is a miracle that curiosity survives formal
education." We believe that the educator's goal should be to nurture,
not trample, individual impulses for exploration. We further believe
that within every field of study, there exists some maneuvering
room to improve student engagement by integrating ideas and problems from students' own lives.

How can you make the curriculum relevant to students? Start by
tweaking it to accommodate young peoples' existing interests and
natural curiosity. Education researcher Grant Wiggins decries what
he sees as a disturbing dearth of student investment and craftsman-
ship in many classrooms—"a far cry from what one witnesses on the

athletic field, on stages, and in vocational wings." This, he asserts, reflects the average classroom's failure to address student interests and thereby allow students to "own" their work.

Too many teachers, instead of encouraging students to relate the curriculum to what they care about, treat students as mere receptacles for others' preprocessed knowledge. Such an "education," laments Wiggins, "remains a forgettable patchwork of adult sayings" (Wiggins, 1989, p. 48).

Echoing Wiggins and numerous others, educator Herbert Kohl rejects the idea that "learning . . . ought to be identical for all pupils. There is no one way to learn, nor are there specific stories or experiments all young people must go through." He urges teachers instead "to respond to [students'] desire to learn about things and not cut off their enthusiasm in the service of getting through the curriculum" (Kohl, 1969, pp. 31, 52).

Does this mean we should focus only on topics that adolescents find interesting? Of course not. That's a legitimately terrifying thought. And besides, the curriculum is what teachers are paid and professionally obligated to cover. When students perceive subjects to be irrelevant to them, however, they tend to resist learning.

As Neil Postman and Charles Weingartner (1969) observe,

> There is no way to help a learner to be disciplined, active, and thoroughly engaged unless he perceives a problem or whatever is to-be-learned as worth learning. . . . [Yet much of the] curriculum in today's schools does not allow inquiry into most of the critical problems that comprise the content of the world outside the school. (pp. 60, 65)

Rather than address issues that have meaning to students, Postman and Weingartner assert, courses cover topics (e.g., the economics of ancient Egypt) irrelevant to those learning them. Most teachers could certainly enliven the subjects they teach by building in problems to which students can relate, and that they would actively like to engage.

Curriculum requirements therefore ought not to be interpreted too rigidly. Rather than serving as dogma to which learners must adhere in every detail, curriculum standards can serve as guidelines for classroom investigation, which can also accommodate student interests.

Why not teach students geography and math by asking them to create itineraries for their own fantasy world cruise or for traveling sports teams or concert tours? Or help them learn geometry and economics concepts by planning a construction project or monitoring personal finances? Or encourage them to master introspection, moral thinking, and the art of narrative by scripting and filming dramatic scenes based on turning points in their lives, or writing letters to people in the past who made a difference to them? Or teach biology and cooperation by arranging group exploration and measurement of the natural environment around the school, or the analysis of a school lunch's nutritional value?

How else can you help generate student interest? Try the following:

- Translate the terms into their language (but beware of trying to use student slang; this can be a near-death experience unless you're doing it blatantly tongue-in-cheek).
- Analogize relentlessly to bridge the gap between the content and students' life experience.
- Ask students what links they see—for example, how the day's topic resembles or impacts their lives, or how they might use what they're learning outside school.
- Bring in outside resources like readings, videos, or guest speakers to illustrate real-world applications of the topic.
- Start with an activity students like, and move step-by-step deeper into less familiar material.

Our website (www.classroomadvisor.com) offers links to additional ideas.

Variety

Variety is also crucial for engaging all students. In our discussion of Multiple Intelligences in chapter 2, "Who Are Your Students?" we mentioned the various strengths and learning preferences that students in your classroom will display. The precise configuration of these strengths will vary depending on the composition of each class, but you can bet that on average, a variety of teaching techniques will both increase the number of students you reach and improve your success with any given student.

As educator Shirley Jordan observes, a great deal of empirical data indicates that "by fourth or fifth grade students show a marked diminution of enthusiasm for school activities, followed by reduced motivation and academic progress." One contributor to this worrisome trend, Jordan (1996) believes, is the fact that "by the middle grades, multidisciplinary learning is replaced by strategies focusing primarily on only the two intelligences required for reading, computing, and answering questions" (p. 30).

In our experience, instructional strategies that engage multiple intelligences tend to yield more engaged, more cooperative, and more productive students. Young people taught to view themselves through a multiple-intelligences lens tend to gain self-respect, feel more empowered, and approach their education with positive rather than aggressive or defeatist attitudes. Anything less cheats students out of a fully engaging learning experience.

Table 2.3 is a good reference for your lesson planning. The right-hand column suggests various types of activities you can build into your classes to capitalize on students' diverse strengths and learning preferences. Our website (www.classroomadvisor.com) provides links to additional resources.

Another aspect of variety essential to keeping students engaged is including an assortment of activities *within* each class period. We recommend changing activities several times each period, with a maximum of 20–30 minutes spent on any single activity. Large, intricate projects are an important part of cultivating higher-level thinking and problem solving, but for typical days, try to build in several brief hands-on activities every lesson. These will help keep students engaged and the class moving.

One young teacher learned this the hard way by assembling for a high school class an extravagant multiday art history lesson that, brimming as it was with visuals and interactivity, he thought should have dazzled students. Instead, it thudded. Why? It asked students to sit in a dimly lit room for 2 hours at 8 a.m. without enough change built in to keep the routine from getting stale. The students didn't fall asleep, exactly, but their energy level just wasn't up to the prolonged periods of concentration he naively expected from them.

A better approach would have been to vary the activities to keep the dynamic fresh and students on their toes. For example: "Now turn to your neighbor and practice this for 2 minutes" or "Now we'll pause for 3 minutes to brainstorm silently five possible reasons for X" or "Now move to a different station and perform task Y for 15 minutes" or "Now let's turn to the photos the TA is handing out and take 3 minutes to observe as much as you can."

Many teachers believe that building variety and creativity into the classroom can be a lot of work. This is true—but not true enough to keep great teachers from putting forth the effort to engage and inspire their students.

Let's look at some common excuses we have heard for uninspired teaching techniques:

- "I don't have time to do all that."
- "I'm not creative enough to come up with all those new ideas."
- "I'm not paid to entertain these kids."

"I don't have time to do all that."

Teachers who complain they "don't have time" are often right. For first-year teachers in particular, simultaneously mastering classroom management, new interpersonal relationships, and the school bureaucracy is a daunting challenge.

For all other teachers, however, lack of time is often attributable merely to disorganization. Chapter 3 lays out numerous suggestions to help run your classroom smoothly, precisely so you can devote your energy to better lesson planning. For most teachers, "lack of time" really means lack of organization or lack of will. What you prioritize will happen.

"I'm not creative enough to come up with all those new ideas."

Those who feel they lack creativity may also be correct; not everyone is comfortable being an inventor. But sometimes this only reflects intellectual laziness (ironic, considering how many teachers bemoan this in their own students). An hour of focused brainstorming—on your own or with colleagues in your department—can yield a small pile of remarkable seed ideas, concepts that with a little nurturing and pruning can sprout into spectacular lessons.

Other teachers feel restricted by the textbooks chosen by their state and school district. Textbooks, by definition, are simplified, homogenized, and often quite dull. This is a legitimate problem, but for a good teacher to allow a bad text to bore students is, in our opinion, a cop-out. If the textbook you're given would have been better written by a troop of chimpanzees, supplement it with other material.

Dozens of books and Internet resources provide creative lessons from teachers around the world. Our website (www.classroom advisor.com) lists some of these. They may need to be massaged to fit your curriculum or your students, or overhauled completely, but a few hours of research can often spare you the dozens of hours of work and great anguish that accompany planning every single lesson yourself. Your first year will contain plenty of challenges beyond curriculum design, and ready-made lessons can sometimes be your salvation.

"I'm not paid to entertain these kids."

Truth or myth? "School should be fun. If students act bored, I should change something." Harry and Rosemary Wong argue convincingly that students who complain about being bored need to stop whining and start working. "If you believe that learning should be fun," they advise new teachers, "you are doing the students a disservice. The student becomes a victim, thinking that everything in life should be fun and that anything that isn't fun is boring" (Wong & Wong, 1998, p. 3).

Point taken. As Greek philosophers might argue, life without reflection, service, and productivity is life wasted. But in our view, life should also be about more than just work—for you and your students. It does not need to be *entertaining*, but it should be *engaging*. So what's the appropriate balance?

Certainly students deserve better instruction than "read the textbook and complete these worksheets." Your grandparents may have endured that kind of schooling, but we believe that with the technology and information available in the 21st century, every subject should be lively and relevant, if not always fun. See the previous sections for recommendations on this.

Level of Difficulty

In our discussion of stretch goals in chapter 2, "Who Are Your Students?" we mentioned how, as with a physical workout, intellectual growth occurs only when the work is sufficiently challenging. If a task is too easy, students will exert minimal effort and quickly grow bored and restless. If it's too difficult, many will give up and also become restless. Either way, you've set yourself up for trouble because from a classroom management perspective, the last thing you want is a roomful of restless adolescents.

Also keep in mind when introducing new concepts that students will need to be able to walk before you can expect them to run. For example, students who don't know how to compute percentages will have difficulty understanding concepts like compound interest, air pollution figures, or polling data. Similarly, if students are largely unschooled in a particular language (of a culture, field of study, or profession), it is unrealistic to expect them to have sophisticated thoughts or conversations about it.

To help ease students into new subjects, create a series of challenges that ladder up in terms of complexity and difficulty. Bloom's taxonomy can help guide this process.

Bloom's Taxonomy

In a seminal exploration of human learning, Benjamin Bloom created a model describing six levels of thought, from rudimentary to sophisticated, which he encouraged teachers to address consciously and continuously. According to Bloom's taxonomy, learners must master lower-level processes before they can succeed at more advanced levels of thought.

Beware of the trap that ensnares many teachers—allowing students to work only at the lower levels because these are less demanding to teach, easier for students to grasp, and faster to assess using traditional standardized tests. Allowing students to stop progressing after reaching, say, only the third or fourth level of the taxonomy denies students the opportunity to develop the most valuable skills—critical and creative thinking and decision making—at the top of the hierarchy.

If you stop teaching once students have learned "what" and "how" without asking them to dissect an issue in detail, ask "why?", imagine alternatives, or make informed judgments about it, you have done only half your job.

An essential part of constructing units and lessons, then, is to build in an ascending series of tasks to move students up Bloom's ladder (see Figure 4.2).

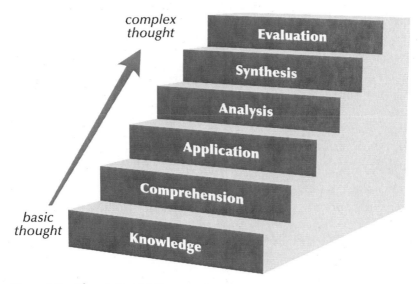

Figure 4.2. Bloom's taxonomy.

The most basic level of thought, according to Bloom, is simple *knowledge*. When students recognize or recall information without manipulating it, they are functioning at this level. Questions requiring knowledge-level answers frequently begin with words like "list," "recall," and "define." Many fill-in-the-blank, matching, and multiple-choice tests demand only this level of thinking.

Bloom's second level of thought is *comprehension*. This type of thinking involves the learner transforming information, often so it can be more easily understood and assimilated. Explaining orally the significance of a statistical table is an example of this level of thought, as is defining an idea in "one's own words." Questions calling for comprehension-level answers might begin with phrases like "give an example of," or "compare and contrast."

The third level in the taxonomy is *application*, which requires students to use some previous knowledge to answer a question or solve a problem. Ideally, the knowledge and/or tool necessary to solve the problem would not be immediately obvious to the student, thus testing her ability not only to apply knowledge but also to select an effective approach. Examples of the application level of thought include students solving proofs in geometry or, in biology, finding a procedure to identify a mysterious cell. Questions demanding application-level answers often begin with words like "solve," or "given (a), produce (b)."

Bloom's fourth level of thought, *analysis*, calls for in-depth exploration of a topic. The goal is to dissect something and discover not only what it does, but also *how* and *why*. Analysis focuses particularly on uncovering assumptions, implications, and motives behind ideas or events. Asking students to describe the intended purpose of a piece of art or predict the effect of industrialization on the environment demands analysis, because it requires attention to detail and exploration beneath the surface of the issues. Questions using the words "infer," "investigate," and "explain in detail" usually require analysis-level responses.

Synthesis, the fifth level in the taxonomy, involves combining knowledge and ideas in a new way to create a product that is "more than just the sum of its parts; the parts are held together in a unique combination—the whole" (Orlich, Harder, Callahan, & Gibson, 1994, p. 120). Like any work of art or invention, a product of true synthesis combines knowledge and imagination, and therefore could not be produced exactly the same way by anyone but its creator. The student who writes a poem or song, drafts a ballot initiative or architectural blueprint, or invents a theory or machine engages in synthesis. The words "imagine," "create," and "design" often indicate synthesis-level activities.

Bloom's sixth level of thought, *evaluation,* asks students to judge the value of the subject under scrutiny. Evaluation requires students first to establish conscious standards on which to base judgments and, second, to document precisely how the topic in question meets or fails to meet those standards. In a sense, then, it combines synthesis (creating unique criteria) with analysis (exploring in detail how the criteria match up with the topic at hand). Evaluation could include deciding who should be president, determining whether a particular novel is "great literature," or judging whether high schools ought to have open campuses. Questions demanding evaluation-level answers often include the word "should," or some variation thereof.

Although there is some debate about whether synthesis or evaluation should occupy the top of the hierarchy, the general point is that each level of thinking builds on lower-level abilities. For example, students cannot truly synthesize without being able to recall, comprehend, apply, and analyze. For this reason, a solid foundation of lower-order thinking skills is essential for students to succeed at higher-order thinking (Orlich et al., pp. 110–122; Hunter, 1976, pp. 45–52; Sebranek, Meyer, & Kemper, 1996, p. 545).

How can you determine whether a task is calibrated to the right level of difficulty for the students in question? One key indicator is the speed at which students move through the material. If students take half as long or twice as long to get through something as you anticipated, rethink the task.

On the other hand, our own students routinely came to us to complain that we made them "think too much." This we view as the highest compliment a student can deliver, and is a good sign that the level of difficulty is right. If your students simply give up, no matter how much support and cajoling you offer, you'll know you've gone too far.

WHAT DOES IT LOOK LIKE? COMPONENTS OF EFFECTIVE COMMUNICATION

Many new teachers quite naturally mold their own teaching styles to some degree on their most recent exemplars: their own college instructors. The *college lecturer* model of teaching typically follows a pattern something like:

*lecture • reading • lecture • discuss reading •
lecture • attend lab • lecture • test*

Although this model can be efficient in certain limited circumstances, our experience and a great deal of research both indicate that the *college lecturer* approach, which heavily emphasizes lectures and reading, is uniquely ill-suited to the secondary classroom. First, it neglects the numerous varieties of intelligence described in chapter 2, "Who Are Your Students?" thus missing opportunities to connect with students for whom sitting still, reading, and listening may not be an optimal way to learn.

Second, the *college lecturer* model depends for success on highly motivated students. Most teenagers, however, will not complete four-year college degrees, and are likely to be neither as intellectually inclined nor as academically skilled as their teachers. Therefore, teaching strategies that may have worked for you as a student promise far less spectacular results among the bulk of your students. College professors enjoy an unusual luxury—their students generally want to be there; many of your students will likely be there under duress.

To demonstrate our point, let's peek into a real classroom observed by the authors. The teacher, Mr. O., stood in front of a roomful of high school students and started a lecture as follows.

Today is April 15. Does anyone know what's special about this day? It's a special day in the United States—tax day. This is the day when you have to file your income tax returns or you pay a penalty to the IRS. Does anyone know what the IRS stands for? No? It stands for Internal Revenue Service. They're the government agency that comes and takes a big chunk of your paycheck. Unless you're very rich. Then you can get away with a lot. You can put your money in a tax shelter and it grows by compound interest.

Does anyone know what I mean by compound interest? It's when you put money in an account and it grows each day, and the more you put in the more it grows. It's a little like bowling. How many of you have been bowling? In bowling, you can get a strike, which is knocking all the pins down in one try, or a spare, which is knocking all the pins down in two tries, or some other score. But if you get a strike, you get to add the score you get from your next two tries to the score for the strike, so your score really multiplies. Let me draw it, here. . . .

Bowling is a great game for your math skills. And it's a lot of fun— it's a very social activity. I've bowled at a bowling alley over on 114th St. for 28 years. They have a great bowling alley at the Air Force Academy. Does anyone know where the Air Force Academy is? Anyone? No? It's in Colorado. Let me show you on this map. . . . It's right here. It's in a beautiful town right next to the mountains. And they have a very famous—does anyone know what's famous there? They have a beautiful cathedral.

My son was married in that cathedral. You have to be affiliated with the Academy to do that. He's a lieutenant in the Air Force. He was a student at the Air Force Academy, which is a very good school. He studied very hard in high school, which I hope most of you are going to do. And he gave the speech at his graduation. Maybe tomorrow I'll bring in the video of his speech, so you can see it. . . .

. . . and so on. Mr. O.'s presentation went on like this for 30 minutes, but you get the idea; we won't torture you further. How many opportunities for improvement did you observe?

Here are five we spotted:

1. Mr. O.'s presentation was a monologue. He filled 95% of the class time with his own voice, and made no real effort to engage students. Occasionally he asked questions, but they were all closed-ended, requiring yes/no or other one-word answers. He

didn't give students much time to think, and when students failed to answer, he answered the questions himself.

2. The monologue seemed to drift forward, sideways, and backward randomly, with no plan, no purpose, and no notice. Adding to the aimless quality, nothing was written anywhere in the room, and the students had no materials to work with or understanding of why they were being subjected to these stories. This kind of teacher may brag about not needing to plan his classes, which in our experience is a likely sign of a charlatan—one who talks a lot but actually teaches little.

3. Mr. O. veered into a series of personal war stories that were not only irrelevant to the curriculum, but also uninteresting to almost anyone but himself. The topics he covered were inappropriate and a waste of class time.

4. He made little effort to check students' comprehension, or even their pulse. He showed little emotion and through most of the lecture failed to look at most of the class, instead locking eyes with and speaking directly to the one unlucky student who chose the front center seat. Partly because of Mr. O.'s perpetual monotone and partly because he failed to relate the topics to each other or to students' lives in any significant way, most of his words bounced right off his audience, rarely if ever soaking in.

5. Mr. O. spoke for far too long. As mentioned earlier, with secondary students we recommend changing activities several times per class period with, as a rule of thumb, 30 minutes as the outer time limit for the duration of any single activity. For lectures, we recommend a shorter time limit: 15–20 minutes. Even if Mr. O.'s story had been essential to the curriculum and thrilling for the audience, 30 minutes would likely have been too long. As it was, students' eyes started glazing over and their heads started to droop before 10 minutes had elapsed, and for the rest of the lecture they waited silently for the end-of-class bell to liberate them.

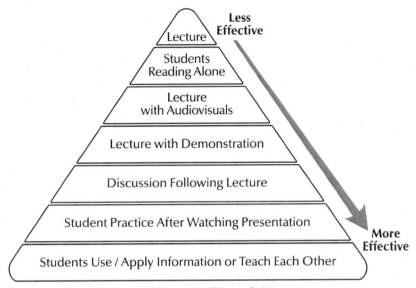

Figure 4.3.   Effectiveness of different teaching techniques.

Luckily, there is a better way. Our recommendations for effective communication in the secondary classroom are informed by two fundamental research findings.

The first relevant finding is a Learning Pyramid popularized by National Training Laboratories, which compares the effectiveness of various kinds of teaching strategies (see Figure 4.3).

The second relevant finding arose through an investigation by researcher Albert Mehrabian into the communication of emotional messages. Mehrabian found that spoken words convey only a tiny percentage (approximately 7% in his study) of the meaning people actually glean from a message. He found approximately 5 times as much (around 38%) was communicated by vocal cues, while the majority (approximately 55%) was conveyed through nonverbal channels. Although these precise percentages may vary by speaker and by context, the underlying lesson is clear: No one is merely a listener; we are all listeners, watchers, and emotional receptors ("Silent Messages," n.d.).

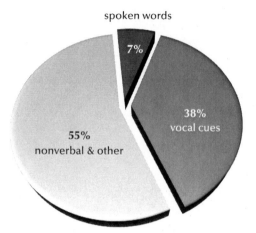

spoken words

7%

38%
vocal cues

55%
nonverbal & other

Figure 4.4. More than words: Findings from Mehrabian's study of communication.

In the classroom, effective communication (on the part of teachers and students) can be understood as several stands interwoven to convey a message.

Table 4.3. Components of Effective Communication

Component	Description
1. Attention	Focus on the person or group with whom communication is intended
2. Energy	Infusion of a message with passion and spirit
3. Words	The portion of a message that would be visible if the interaction were transcribed on a written page
4. Vocal cues	The volume, pitch, inflection, tempo, and rhythm of speech, used to layer spoken words with emphasis, emotion, and subtle shades of meaning
5. Silence	Pauses that can provide moments of anticipation, tension, and humor, as well as time for students to think, ask questions, and give feedback
6. Visual cues	The signals, illustrations, and other visual reinforcers of your message
7. Body language	The posture and gestures with which a message is delivered, useful for conveying energy as well as punctuating and highlighting spoken words
8. Movement	Your proximity to your audience, often deliberately varied to accent spoken words, boost group energy, and engage all audience members

1. Attention

Delivering appropriate attention to students is essential both to absorb the messages they're continuously sending (consciously and subconsciously), and to model the behavior you want reciprocated.

There are several attention-related behaviors we encourage teachers to monitor in themselves. One of these is favoritism. Sometimes this reflects hidden biases—as with teachers who interact more with boys than girls or vice versa, or teachers who hold different expectations of (and behave very differently toward) students of different ethnic groups. Less pernicious but still unsupportable are tendencies like focusing disproportionately on students who are loud or popular or attractive.

Also be aware of many teachers' propensity to face and interact with one side of the room much more than the other. This can result in lopsided levels of attentiveness and uneven learning among students. A related problem: Some teachers only direct their attention to students who are "teacher responsive"—i.e., inclined to pay attention to the teacher no matter what's happening in the room. We have seen classes where teachers deliver lessons only to a handful of students (typically at the front of the room) because those were the only ones paying any attention.

This is a well-established method for starting a vicious cycle, in which teachers reason, "Well if they're not going to pay attention, I just won't teach it to them. That'll show 'em." And in response, students think, "This teacher isn't even talking to me, so why should I pay attention?" It goes only downhill from there.

Encouraging attentiveness in students is also crucial. Adolescents often interpret *communication* to mean merely *sending* a message, and believe that great communicators are those who can speak in the loudest, cleverest, or most compelling way. In reality, of course, oratory is only one aspect of communication. The act of speaking is important, but so are the acts of inviting, receiving, interpreting, and responding to messages.

The communication skill we have found most commonly lacking in secondary students is the ability to *listen*—openly, respectfully, and responsively. See the sidebar "Teaching Listening Skills" for suggested techniques to help students improve their capacity and willingness to listen. This is an invaluable but underappreciated technique not only for improving students' academic performance, but also for cultivating a custom of decorum and mutual respect in your classroom.

We find it useful to remind students (sometimes frequently) of the aphorism "We have two ears and one mouth so we can listen twice as much as we talk." Of course, good listening should be something you model as well. As with any behavior you seek to encourage in students, don't expect it from them unless you're willing to display it yourself.

TEACHING LISTENING SKILLS

Most people seem to think they are good listeners (much like most people seem to think they're above-average drivers, a statistical impossibility). In reality, of course, many of us are lousy listeners. We're often so obsessed with ourselves, our interests, and our problems we couldn't care less what the person talking to us is "blabbing on about"—even if the person in question is our own spouse or child. Or, if we are tuned in, we're more focused on what we're going to say next than on what the other person is telling us.

To help students understand what effective, active listening is and how to practice it, the Canadian Association of Student Activity Advisers (CASAA) puts an adolescent-friendly spin on some common "better listening" techniques. "If you are really listening intently," CASAA notes, "you should feel tired after your speaker has finished. Effective listening is an active rather than a passive activity."

CASAA's first technique for effective listening is:

We have spent a lot of our modern lives . . . tuning out all of the information that is thrust at us. It therefore becomes important to change our physical body language from that of a deflector to that of a receiver, much like a satellite dish. Our faces contain most of the receptive equipment in our bodies, so it is only natural that we should tilt our faces towards the channel of information.

Second, in many Western cultural contexts, communication improves when the listener makes eye contact with the speaker. "Your eyes pick up the non-verbal signals that all people send out when they are speaking," CASAA points out. Additionally, a "speaker will work harder at sending out the information when they see a receptive audience in attendance. Your eyes help complete the communication circuit . . . between speaker and listener."

Third, CASAA urges awareness and use of nonverbal signals. "Your face must move and give the range of emotions that indicate whether you are following what the speaker has to say." This will help the speaker adjust the message, as necessary, to ensure its accurate transmission.

Fourth is the point we made at the start of this section:

It is extremely difficult to receive information when your mouth is moving information out at the same time. A good listener will stop talking and use receptive language . . . [to] follow and encourage your speaker's train of thought.

Fifth, CASAA encourages listeners to adjust their pace of thought "to concentrate on what the speaker is saying." This is not always easy because the listener's mind usually moves faster than the speaker's mouth, and can tend to race ahead or off to other ideas. Slowing one's pace of thought to embrace and savor a speaker's message is a critical skill that many people (including the authors of this book) require decades to learn. Start early.

Finally, effective listening requires a willingness to entertain alternative perspectives and refrain from judging or attacking the speaker. As CASAA rightly observes, "You cannot fully hear [others'] point of view or process information when you argue mentally or judge what they are saying before they have [finished explaining themselves]. An open mind is a mind that is receiving and listening to information" ("Listening Skills," n.d.).

Our website (www.classroomadvisor.com) includes additional resources on teaching listening skills, including a role-play that encourages students to reflect on the components of good listening.

2. Energy

Great teachers assume many forms, but in our experience they have this in common: They love the subjects they teach and share their enthusiasm. In the closed system of the classroom, moods can be highly contagious. The happy result when the teacher has a positive attitude: Students tend to absorb this optimistic spirit and thereby enjoy higher rates of success.

Of course the inverse is also true—a bad attitude tends to breed more of the same. We've had to perform major midyear interventions in classrooms where students seemed to hate their teacher, and the feeling was reciprocated. The solution was neither simple nor pretty. We urge you to monitor yourself carefully to avoid ever embarking on this path.

COMMUNICATION ESSENTIALS

The bottom line here is that your energy will reverberate through your class, buoying it or dragging it down. And the effects can range from extreme, as described above, to more subtle. If you're excited, your students will perk up; if you're bored teaching whatever the subject is, don't expect them to be less bored learning it.

> I've come to the frightening conclusion that I am the decisive element in the classroom. It's my daily mood that makes the weather. As a teacher, I possess a tremendous power to make a child's life miserable or joyous. I can be a tool of torture or an instrument of inspiration. I can humiliate or humor, hurt or heal. In all situations, it is my response that decides whether a crisis will be escalated or de-escalated and a child humanized or de-humanized.
>
> —Haim Ginott

Energy in the classroom takes many forms—motion, sound, and stillness among them. Subsequent sections detail each of these, but here we touch briefly on three aspects they share: focus, pacing, and drama. Adjusting these dimensions of energy flow will modulate the classroom experience in significant ways.

By *focus,* we mean the direction and target of energy flow. Your position as the teacher should allow you to become the center of gravity in the classroom whenever you choose to exercise that power. There are many circumstances, however, in which your purpose would be better served by diffusing students' attention throughout the class, or spotlighting a particular student or group, than by drawing all the attention to yourself.

Pacing determines the tempo of action in the classroom, which is driven partly by the rate of energy flow. Setting the right timing, speed, and duration for each activity is important. If you push forward too fast, you risk leaving students confused and flailing in your wake. On the other hand, moving too slowly could invite distraction. Don't be afraid to adjust the pacing as the class is in motion; this can keep students both plugged in and on their toes. Our previous discussion of assessment offers additional guidance on this.

The concept of *drama* as a tool in your teaching arsenal describes the purposeful combination of stance, gesture, motion, words, and vocal quality to achieve emotional resonance among your students. As novelist Gail Godwin famously observed, "Good teaching is one-fourth preparation and three-fourths theater" ("Teacher Quotes, Teacher Sayings," n.d.). Although making every moment a histrionic spectacle would quickly fatigue both you and your students, a certain degree of theatricality can give your classroom a needed jolt or help brighten up a dull lesson by sparking interesting questions, or injecting a bit of humor, or spinning a flagging discussion in a new direction.

Sometimes student energy levels will droop or explode with little notice or explanation. Sometimes an extraordinary external event (e.g., tragedy befalling a classmate) will be at fault, in which case we recommend consulting a counselor or administrator for guidance; the appropriate course of events may be to take a time-out from the lesson at hand and regroup. In other cases, the time of day or the weather may be to blame, in which case we encourage you to be patient with students, and consider adjusting your activities—either to overcome or to better accommodate their natural energy rhythms at those times.

One useful way to influence students' energy levels is through control of the physical environment—including music, lighting, color, scent, air movement, and temperature. If you've ever been to a massage therapy session or meditation shrine, you have some idea what we mean.

If your goal is to settle students down, try turning fluorescent overhead lights down or replacing them with indirect lights (if your school allows them) and adjusting window shades to provide more indirect light. Put on soft classical music or soothing nature sounds in the background. And try to immerse students in mellow, calming colors—pastels, beiges, and nature tones like muted blues, browns, greens, violets, and grays.

If you want to perk students up instead, try opening the window shades or turning up the lights. Get air moving with a fan or a natural cross breeze. Put on upbeat music and surround students with sharp, intense colors—reds, oranges, yellows, and bright blues, greens, and purples. Of course, activities that force students to move around will increase their energy level as well.

3. Words

Many teachers, verbally gifted themselves, rely mostly on verbal communication in the classroom. It's quick, it's cheap, and it's easy to reproduce. However, as Mehrabian has demonstrated, much of what people glean from in-person communication is not transmitted through the actual words they hear. Therefore, teachers who complain that their students "never listen" should perhaps reassess their own communication styles.

Every teacher lectures occasionally; when lecturing is unavoidable, maximize the impact by following three guidelines: make it short, make it dynamic, and make it visual.

First, brevity is crucial. As mentioned earlier, we recommend spending a maximum of 20–30 minutes on any activity (for lectures, we urge you to err on the shorter side of that range).

Also note that one way experts measure student engagement is by calculating the portion of a class period consumed by "teacher talk" versus the portion devoted to student voices. Your "teacher talk/student talk" ratio reveals volumes about who's at the center of your classroom. Although of course you will be the expert on many matters, and we certainly do not advise encouraging an entire class to wallow in mutual ignorance for the sake of hearing students' voices, students cannot become articulate thinkers, presenters, or debaters without practicing. This means good teaching sometimes requires less talking on your part, not more.

Classroom veteran Gary Rubinstein illuminates an additional reason to rein in your verbosity. He reports that one of the most effective (and difficult to master) teaching skills is to

> learn to say, "Shut up!"—not to your students, of course, but to yourself. . . . [A] mentor of mine once told me, "Teachers have only a certain number of words they can say in the year before their classes tune out. New teachers usually use them up in the first month." (Rubinstein, 1999, p. 73)

Second, speakers who enliven their talks with gestures, varied vocal tone, movement, and other tools mentioned in this section tend to hold students' attention more than flat speakers who use none of

the above. Students should feel the passion behind every presentation; otherwise, consider that there may be a different, more effective channel to reach students with the message in question.

Third, illustrations, models, demonstrations, and other visual representations tend to enhance and reinforce verbal explanations, particularly for learners who are more visual than auditory. We discuss
this further below, in the section on visual cues.

Anytime you talk to students—whether in a lecture or in a less formal interaction—analogies that reference things they already know
can help bridge the gap between your world and theirs. The better
you know your students, the easier these will be to generate. Have
you visited your students' homes, or at least their neighborhoods? Do
you know their likes and dislikes? The student survey mentioned in
chapter 2 and on our website (www.classroomadvisor.com) can help.

Also keep in mind that teachers sometimes use words that students
don't understand. These can provide excellent teachable moments, of
course, and any teacher who loves language can enjoy exploring with
students various aspects of etymology and the linkages among words.
This is good pedagogy. Be cautious when speaking as you would to
your most educated peers, however; if your entire vocabulary is too
complex for your students, they'll either give up trying to understand
you, or expend a great deal of energy just trying to keep up. In either
case, this can make it difficult for them to excel in your class.

4. Vocal Cues

Recall any brilliant verbal performer—perhaps a great speaker like
Martin Luther King Jr. or John F. Kennedy, or a skilled actor like
Katharine Hepburn or Meryl Streep. What do you notice about their
delivery that makes it effective? A well-honed message? Certainly.
Thorough rehearsal? Definitely. These two elements are critical for
any speaker, including teachers. But here we want to emphasize the
qualities of speech that make an audience want to either follow
along or fall asleep.

Components of speech like volume, pitch, inflection, tempo, and
rhythm layer spoken words with emphasis, emotion, and subtle shades

of meaning—whether we intend them to or not. Expert use of these can buttress your arguments (including the importance, excitement, or inherent fascination of the content you're teaching); inept use can weaken your overall message.

We encourage you to enhance your verbal delivery by adjusting the volume, pitch, and cadence of your voice. Don't be afraid to blast students awake with a roar when necessary, or to prolong emotional tension with a slow, dramatic whisper.

Also beware of the potentially debilitating effect of unskilled vocal expression. Consider these two hypothetical teachers:

Teacher A speaks very softly, until she gets nervous or angry, at which point she usually reverts to a loud and high-pitched squeal. She also tends to speak slowly and often finds students' eyes and posture drooping. She is convinced that most students are largely unengaged when she speaks.

Teacher B speaks with a deep, booming voice, typically at very high speeds, which leaves many students feeling as if they're being assaulted by a hurricane. When he gets excited, he gets so loud that students often ask if he's angry when he's not.

Which of these would you rather have as a teacher? Probably neither. The lesson here? Vocal cues make a big difference in teachers' effectiveness and students' levels of engagement. Take care to avoid the common problems shown in Table 4.4, which can easily overwhelm or undermine your intended message.

Table 4.4. Vocal Cues and Their Effects

	High	Low
Pitch	High-pitched voices tend to convey helplessness, nervousness, and tension	Low-pitched voices tend to convey strength, calm, and maturity
Volume	High-volume speakers are frequently perceived as aggressive or overbearing	Low-volume speakers are frequently perceived as timid or polite
Tempo	High-speed speakers leave students' eyes glazing over, as they let the words wash over them	Low-speed speakers leave students' minds wandering, as they lose interest in what the speaker is saying

Note: From "Nonverbal Communication" (n.d.).

5. Silence

Effective speaking is typically not a continuous flow of words. Rather, it is a thoughtful combination of carefully chosen phrasing and periodic pauses, which provide moments of anticipation, tension, and humor, and also allow quiet moments for reflection.

Don't underestimate the value of quiet reflection. In their zeal for inquiry, eager teachers sometimes unleash a barrage of questions on students without considering the quality of those questions or the potential for thoughtful student response. When presented with a new concept, most people need time to mull it over, consider various sides, and reason their way to a conclusion. Answering questions thoughtfully *and* instantaneously is simply impossible for most students.

Allowing adequate *wait time* for students to reflect without interruption after questions is therefore critical, but not always easy. Standing in front of a roomful of people—especially if you're a new teacher—typically generates a small dose of adrenaline. This will increase your heart rate and your brain function, which can make time seem to slow down. The unfortunate side effect: You may ask a question, wait for what seems to you like hours but is actually about 1.5 seconds, then jump in with an answer because no one has spoken up and you want to move the class along. Needless to say, this dampens student participation in conversation.

Many students, accustomed to this pattern, simply outwait the questioner. They have faith in this technique because most of their academic histories have proven that if they wait long enough, someone else (often the instructor) will grow uncomfortable or frustrated with the silence and provide an answer for them.

The teacher can thwart such a strategy using two techniques. First, if the question is especially complex or worthy of substantial class time to explore, you might give students time to prepare written thoughts on the matter. Ask them to *think in ink* by answering the question first in their class notebooks, for example. While they are writing, you can walk around the room and mark next to any notebook entries you find particularly insightful. Then when you ask for volunteers to share their answers, there will be at least a few students willing to speak out.

The second technique is simple to articulate but notoriously difficult to practice: ask the question and then wait them out. Smile and maintain eye contact with all students, clarify the question if necessary, but refuse to provide any answers. During the waiting process, students might stir, wanting to break the building tension with movement, noises, or unrelated chatter. These tendencies should be squelched. The teacher must make clear the students' alternatives: generate ideas, or continue to suffer in the growing, stultifying silence. After a few rounds of this, they'll learn the futility of trying to wait you out and should begin to speak up more regularly.

6. Visual Cues

The saying "Hear and I forget, see and I remember, do and I understand" makes clear the value of reinforcing messages through multiple channels of communication. Write important things down. As discussed previously, augment spoken words with illustrations, models, demonstrations, and other visual representations. That's why you have a blackboard, whiteboard, or projector.

Don't be shy about this, even if you draw like a 3-year-old or serial killer. You don't have to be a great artist to create a useful illustration. If you prefer you can always prepare illustrations in advance.

Also encourage students to draw their own pictures or diagrams in their class notes. These can not only help you ascertain how well students have understood the course material, but also give you student-centered models for explaining challenging concepts in the future. You could even invite students to reinforce each others' learning by sharing their illustrations.

Our website (www.classroomadvisor.com) includes additional tips and resources to make your teaching more visual.

7. Body Language

Recall Albert Mehrabian's finding that in the messages he studied (emotional messages), body language and other nonverbal cues contained the bulk of the power—more than verbal cues, and far more than the content of spoken words. Nonverbal cues, although likely less dominant in less emotional communications, color the meaning of most messages. Such cues include eye contact, facial expressions, gestures, physical mannerisms, and posture.

In the United States and many other Western cultures, making eye contact during conversation conveys respect and interest in making a connection with the other party; conversely, avoiding eye contact tends to be interpreted as disrespect or dishonesty. If you're uncomfortable speaking in front of a group and making eye contact with everyone, try this trick: Focus on a couple of friendly faces (preferably on different sides of the room), and sweep your eyes across the audience from one to the other. If the faces you chose are far enough apart, you will look perfectly natural moving your attention from one to the other and back, and no one will figure out how mortified you are inside. Eventually, with practice, your discomfort will fade and you'll be working the crowd like a pro.

Facial expressions also influence the impact and credibility of your words. If you are not a facially emotive person—for example, if people tell you it's strange that you wear the same deadpan expression for every occasion from your pet's death to your wedding—consider the advice of communication specialist Dr. Dilip Abayasekara (2005):

> The speaker's job isn't done unless he connects with the mind and heart of the members of the audience [that requires] a face that tunes itself to the message. . . . Let your thoughts, your mouth, your words, and your heart all be connected to your facial muscles [until] your face feels every vibration and meaning of your words. When that happens, your face will become congruent with your message.

Gestures are also a useful part of effective communication; they can be used to project attitudes and feelings, or at least to empha-

COMMUNICATION ESSENTIALS

size your point. Of course, gesticulating too often, too rapidly, or too wildly can distract your audience and make you look like a hyperactive cartoon animal. Much as moments of silence bring welcome respite from a shower of words, occasional stillness can help offset a flurry of gestures. Use your judgement here, and if your students start making fun of you, you'll have a sense of what's excessive.

If you don't know what to do with your hands when speaking, and therefore revert to physical mannerisms like clicking a pen incessantly or gripping the sides of a podium, let us again direct you to the advice of Dr. Abayasekara (2005), who urges speakers to

> get so wrapped up in your audience and your message that you have no time to become self-conscious. Then your hand and arm movements will flow naturally by themselves [and] be connected to the words and feelings of your message. Left alone, without conscious control, they will move in harmony with your message and help the audience connect intimately with the meaning of what you are saying.

Another element of body language is posture. We have found that in teaching (and in life), good posture can actually give you energy, while poor posture tends to sap it. This could be partly because over time, poor posture can lead to numerous health problems—including back and muscle pain, nerve damage, leg weakness, and circulation problems. The posture-energy connection might also be traceable to the positive feedback loop that good posture establishes with students. Think of all the characteristics posture can connote about the person displaying it—passion or apathy, competence or ineptitude, belligerence or intimacy, and the list goes on. Teachers who practice maintaining an erect stance convey confidence and alertness, while those who slouch through the day often communicate fatigue and inattentiveness.

Body language can send important messages from students to you, as well. Not every student will tell you every time he's in a good or bad mood, so watch for body language that will give you clues.

A boy who slips into your room with his head down and slumps silently into a desk, speaking and making eye contact with no one, can reasonably be interpreted to be in a bad mood. Recognize this, and realize that there's probably a reason. It could be a fight with a family member, a breakup with a significant other, trouble at work or in another class, general financial or life stress, or any number of other reasons.

Sometimes the best answer to this challenge is to talk with the student and cajole him into at least trying to work. At other times, this emotional interference could make his affective filter so dense he won't be able to focus on classwork. In some cases you may prefer to move him to a back corner where he won't provide poor modeling for the rest of the class, and leave the situation alone. Everyone has bad days, so expect times when your best efforts to engage students may fall flat or actually be counterproductive.

8. Movement

"Did you ever wonder," asks teacher Richard Trimble, "why it is sometimes difficult to stay awake during a church sermon? The answer is easy—the pulpit is the problem" (Trimble, 1990, p. 56). A pulpit or lectern not only restricts a speaker's movement, but also inserts a physical barrier between speaker and audience. If you're seeking an aura of formality this might be appropriate, but many classrooms benefit from more open communication.

As discussed earlier, we do not recommend lecturing as your only—or even your primary—teaching mode. When you do lecture, however, keep it lively.

In our experience, great teachers move around frequently, often spending the bulk of the class prowling around all corners of the classroom. They do this for three excellent reasons:

1. to keep their energy up
2. to maintain the interest of students
3. to patrol for incipient misbehavior

Be aware of your own bodily rhythms. Don't deny your afternoon classes an energetic lesson just because you're a morning person and know you shouldn't have had the fries *and* the pizza for lunch. Physical movement is a great cure for the trapped-in-the-classroom blues your body will from time to time experience, whether your brain is consciously aware of it or not. As with vocal cues and gestures, varying your physical location can minimize monotony, thereby helping both you and your students maintain focus.

If the class is feeling particularly lethargic, try the "Okay, I can see we're all a little tired; let's all stand and do 60 seconds of coordinated activity" trick. Inform any student who complains "that's too kindergarten" that this type of activity is a very popular team- and energy-builder in many businesses—taking forms ranging from morning calisthenics at numerous Japanese firms to the (in)famous Walmart cheer. Virtually any controlled activity (clapping, stretching, modified jumping jacks, bouncing on toes) will work to boost the energy level of a droopy class, and after a few groans, you may be surprised how much your students—even the ordinarily cynical ones—appreciate it. Just don't be surprised if, the next time they feel their own energy flagging, they ask to do it again.

If moving from the front of the classroom feels unnatural to you—something akin to abandoning your post (or perhaps your "rightful perch"?)—keep in mind that unless you're actually writing on the board, most of what you do can be done from anywhere in the room. Questions can be asked, books read, and lectures delivered from the far corner as well as from the front.

As mentioned previously, movement is also invaluable in monitoring student behavior. Your circulation throughout the classroom can help keep students engaged and out of trouble.

5

CLASSROOM MANAGEMENT I: PREVENTION AND MINOR TROUBLE

CLASSROOM MANAGEMENT IS PROBLEM PREVENTION

Many teachers use the term *classroom management* to describe the process of disciplining students for misbehavior, intervening in conflicts, and otherwise solving problems as they arise. In reality, however, that's *crisis management*; classroom management is more proactive.

We define *classroom management* as the establishment and maintenance of problem prevention systems, including the regulation of time and space and the active engagement of students as detailed in the previous chapters.

Problem prevention, we have found, consists of eight key elements:

1. Keep students busy.
2. Be alert.
3. Be engaging.
4. Be consistent.
5. Get to know your students.
6. Don't try to be students' best friend.
7. Don't try to be students' worst nightmare.
8. Acknowledge good behavior, not just bad behavior.

1. Keep Students Busy.

Entropy is the natural principle that all organized systems tend inevitably toward chaos unless energy is applied to channel them in a particular direction. This is never truer than in a room full of teenagers. Youthful energy abhors a vacuum. Or, as your grandmother might have put it, "Idle hands are the devil's workshop." Well, your grandmother was no fool.

Criminal justice experts reveal that most crimes committed by teenagers are crimes of opportunity. This bodes ill for the unprepared teacher, because the typical classroom contains 30 or more pairs of hands waiting for any idle moment to get into trouble, and only one person with the authority to keep them all focused: you.

Unless you regulate their time, your students will fill it with mischief and force you to squander energy getting them back on track multiple times a day. But how can one person control the actions of 30 teenagers? The answer: keep them busy! The best way to keep students on task is to *overplan*. If your class is 60 minutes long, plan for activities to fill 2 hours.

Even diligent students will sometimes take longer to finish a lesson than you had anticipated. That's not a huge problem; at worst it may force you to trim a bit to meet your long-term timeline. A more serious issue will arise, however, if you prepare something for the hour that the class finishes in only 30 minutes. Then what? You'll be left scrambling to fill the remaining time with an educationally valid activity that doesn't look thrown together and doesn't put your students to sleep.

> *If you're underprepared and there's 20 minutes left in class and you're just standing there—that's when mayhem happens.*

> —J. Jobes, personal communication

That having been said, "busywork"—assignments created solely to occupy students' time without engaging, motivating, or enlightening them in any significant way—is not only distasteful (and, in some teachers' minds, actually immoral), but also counterproductive. Students often respond to the disrespect that busywork implies with less subtle forms of disrespect.

2. Be Alert.

Misbehavior abounds in a distracted teacher's classroom. One teacher we interviewed was shocked to learn that her students were sniffing and even smoking substances in the corner of her classroom *while her class was in session.* She was busy helping students in one corner and had no clue such activity was occurring behind her back, until her principal called her in to discuss the matter. A concerned student—possibly believing the teacher had willfully ignored the occurrence—had reported this activity to the school administration.

Perhaps worse, however, was the elderly substitute teacher—a fixture in the home district of one of this book's authors—who fell asleep while showing his class a video. He was awakened by a security guard and an administrator responding to a complaint from a student who'd sneaked out to contact them. This student was distressed by the sex act that occurred in the back of the room during the teacher's nap. The substitute teacher was not invited back to that district.

Although situations like these are thankfully not typical, they are useful reminders that the price of a well-run class is eternal vigilance. The best classroom managers are legendary for having eyes in the back of their heads. They separate talkative friends and put likely troublemakers in easy-to-watch places. They circulate through the room regularly, and even while involved in paperwork or conversation, they listen continually for indicators of potential trouble—including too much silence. Sometimes they sit behind students to keep an eye on them, and sometimes they place reflective surfaces (e.g., small mirrors or a computer screen) so they can see the class when they appear to be looking away from it.

> *I listen in on everything because that's how you learn what's going on. Kids get away with a lot because a lot of teachers don't have a clue what the kids are talking about. They have*

a code they talk in, and you have to listen carefully and ask questions if you want to know what's going on. Otherwise, they'll try to put all kinds of stuff over on you.

The kids call me "Radar" because I hear everything that goes on in this room. I can be way over in the corner and somebody will be whispering over on the other side and I'll say, "What's that? I don't want to hear that in my classroom." And they're not even clever about it. They don't even think about denying it. They'll be like, "Aw, Ms. Davis! How'd you hear that? We were trying to whisper."

—C. Davis, personal communication

TEACHING DILEMMA: CLASS DISSOLVES INTO CHAOS WHEN TEACHER TURNS HER BACK

One of my ninth-grade classes is chaos. They're okay when I'm facing their direction, but as soon as I turn away to get something from my desk or to help a single student, things unravel. They stay in their seats, but they just go crazy— throwing things, hitting each other, all this immature stuff. I'll turn around to try to catch them but they're quick. And I think I know who's the head troublemaker, but my administrator demands proof before he'll do anything.

SUGGESTED SOLUTION A: CHANGE YOUR HABITS

Ask yourself some questions: If you have more than one ninth-grade class, why is this one the difficult one? Is it related to the time of day? Many adolescents get especially squirrelly at particular times—say, just before lunch or during the last period of the day. Elementary schools typically build in recess periods to allow children to work off excess energy and focus better for the time they're in class. Unfortunately, most secondary school schedules omit this useful break period.

To compensate, you may need to build in a variety of activities to accommodate your students' different energy levels and learning styles (see chapter 2, "Who Are Your Students?" and chapter 4, "Communication Essentials" for more on this). Also try starting or punctuating class with a "quiet time" activity to settle students down. Or try an activity that siphons off energy by allowing students to be noisy and boisterous for a short time; just be sure you can keep a lid on it and bring students back into class mode afterward. You'll quickly figure out what works for the dynamic of your class.

Also keep in mind the power of the seating chart. Try breaking up troublesome knots of students. Situate instigators and other particularly challenging students near you or in the back, where they can't give visual cues to other students.

Practice MBWA—management by walking around. Student adrenaline levels rise when a teacher approaches, even when there is no crime afoot. This adrenaline, in small doses, is great for combating sleepiness. Also the need to swivel the head on the neck, to track the movements of an ambling teacher, helps keep blood flowing and brain function high.

Lastly, try to reconfigure your room and adjust your work habits so you are not facing away from students so much. When you do sit down, always face the students. As discussed in chapter 3, "Preparing for the First Week of School," positioning yourself in plain sight can help prevent trouble. When students see that all you have to do is glance up to catch them making mischief, they'll often keep themselves in check.

Other times, you may prefer to sit to the side or in the back, so students never know when you're watching and you can catch and correct misbehavior. Planting yourself in a different seat from time to time can also throw would-be troublemakers off-balance. Standard practice in premeditated mischief is to scan to be sure the teacher isn't watching; if troublemakers are used to looking for you in a particular spot, having to look around the room to find you will take extra time and could create unusual movement that should catch your eye and give you early warning.

SUGGESTED SOLUTION B: SEEK DEEPER INSIGHT

Consider whether this combination of students is just a troublesome mix of personalities. If a few students have secret conflicts with—or perhaps unrequited crushes on—each other, this can color the character of your class as a whole. You may be unaware of this because it's usually unrelated to you, but ask around.

Pull aside a student who's often a bystander to the trouble for an informal chat. We don't recommend grilling the student about who did what, as fingering perpetrators violates unwritten student codes against "snitching." Instead, ask for the student's insights. Try not to appear needy; just pose a few open-ended questions about what the student has observed and what she might recommend to improve the situation. Learning from a student who's close to whom and what's going on outside class can reveal volumes of interpersonal drama you've been missing. If you're lucky, the student may even tell you how another teacher solved the same problem.

In any case, we always recommend consulting other teachers—particularly those who have your most challenging students in their classes. They may have seen behavior patterns you've missed, and they can likely advise you which students to watch closely, who should not be sitting near whom, and who should perhaps be transferred to a different class (presuming this is an option at your school).

SUGGESTED SOLUTION C:
SEEK OUTSIDE ASSISTANCE

If all else fails, try inviting a trusted colleague to observe your class for a period and give you suggestions. We do not recommend inviting in administrators because students often fear to misbehave in the presence of administrators, which defeats the purpose. Alternately, if your students act crazy in front of an administrator and you look powerless, you could be opening yourself to charges of incompetence. Invite a colleague.

In an extreme situation, you might consider videotaping your class to assess your own performance. Coaches videotape athletes' practice sessions, actors videotape rehearsals, and jobseekers videotape mock interviews, so why shouldn't teachers videotape their own (and their students') performance? This can help you spot patterns in your behavior that might be causing problems, and if you catch students misbehaving on camera, even better.

We have found that *showing* students their behavior—particularly when their parents or administrators are in the room—impacts that behavior more profoundly than simply carping about it. As one teacher suggests, "The first step toward taking responsibility for your actions is to see them clearly" (R. Cornner, personal communication).

However, although video surveillance can be effective in certain extreme situations, many argue that if you need a camera to keep an eye on your students, maybe you should find another profession. Indeed, what would compel teachers to improve their classroom management skills or students to develop self-discipline if they could all rely on technology to do it for them?

3. Be Engaging.

Chapter 4, "Communication Essentials," discussed many ways to engage students. Here we will stress one underappreciated technique for maintaining stability in the face of rising chaos: movement.

Quick quiz: A student in a far corner of the room is causing trouble. Which should you do?

1. Shout across the room to tell the student to stop.
2. Throw a piece of chalk (or whatever else you happen to be holding) at the student to get his attention.
3. Wait for the student to settle down on his own so you can resume teaching.
4. Ignore it and continue the lesson for whoever wants to pay attention.

Our recommendation: None of the above. Instead, go stand next to the student and continue with whatever teaching activity you were engaged in. If you were talking, continue talking. If you were listening to another student, continue listening. If the student continues with his disruptive behavior, put your hand on the student's shoulder. Most students will get the clue after this, even if their response is something along the lines of, "Eww—don't touch me! Why are you touching me?" In such cases, a simple response like "I was trying to avoid embarrassing you by calling out your misbehavior in front of the class, but you didn't seem to get the message" will usually suffice.

If you never visit the back of the room, you will never know who is secretly reading a comic book or sending a text message to a friend, behind his English book. Can you imagine any other misbehaviors that might be occurring out of your normal range of vision?

Keeping students engaged also requires connecting to them on multiple levels. Chapter 2, "Who Are Your Students?" and chapter 4, "Communication Essentials," present various options to further this goal. To these we would now like to add: Don't be afraid to laugh with students.

When a student blurts out a smart remark, what's the best response? Is it funny? If so—presuming it's not denigrating anyone—feel free to laugh. Laughing together is therapeutic. It can defuse otherwise tense situations and show students you're human. In fact, humor is one of the most powerful social lubricants that's legal in the classroom.

What if a student comment is neither funny nor helpful? Don't get angry—you'd be playing right into their hands because, frankly, what teen doesn't love to see an authority figure lose his cool? Some teachers bristle visibly and clench up when students try to disrupt class with inappropriate humor. Our advice: Decisively choke off discussion, as described later in this chapter under "Classroom Misdemeanors," and move on.

> *One of my personal rules is to always have fun. . . . If you can't have fun in the classroom, why bother? Why should I even be teaching? If I couldn't laugh, I'd be totally ineffective as a teacher.*
>
> —L. Thlick-Katchadourian, personal communication

4. Be Consistent.

Teenagers delight in testing people, and in particular they will test your resolve in enforcing your rules. Expect students to beg, bribe, or even threaten you in an attempt to weaken your commitment. Frequently, they'll try to distract you from your course of action or delay the implementation of consequences for their misbehavior. If this fails, they may loudly challenge your rationale or try to negotiate away a negative consequence.

If you're young and friendly, you'll be especially vulnerable because some students will shamelessly turn these qualities against you. They'll pout, cry foul, and/or create a scene to try to manipulate you, because they're betting you'll want to be liked more than you'll want to be a disciplinarian.

How should you respond?

1. Anticipate and be ready to confront common student ploys—see the examples in the section, "What Do I Do When the Whining Starts?"
2. Remain pleasant but firm. Never change your day's plans without a very good reason. (Hint: complaints like "That sounds boring!" are generally not a good reason.)
3. Enforce your rules. Always.

If students balk at following class rules, remember what we suggested in chapter 1, "Creating a Classroom Culture": establish a rule that says, "Follow the teacher's instructions immediately, and ask questions later." Lean on this as much as necessary until students learn that you're neither joking about nor willing to compromise on this. If you enforce your rules with 100% consistency, what at first seems impossible will miraculously come to pass: Students will recognize the futility of arguing with you and will begin to cooperate. You will have left them no choice.

> *Nine times out of ten, behavior problems are my fault. I escalate it or I don't see everything or . . . I only deal with one party because sometimes it's easier to shut one guy up and let the other guy go.*
>
> —J. Jobes, personal communication

Children Crave Limits

Ironically, despite their endless complaining about how "restrictive" and "boring" your rules make their lives, most young people secretly crave limits and predictability. A sure way to create a classroom full of neurotic, on-edge students is to set no clear boundaries and to be totally unpredictable in your behavior. Students who know what will happen if they push Button A or pull Lever B will be much calmer and more productive because they will feel safer. As one veteran high school teacher puts it, "students like the safety and security the rules guarantee. They're comforted by the structure we can provide in the classroom" (C. Langer, personal communication).

Even the loudest complainers don't *really* want to live by the law of the jungle. They understand that adults' rules are often the only thing standing between them and the amazingly stupid—and potentially dangerous—stunts adolescents concoct under the influence of teen bravado and peer pressure. Show us a teen who never silently thanked her strict parents for providing an excuse to tell friends no, and we'll show you a teen with more chutzpah than sense.

TEACHING DILEMMA: TEACHER GIVES IN TO STUDENTS "JUST THIS TIME"

This year our school started a daily silent reading time, but I have a few students who simply will not cooperate. All they want to do is talk. It doesn't matter how many times I ask them to quiet down; they always promise that if I cut them a little slack now, they'll be good later.

At first I let them talk just a little. They weren't distracting their classmates too much and it took so much energy to stay on top of them, it didn't seem worth it. I figured I'd let them talk a little, and get serious about the rule another time. But that time never came, and the problem has gotten worse.

SUGGESTED SOLUTION

Oops. This kind of reasoning will lead you onto a very slippery slope. This is the most difficult time to stand firm, but also the most essential. When students protest any of your class policies, pause politely to hear out their arguments and succinctly explain the reasoning behind your edicts if you will, but do not get drawn into an extended discussion and *do not give in.*

Sometimes, instead of challenging you openly, students will try to undercut your rules or routines by taking advantage of loopholes or wearing you down with repeated failure to comply. Children practice these stealth attacks from an early age; consider this interaction observed between a toddler and his grandmother:

Toddler:	Grandma, can I play your piano?
Grandmother:	Later. We're having dinner in a minute.
	(30 seconds elapse)
Toddler:	Grandma, please can I just touch your piano? I'll be quiet.
Grandmother:	Later.
	(another 30 seconds elapse)
Toddler:	Grandma, can I just sit on the bench?
Grandmother:	Okay. But just sitting. No playing.
	(another 30 seconds elapse)
Toddler:	Grandma, can I take the cover off?

Is there any doubt where this is heading? Although this toddler is perhaps unaware that he is exploiting a sophisticated foot-in-the-door persuasion technique, he clearly senses that his caregivers are not always 100% consistent, making "no" just the beginning of negotiation.

Adolescents, occasionally even more devious than toddlers, require similar handling skills. "No" should be your habitual first response to any unusual student inquiry. Particularly if you're a new teacher, the worst response you can give students who ask, "Can't we change plans and ignore that rule today?" is, "Well, gee, I hadn't thought about it. I guess so."

On the bright side, that response is honest and accommodating. The problem: You'll be seen as a pushover, and it sets a bad precedent. Remember, just say no. And say it decisively. Then if you think about it later and decide you were too harsh, you can always adjust your stance. But in teaching as in parenting, it's a lot easier to change a no to a yes than vice versa.

One useful technique in the face of particularly persistent nagging is to say, "If you feel really strongly about this, ask me again a week from now. Meanwhile, let's get going." Any student who can even *remember* what she was asking about a week in the future may have a good point to make. And in the worst-case scenario, that will buy you time to consider the request without the pressure of a ticking clock and a roomful of onlookers.

What you absolutely want to avoid is for students to learn that if they push hard enough you'll cave in. If at this critical juncture you give them an inch, your rules, like this teacher's silent reading time, will quickly become irrelevant and your students will be walking all over you by the end of the week.

5. Get to Know Your Students.

Building bonds of mutual respect is fundamental to maintaining influence over your class, and getting to know your students is an essential step in the process. As discussed in chapter 2, most students won't care nearly as much about the subject you're teaching as you do.

All students, however, care a great deal about themselves. As with any relationship, student-teacher rapport depends on a kind of quid pro quo—that is, "You show me you care about me, and I'll think about listening to you." You don't have to love every student, but you can find something in every student to love. Sometimes it takes a bit of searching, but the payoff is almost always worth the effort.

With teens, more than with most adults, respect must flow both ways. Teachers who demonstrate an interest in students as individuals (not just as students) earn more respect and more cooperation than teachers who remain blissfully oblivious to their students' "real lives."

One cannot get to know young people in a crowd. Youth is shy and a teacher gets his best results both in the classroom and out when barriers are down, and it requires wooing before the barriers come down.

—Eleanor Roosevelt, 1930

In addition, as discussed in chapter 4, "Communication Essentials," to excite students about the class content you're teaching you must draw connections between it and your students' realities. You may occasionally have to bend over backward to find a link, but one *always* exists and the more you know about your students, the easier this will be.

Of course, never forget one of your most potent classroom management tools: your relationship with parents/guardians. Parents are natural storehouses of information about their own children, and can tell you all about their tastes, their friends, and particularly what motivates them and what doesn't—if you ask. Most parents will be happy, even flattered, that you care enough to inquire.

Be aware that students frequently play parents and teachers off against each other, relying on both parties' isolation and busy schedules to warp the information flow between them. Regular contact with parents—ideally, not just the parents of chronic misbehavers but *all* parents—can help preclude this maneuver and prevent problem behavior in the first place. Show students you have a close rapport with Mom, Dad, Grandma or whomever, and witness a near-miracle: Troublemakers whose relative anonymity shields them from consequences in other teachers' rooms will police themselves in your presence.

Some teachers actually visit every student's home in the first few weeks of school. This is easier for elementary school teachers (who have fewer students than secondary school teachers), but there is no reason every teacher cannot have significant contact—even through a 5- or 10-minute introductory phone call—with most parents at some point in the first month or two of school.

The few hours thus expended may produce the greatest return on investment you'll ever earn as a teacher. The effort will show initiative and concern on your part, and make you more than an abstract name in parents' minds. This seed of a relationship will, in turn, make your life immeasurably easier; parents will be quicker to respond to your future calls and more willing to give you the benefit of the doubt in any conflict with their children. And, believe us, the students will never forget it.

THE POWER OF A "DRIVE-BY VISIT"

If a student keeps giving me problems or if I can't get a parent on the phone, I'll do a drive-by visit. I'll go knock on their door at home, unannounced. I only had to do that one time, because the next day the word got around. "She'll go visit your house!" They're amazed, like nobody's crazy enough to go to all that trouble.

But I was very well received by the parents. I told them, "I'm here because I'm concerned. Otherwise, I wouldn't be here. This is what's happening with your child. . . . This is what I have done, and this is what I need you to do." That student's behavior was very different the next day.

—C. Davis, personal communication

Note: This tactic may not be welcome or appropriate in all settings. What works in certain urban or rural schools may not be received the same way in certain suburban settings, and vice versa. In any case, visiting parents at home can be tricky because you might run the risk of your actions being misconstrued. For example, a neighbor who sees a teacher visiting a child's home could draw unsavory conclusions, or a parent could interpret your actions as crossing an invisible line between personal and professional space, depending on the cultural context. As always, use your best judgment.

6. Don't Try to Be Students' Best Friend.

Wanting to be liked is natural. And, as we just discussed, making connections with students is a valuable motivator. If you are a first-time teacher, however, beware of allowing the entirely healthy impulse to connect with students on a personal, emotional level to violate your appropriate professional distance from them. It's fine to be *friendly* with students, but don't try to be *friends* with them.

Many teachers, especially new teachers, have concerns like, "I don't want my students to call me bossy." Well, guess what? In the classroom, you are the boss. Bosses coach, encourage, monitor, reward, and sometimes issue directives. This may be interpreted as "bossy" by some, but that's just one reading of reality, not the reality itself. And if you fear every student's potential negative reaction to every action you take, you've lost before you've started.

Another common fear we hear is, "I don't want them to talk behind my back." We don't know a lot of people who eagerly anticipate this, but in the profession you've chosen it's inescapable. Don't take it personally. They say all kinds of nasty things about their parents too, but that doesn't mean they don't love them. It doesn't even mean your students believe everything coming out of their own mouths. Sometimes they just need to vent; other times complaining about teachers is how they bond with each other. In teaching, a little bit of thick skin goes a long way. For severe situations, see the teaching dilemma "Students Make Derogatory Personal Remarks About Teacher" later in this chapter.

The bottom line: Your students don't need a friend in you. They need a guide, a coach, a mentor. It's your responsibility as the teacher to be above teenagers' basest instincts and show them how to think and behave in a civilized society. As one classroom veteran explains, "The kids don't need you to be their buddy; they need a role model. If you can live up to that, the students will do more than like you. They'll respect you" (R. Cornner, personal communication).

Living up to this can be tricky at first because students often attempt to blur the line between themselves and their teachers. Particularly if you look or act young, students may inquire about your personal life, relate serious and intimate personal issues, flirt with you, invite you to parties, and so on. Sometimes this will be just because they like you; many times, they will perceive you as a safe target on which to practice their relationship-building skills. As the professional adult in the situation, the responsibility falls to you to mark certain territory clearly *off limits.*

When faced with student questions, offers, or advances that strike you as odd or make you even slightly uncomfortable, listen to your instincts and err on the side of caution. If in doubt, stop the conversation immediately with a simple, straightforward response like, "I don't think that's an appropriate topic of conversation for a teacher and student." If the student persists, don't hesitate to use more assertive phrasing. Temporary hurt feelings are a lot better than letting the situation get out of hand. The danger of losing your teaching credential and/or facing legal action is very real.

TEACHING DILEMMA: NEW TEACHER TRIES TO BEFRIEND CLASS, COMPROMISES AUTHORITY

When I started teaching, I didn't want to be the mean guy. I was determined to be a cool teacher. I wanted to liberate my kids from the factory-model school and create a more student-centered class. I spent hours writing interactive lessons and the student response was great. They talked more, laughed more, moved around more, and enjoyed themselves more.

But now some students are complaining that my class is too noisy, too chaotic. They don't think a lot of learning is going on. Some days we make progress, but other times we seem to be traveling in circles. Now some students are talking back or starting to ignore me, or just slacking off. I can see a lot of them getting frustrated. The problem is I'm always scampering around putting out fires and can't really address their concerns.

SUGGESTED SOLUTION

Don't start down this path. This teacher began as every kid's dream babysitter—friendly, creative, and fun-loving. This attitude might be great in a camp counselor or cruise director but in a teacher, it's an invitation to disaster. In a quest to be "cool," this teacher sacrificed discipline. Because of this, his students took him less seriously than they did his colleagues which, paradoxically, led them to respect—and thereby appreciate—him less, rather than more.

This well-intentioned teacher went wrong by removing the restrictions of childhood without preparing his students to assume the responsibilities of adulthood. Like a parent who hands a child car keys without instruction in vehicle operation, this teacher failed to provide the structure and hands-on supervision required to channel the raucous energies of youth into productive industry.

Variety and creativity are admirable and important classroom goals, but a point made in chapter 3, "Preparing for the First Week of School," bears repeating here: The wise teacher seeks order first, then creativity.

7. Don't Try to Be Students' Worst Nightmare.

At the other extreme are teachers who believe smiling before December is a sign of weakness. One urban teacher transplanted from the world of business describes the logic of this philosophy: "You've got to come out hard at the beginning of the year. Be the meanest SOB they've ever seen. Because if you come out nice, trying to be their friend, you can't go back to hard" (J. Jobes, personal communication).

This approach has merit, particularly with a roomful of tough kids. Beware of taking it to an unreasonable extreme, however. Some teachers, interpreting "strong discipline" to mean absolute control of their classrooms every moment, consciously cultivate reputations as tyrants.

Like many others who should know better, authoritarian teachers fail to recognize the long-term costs of the short-term compliance they achieve. Management by terror may temporarily boost your influence, but will eventually undermine loyalty and productivity among your charges. One media executive sums up the dangers of this technique: "Although ruling by fear is common in Hollywood, it never works in the long run, and I don't like the effect it has on people" (Medavoy & Young, 2002, p. 165).

In the end, classroom despots forget that those who live by the sword often die by the sword. Their autocratic style makes them magnets for student anger and resentment. And any time students leave a class more hostile toward the subject than when they arrived, their parents begin to wonder—quite rightly—what's going on. Call it karma, divine justice, or simply the law of cause and effect, but tyrants tend not to have friends when they need them.

Portrait of a Petty Dictator

> *[Every school has teachers who] think they know everything and don't give students any leeway whatsoever. Even if a kid is trying to do something good, trying to help out another student, these teachers will jump all over them. "Stop talking. What are you doing over there? I told you to do your own work!"*
>
> *Their kids are sitting in rows and the kids are terrified to get out of their seats. Even if they have to pee their pants they're not going to even move. They're not learning because they're so threatened; they're just trying to follow along.*
>
> —L. Thlick-Katchadourian, personal communication

What do teenagers want more than anything? Ask them and they'll tell you. Right after love and money—not necessarily in that order, unfortunately—they want respect. For most teens, self-respect demands saving face.

From that fact follows this rule: The fastest way to polarize a class and create enduring resentment is to humiliate students. Try to recall a teacher, coach, or boss who belittled you or others—whether through insults, sarcasm, general arrogance, or some other odious behavior. Now imagine being a child under that person's control for 9 months. Then imagine being a teenager who has to cope with puberty, identity formation, peer pressure, and the academic demands of school . . . not to mention an insecure, overbearing teacher whose idea of fun is making you look like a fool in front of all your friends.

If bad teenage attitudes irritate you, you're not alone. But try not to return it in kind. You are the responsible adult in the room, so act the part. Heed Gandhi's observation that "an eye for an eye makes the whole world blind."

Also be aware that most adolescent attitude stems from insecurity. Trust us: No matter how talented or popular a student is, she will be insecure about *something*. Yes, this applies even to the attractive ones. In this, adolescents are not unlike adults, only most teens haven't yet learned to live with their insecurities so they try even harder to conceal them. Keep in mind that adolescents are growing into not only their bodies but also their personalities.

Although your students may look and act tough or blasé or scornful, generally *they are pretending*. In some urban settings, we've taught students who would have terrified us if we'd first met them on the street. But slowly we earned their respect and trust and peeled back their facades to discover that most were simply applying a well-known sporting principle, "The best defense is a good offense." Many young people learn to pose and posture just to survive in the outside world.

Also keep in mind that, although the gangbanger or teen mother in the second row may have seen and done things you couldn't imagine, in the classroom they're no match for you. You have too much on your side. Your age, your experience, and the power and prestige vested in you as a teacher give you the automatic advantage in any one-on-one confrontation. By design, you have the entire weight of the educational institution behind you.

This has two major implications. First, if you play by the rules, you will win any conflict with any student. Confident teachers, knowing this, feel no need to beat their chests and continually intimidate their students. Instead, they demonstrate their power once or twice early in the year to strike fear into the hearts of potentially unruly students, and act normal thereafter. As one middle school veteran puts it, "Make clear to students that you are a dormant volcano, and they won't mess with you" (J. Stanford, personal communication).

Second, a teacher-student relationship is inherently one of disproportionate power, and with great power comes great responsibility. Do you want to embitter your target and onlookers through a humiliating spectacle as you grind your biggest troublemaker into the dust? Or would it be wiser to temper your disciplinary actions with mercy and let other students admire you for your maturity, restraint, and sense of justice? The last of these, in particular, is highly prized by teens—many of whom harbor a perpetual sense of being wronged by the world.

If you find sadistic impulses rising with your temper, recall Dorothy Nolte's poem, "Children Learn What They Live":

> If a child lives with criticism, he learns to condemn
> If a child lives with hostility, he learns to fight
> If a child lives with ridicule, he learns to be shy
> If a child lives with shame, he learns to feel guilty
> If a child lives with tolerance, he learns to be patient
> If a child lives with encouragement, he learns confidence
> If a child lives with praise, he learns to appreciate
> If a child lives with fairness, he learns justice
> If a child lives with security, he learns to have faith
> If a child lives with approval, he learns to like himself
> If a child lives with acceptance and friendship,
> He learns to find love in the world

8. Acknowledge Good Behavior, Not Just Bad Behavior.

The most effective classroom managers do not focus solely on punishment, but recognize and reward effort and good conduct at every opportunity. Madeline Hunter, among others, bemoans the irony of teachers who direct more attention to student misbehavior than to appropriate behavior.

Hunter describes a hypothetical teacher who ignores the good behavior of most students, and consistently addresses the disruptive antics of a particular boy. The teacher then largely ignores the boy on the one day he is well behaved. To no one's surprise, this student reverts to his old misbehavior the following day. The moral: Most young people crave attention and for some, negative attention is better than no attention at all (Hunter, 1990, p. 19).

This is not a phenomenon occurring only in young children. Psychologist Perry Buffington observes that as children become teenagers, many parents and teachers "become more critical and challenging and less trusting. Their fears and doubts are communicated both subtly and clearly in their speech, behavior and expressions of emotion."

Problem behavior may seem inherent in children of a certain age, and if you expect to find it, you likely will. But what if you changed your expectation—and started looking for good behavior instead of bad? "Make it a point to notice [a] child when she is good," Buffington (2003) advises, "and you'll find that the little devil has no need to come out and play" (pp. 13–14).

Although elementary teachers typically excel at recognizing good behavior, secondary teachers often neglect it. Perhaps they believe their students have somehow outgrown positive reinforcement, or that grades alone should be sufficient incentive to work hard. For many students, however—age notwithstanding—this is simply untrue. Chapter 4, "Communication Essentials" further discusses positive reinforcement techniques.

Following the recommendations presented so far should stop most disruptive behavior in your classroom before it starts. Since no teacher escapes the profession without a few battle scars, however, the rest of this chapter offers recommendations for coping with trouble when it arises.

CLASSROOM MISDEMEANORS: INCIVILITY, DEFIANCE, WHINING, AND MANIPULATION

Incivility

If words like self-centered, obstinate, irrational, hyperactive, insecure, and rude come to your mind when thinking about adolescents, you're in good company. As a teacher, expect to encounter a staggering dearth of basic civility—a term that is alien to many teens, but which we typically define for them as "behaving in a way that would not embarrass your grandparents." The teacher's eternal challenge is to help students recognize when their behavior is obnoxious, as the first step on the long road to less odious habits. The examples below illustrate what we mean.

TEACHING DILEMMA: STUDENTS CONTINUALLY USE PROFANITY

All my classes have at least a few students who can't seem to stop swearing. I think it's inappropriate in school and tell them this, but they don't seem to care. I don't know if it bothers other students but it bothers me.

SUGGESTED SOLUTION

Some teachers view profanity from students as an inevitable part of life; others find profanity annoying and believe it has no place in school; still others are profoundly offended by it. If you choose to spend energy fighting profanity, you might try one of these techniques.

SUGGESTED SOLUTION A: "DON'T TRY TO PLAY ME. I'VE SEEN IT ALL."

If you believe the students are deliberately trying to shock you and not just swearing out of habit, try telling them, "There's nothing you can say to shock me. There's nothing you can talk about that I haven't heard about. The games you try to play, I played them all before, because I was your age once. So when you try to do and say things to shock me I'm not going to be shocked. But there are certain things I'm not going to allow in this classroom."

SUGGESTED SOLUTION B: "IMAGINE YOU'RE AT GRANDMA'S HOUSE, NOT ON A STREET CORNER."

If you can pull it off, act like a little old lady (or gentleman) with virgin ears who really, *really* would prefer not to have to hear language like that. Students' sense of respect will often cause them to be a bit more considerate after this.

Alternately, you might sit your profanity-spewer down one-on-one and say,

> You know, I know the words I heard you using in class. I've heard them plenty and sometimes I've even used them myself. Those words might be fun for you because they're new or because they can be shocking. But adults understand there's a time and a place for those words, and my classroom is neither. I'm especially concerned because I can see the other students in here really look up to you, and I hope you'll try to set a better example.

SUGGESTED SOLUTION C: "SAY THAT AGAIN PLEASE, WITHOUT AN AUDIENCE."

Write down what the student said, word for word, on a discipline referral form. Then sit the student down privately after class and ask the student to read what he said. We have watched students blush just to see those words in print. Rare is the student who thinks reciting profanity one-on-one to a disapproving teacher is either enjoyable or "cool."

Then ask the student what he would like to see done with the discipline referral form. Typically, you can forge a simple win-win agreement: you will not send the referral to the office or to the student's parents, provided that the student does not repeat the behavior. Case closed.

TEACHING DILEMMA: STUDENTS MAKE
DEROGATORY PERSONAL REMARKS ABOUT TEACHER

My first year teaching, a few popular students in one class kept making derogatory comments about me personally. Because they usually muttered these comments in the back of the room, I ignored them. When they tired of it and stopped I thought I'd won, but they resumed soon afterward. Eventually the comments started to affect my self-confidence, which dragged down my teaching. I was afraid the comments were tarnishing my image in the eyes of the other students and I was starting to feel miserable in that class. I couldn't talk to the principal or the parents because I didn't want them to think I was weak. I couldn't talk to other teachers because I was embarrassed about what the students were commenting on. And I couldn't talk to the students because I didn't want them to know they were getting to me.

SUGGESTED SOLUTION

Many adolescents, cursed with limited imaginations, believe the only way to build themselves up is by tearing others down. And, like pack predators, they are typically drawn to those they perceive as "weak." In chapter 1, "Creating a Classroom Culture," and chapter 6, "Classroom Management II," we suggest how to intervene when students attack students.

But what if students attack you? Are you physically small, soft-spoken, or of extraordinarily gentle temperament? Is there something about you that's noticeably different from what teens in their narrow experience might consider "normal?" If so, they may perceive you as a tempting target for ridicule.

First, if this happens to you, try not to take it personally. Keep in mind that children of all ages like to poke at anything—bug, slug, or teacher—likely to give them an interesting reaction. But how should you react? For example, if a student remarks on what a big nose you have, you have several options:

1. Pretend you didn't hear.
2. Insult the student back.
3. Make a general comment about how "poor upbringing has made children so rude these days."
4. Tell the student directly that the comment is inappropriate, then move on.
5. Silence the student with a look of death and move on.
6. Make your own joke about your nose like the ones you've probably heard your whole life, and then move on.

Let's examine these alternatives.

For minor incidents, *pretending not to notice* might eventually extinguish this behavior by denying your attacker the attention he craves. If, however, the comments win attention from classmates, your silence could simply embolden him to continue. In that case, you will not appear to be in charge, and the insults could start to taint students' general perception of you, as the teacher in this dilemma discovered.

Returning the student's insult will likely escalate the situation, make you look petty, and possibly get you in trouble with your administration and the student's parents. One rare exception: Some of the best teachers we know engage in playful banter with students, which is understood by all to be a game and not a problem as defined here. If you are one of those teachers and this is one of those situations (i.e., if you're confident that your students are merely teasing and not attacking), feel free to engage. Otherwise, we do not recommend this tactic.

Making a general comment to the class about "kids these days" not only fails to address the problem directly, but could also give you headaches down the road when students go home to tell Mom and Dad what bad parents you said they were.

Opting to *tell the student directly that the comment is inappropriate* is always a safe bet. It avoids the potentially nasty edge and passive-aggressive quality of the previous option, while firmly putting students in their rightful place and reinforcing your role as the leader and keeper of order, who is above scrutiny for irrelevant personal characteristics.

Some teachers, particularly those whose voices get shrill or tremulous under pressure, prefer *silencing the student with a look of death* because it reveals nothing about whether the student's attack has affected them. When delivered properly it also conveys the "shut up before you get yourself in trouble" message better than words ever could because it leaves so much to students' imaginations (see also "The Stare," later in this chapter).

If it suits your personality and the circumstance, you might try *turning the whole thing into a joke.* This tactic halts both your attacker and the unhealthy classroom dynamic, and while the class is laughing you can steer them back on track. A little self-deprecating humor can also transform you in students' minds from a potential victim into a self-confident professional who is not only above such pettiness but also in complete control. In effect this approach tells students, "I've heard every nose joke ever told and they bounce right off me so don't even bother, kid. I'm the teacher and I'm indestructible."

Defiance

Children of many ages take joy in liberal—some might even say indiscriminate—use of the word *no*. Few other words are so ideally suited to the adolescent mindset, succinctly conveying petulance while offering a potent adrenaline rush—the invisible thrill of raw, obstructionist power. And few other words so enthrall onlookers by their instant effect on a teacher's blood pressure. Unless, of course, you choose not to play along.

When a student openly defies you, determine whether you're witnessing some kind of profound, entrenched resistance or merely a momentary temper tantrum. The former scenario, common in teachers' imaginations but quite rare in reality, we will discuss in the next chapter. For the latter—a temporary flare of obstinacy—the best response is to "take your sail out of their wind" (in Rudolf Dreikurs' memorable phrase) by keeping your cool.

Don't get sucked into arguing with the student—as in, "Yes you will." "No I won't." "Yes you will. I'm the teacher and I said you will." "No I won't, and you can't make me." *Don't* launch into a protracted lecture about the costs and benefits of the student's choice. And *don't* berate the student—as in, "Yeah, I figured you probably couldn't do it." (Don't laugh; we've heard teachers actually say this.)

Instead, when faced with any form of "I'm not doing that," consider one of the following responses, each appropriate with the right student in the right circumstance:

- *The slyly humorous approach.* "Is that a new attitude you're wearing? Maybe you should try on a different one. I preferred the one you had on yesterday; want to put that one back on?"
- *The matter-of-fact "as long as you understand the consequences" approach.* "Are you sure? Because if you insist on not doing this work, you won't be getting the points for the assignment. And the impact on your grade won't be pretty."
- *The compassionate but firm approach.* "I understand you might be having a bad day, but I don't want you to fail this assignment or set a bad example for the other students, because we both know you can do it."
- *The "get the kid out of the limelight and get the class back on track ASAP" approach.* "Why don't you take a time-out and give yourself some time to think a little more about what your best choice would be here."
- *The "what would your parents think?" approach.* "Why don't you stay after class today so I can help you get caught up on this project? That would keep your grade up and make both me and your parents happy."

If your chosen tactic fails to disarm the student and you face continued defiance, engage your *discipline hierarchy* (discussed later in this chapter) and announce that your attempt to cajole the student was a formal warning—Strike 1. If you are issuing a behavioral directive (e.g., "sit down," "please move over here," "stop touching him," etc.), the student's refusal to comply will likely constitute a violation of the school disciplinary code, filed under "insubordination."

What Do I Do When the Whining Starts?

Anyone who's spent time around a 2-year-old knows how irritating whining can be. Now imagine a 2-year-old who thinks he knows everything. Then picture a roomful of them. This is what secondary teachers cope with every day.

One common fear: What if whining erupts from every corner at once? Although rare in a well-managed classroom, it happens. If complaints pop up so furiously that you can't swat them all down and the room seems ready to dissolve into general rebellion, do what sports teams do when pressed against the wall with no apparent escape: take a time-out. Stop whatever you're doing and ask the group for an explanation. Simple language like, "Okay. Time out. What's going on?" works as well as anything.

Sometimes the group will have a legitimate complaint—perhaps you neglected to give a critical instruction (like what students should do when they complete Step 2), or failed to consider an extenuating circumstance (like the fact that you just assigned 6 hours of homework over homecoming weekend), or forgot a previous promise (like how if they all passed the last test you'd spare them homework for a night). If this is the case, all you have to do is change course and apologize for your oversight. Don't neglect this last step—your students won't forget your humility, and some may even absorb a bit of civility from your example.

Other times student complaints will feed on each other, building momentum in an effort to overwhelm you like a tsunami. If this happens, stop the class and tell them simply, "I sense that a few of you would like to throw us off track, but it's not going to work." Give a short explanation to address their general complaint if you like, and then plunge ahead. The grumbles will fade and you will have reasserted control.

Or try a more humorous approach. Adopt the pose of a musical conductor, directing the moaning and groaning like the sections of an orchestra—more screeching here, less bellowing there. "Okay, let's get the complaining over with. Right now. Come on. Jason? I know you have a complaint. Let's hear it. Veronica? Good. More. Come on, is that all you've got? I know you have more." This may sound ridiculous, but try it. It's fun to ham up and, like the mere act of smiling, will help put you in a good mood. Soon your students will tire themselves out and will probably start to giggle, at which point you can steal their ammunition by addressing all their complaints quickly and decisively before moving on to the day's lesson.

Common Manipulative Ploys

Students also employ certain common verbal maneuvers against naive teachers. In case ignoring these fails to quell them, the suggested responses listed in Table 5.1 have all proven effective in difficult classrooms. Depending on your personality and the population you're facing, these may or may not work for you, but they should give you an idea of the arguments stockpiled in students' arsenals.

In case you do not find a response listed here suitable for your situation (or your personality), we have left space for you to compose your own responses. Keep the content and change the phrasing, shift the focus slightly, or start entirely anew if you like. For example, if tongue-in-cheek delivery is not your forte, you might need to make more direct, less ironic, statements. You're the only one who knows the dynamics of your class so, as always, choose what fits you best.

Some of these responses are better delivered one-on-one; others are suitable for broadcasting because they set examples for the entire class. What works for you will vary with the circumstance, the students involved, and of course your style. Also note that although some of these responses are earnest, others are meant to be delivered with some signal in tone or body language that they are humorous. *In no case* do we recommend speaking any of these words with hostility; the whole idea is to avoid rancor, make your point memorably, and quickly move on.

Table 5.1.   Common Verbal Maneuvers and How to Respond

When Students Say	Consider Responding
"Oh come on, please? Can't we try it just once?"	"Once is once too much." or "I said that a lot when I was your age. The problem with that argument is that 'once' is never really just once. Once today becomes twice tomorrow, and it's no secret where you all would like to take it from there. Nice try, though." or
"I don't like this seat."	"That's unfortunate, but that's where you chose to put yourself with that behavior. If you show you can behave better for a week in that seat, I'll consider moving you out of that corner." or "That's too bad. It's not a choice." or
"She was talking too. How come she didn't get in trouble?"	"I'll handle her separately. Your job is to take care of your own business. And your business is this work. That's a full-time job on its own." or "I didn't notice her doing that. But the next time she's being as disruptive as you just were, you let me know. Then I'll handle it." or
"He started it!"	"And you played along. You sank to his level, so now you're both in trouble." or "Next time you see a problem arising, just raise your hand and ask to move your seat. I'll bend over backward to help people who want to avoid trouble and get work done." or

Table 5.1. *(continued)*

When Students Say	Consider Responding
"This is boring!"	"I'm sorry to hear that, because I put a lot of effort into making this lesson relevant to you. If you'd like to drop by after school for a few minutes, I'd welcome your ideas for making this subject more exciting."
	or
	"Have you ever heard the saying, 'If you're bored, you're boring'?"
	or
"This is stupid. Why do we have to learn this?"	"Because the adults of this state voted for a State Board of Education that consulted with a lot of experts who determined that this is important for everyone to know. So you can choose not to care about this but unfortunately I can't change it, so I hope you can 'not care' quietly."
	or
	Tell a true story like this one to demonstrate the real-world utility of your subject matter: "Let me tell you how knowing geography could have saved a 23-year-old friend of mine a lot of trouble. I talked to him one day about a party we were supposed to go to that weekend. But Saturday came and went, and he didn't show up and hadn't answered his phone for days. I was about to start calling hospitals when he called on Wednesday to tell me he missed the party because he had offered to drive someone from Colorado to Michigan. The only problem is he didn't realize those two states were not adjacent, or even within 1,000 miles of each other."
	or
"Why can't we do blah blah instead?"	"Because I have a professional responsibility to teach certain content and skills and address certain learning modalities. The activity you're suggesting fails to fulfill the learning goals I've targeted in planning this lesson."
	or
	"*Blah blah* is not on the menu today. Sorry."
	or

Table 5.1. *(continued)*

When Students Say	Consider Responding
"Ms. Whoever is letting us go outside to play games today."	"Well I'm sure she has a good reason, but we need to finish this project by Friday, so we don't have time for that." or "Great! When you get to Ms. Whoever's class, you'll have to write back and tell me how that is." or
"We've been good for the last half-hour. Can you please take away our punishment?"	"Absolutely not. Half a period of bad behavior plus half a period of good behavior does not equal zero. Consistent good behavior is the minimum acceptable standard in this class." or "For the first 20 minutes of class you were so loud you distracted people who were trying to work, you gave me a headache, and you embarrassed me (and yourselves) in front of a visitor. So after careful consideration, the answer is no." or
"Can't we just have a free day?"	"No, because a 'free day' is not really free. If we had a 'free day' every time a student asked me for one, we'd take so long to get this work done that we'd have to keep you at school until 9 at night and all through the summer just to get finished. I don't know about you, but I have a feeling your classmates wouldn't really enjoy that. Am I right?" or "No, we cannot have a 'free day.' We cannot 'just kick it.' We cannot watch TV. Do you have a TV at home? Then watch yours at home, because we're not watching TV in this classroom. Class time is work time, period." or
"Your third period class didn't have to do all this work. How come you're making us do it?"	"Maybe I hold this class to a higher standard because I know how capable you are. Maybe you're at a different place in the work. Maybe third period has been extra well-behaved all week. Or maybe *your* work is your business, and the other class's work is not."

Table 5.1. *(continued)*

When Students Say	Consider Responding
	or
	"This is not third period."
	or
"I didn't understand what this assignment was all about."	"I'm sorry to hear that, but it's a little late since the assignment is due today. If you ask before the deadline next time, I'll be happy to help. That's what I'm here for."
	or
	"Well, hand in what you've got and we'll see. Maybe you did better on it than you think. If not, since this is the first time this has happened we can consider extra work you might be able to do to make it up."
	or
"You never told me that was due today!"	"I mentioned the due date in class, wrote it on the board as I always do, and it's on the homework website. But why don't you come by after class and I'd be happy to help you figure out better ways to manage your schedule so you don't lose track of important things like this in the future."
	or
	"Hmm. . . . I know you weren't absent the day I gave this assignment. I also know Jason and Monica and Ming are sitting all around you, and they all did exactly what I asked. So if you were in my shoes, what conclusion would you draw?"
	or
"That's not fair!"	"If you feel sincerely that this is a problem for you, why don't you take time—not now, but after class—to write me a note about it or drop a card in the class suggestion box, and I'll be happy to discuss it with you later. For now, though, this is how it's going to be."
	or
	"Not fair? Wow. Imagine how you'd feel if you were _____." [Insert a truly persecuted historical figure or group; you might even ask your TA to cull photos of

Table 5.1. *(continued)*

When Students Say	Consider Responding
	(continued)
	tragedies from magazines and make placards of these so you can flash them at the class and elicit a brief comparative discussion—i.e., there's "suffering" and then there's SUFFERING—whenever complainers need help putting petty grievances in perspective.]
	or
"You used to be my favorite teacher. Not any more."	"Does this mean my royalty checks will shrink because you're going to stop wearing _____?" [Insert any popular, celebrity-endorsed fashion item with your name substituted in place of the actual brand name. The more absurd, the better.]
	or
	"I'm sorry to hear that. I'll be heartbroken to give up the trophy. But I'll always cherish our time together!" [This works well as a deadpan throwaway line, or if you feel the urge, collapse to your knees and deliver it through faux tears. It may sound hokey (and it is) but half of great teaching is theatrics, and the more outrageous your response, the more they'll enjoy—and remember—the point.]
	or
"I'm going to tell my parents / the principal!"	"Good. Why don't you stick around after class and we can call them together; that way we won't forget to mention all the problems that have led us to this point."
	or
	"That's your choice, of course. But when they ask me how your behavior has been all week, what do you imagine I'll tell them? Or would you rather invite them to class to see for themselves how you're doing, and how you're planning to improve?"
	or

If you think of other common student remarks and/or alternative response strategies—for complaints listed here or your own—please share them with other teachers on our website: www.classroom advisor.com/forum.

FOUR BASIC TENETS OF DISCIPLINE

Here we recommend a series of precise steps to take when students break the rules. First, however, we want to emphasize four basic tenets of discipline that should make your life exponentially easier:

1. Remember that delivering consequences is a necessary evil; try not to look like you enjoy it.
2. Consistency is essential.
3. If you're not sure who did it, don't assume.
4. If a few students gang up on you, turn the tables.

1. Delivering Consequences Is a Necessary Evil; Try Not to Look Like You Enjoy It.

Like it or not, you are a model for students, and an essential factor in their lives because some kids have very few good role models. Remember that as a teacher you are continually onstage, starting the moment you set foot on school property (or sometimes earlier if students see you, say, dropping by a local coffee shop before school).

The focus on you will intensify when you're delivering consequences in the classroom. In such high-tension moments, both the offending student and any onlookers will learn a great deal from your words, vocal tone, body language, and actions. Make certain all are aligned to send the same underlying message—and we recommend that message *not* be, "Okay kid, you asked for it. You've pushed me so far that my sadistic side is coming out," but rather something dispassionate and professional like, "I don't enjoy doing this, but you chose to break the rules so for everyone's sake I must live up to my responsibility to enforce them."

This demands that you make every effort to remain calm no matter what the student does. A student may yell, swear at you, or throw things in a hormone-driven bout of temporary insanity, but as long as he's not endangering himself or another student, there's no need for you to respond in kind. The last thing you want is to escalate a discipline situation with a power struggle, so don't lose your cool no matter how students try to provoke you; instead, silently count to 10 and take that time to plan your response.

Sometimes you really may not know what to do with a troublesome student, or you may realize that you are too upset to make a good decision in the moment. In such situations, consider this stalling tactic. Tell the student, privately and with an impassioned look on your face, some version of the following: "I am too angry/hurt/upset/disappointed/whatever to talk to you about this right now. I need time to calm down so I don't say or do something I'll regret. We'll settle this tomorrow when I am calmer."

This doesn't let the student off the hook, but it does give the student time to stew in her own juices for 23 hours while you ponder what to do. If the student did not acknowledge the mistake immediately, there's a good chance she will after thinking about her actions, and what you are likely to do in response. The student will often return to class humble and contrite the following day, which makes everyone's life easier, and often allows the matter to be settled with a sincere apology and a handshake. We have found that, contrary to conventional child-rearing wisdom in certain circles, treating adolescents as the adults you would like them to become rather than as criminals-in-the-making frequently makes them more cooperative and accelerates their maturation.

Also be aware that everyone has a bad day from time to time—including perhaps even you. Students who misbehave one day do not need to hear about it from you for the rest of the week. In fact, this is counterproductive because as discussed previously, students tend to live up to consistent expectations, low or high.

To encourage improved behavior for the long term, treat every day as every student's chance to make a fresh start. Some students will require several fresh starts, to be sure, but keep trying. If you welcome your former offenders back with a smile and the same high expectations you've always held, before long they will become just what you desire—*former* offenders.

2. Consistency Is Essential.

When delivering consequences, beware of a trap many new teachers fall into: inconsistency from day to day or from student to student. Don't crack down harder one day just because you're in a bad mood, for example. And avoid giving extra leeway to students who are ordinarily well-behaved. Giving a mere slap on the wrist to a rule-breaker who rarely causes trouble will elicit howls of self-righteous protest from students with a finely honed sense of justice. Note that some leeway is built into the discipline hierarchy recommended here, but it does not depend on the teacher's whim; it applies equally and consistently to all students, every day.

Of course, treating all students fairly does not necessarily mean treating all students the same. Fairness may require differential treatment for students with different needs. How should you address the student who seems to need extra help attending to and following the rules? Make your warnings visual. Make them personal. Create a special system of signals with that student. Narrow the physical distance between you and especially troubled students, seating them near you if necessary.

3. If You're Not Sure Who Did It, Don't Assume.

If you know who's responsible for a disruption, isolate that person. If you can't immediately determine who's at fault, be patient. Watch students' reactions. Do certain students display inordinate glee at the prank? Students often give away the identity of the trouble-maker with glances they cannot control. You may not find proof of wrongdoing, but you will get definite clues about which students to watch in the future.

Beware, however, of accusing students of wrongdoing just because they have a history of bad behavior. Deon may have gotten into trouble in the past and his friends may seem to live in the discipline office, but that doesn't mean Deon is guilty every time anything goes wrong in his presence. Assuming the worst about a student—any student—engenders resentment and mistrust, and hinders that student's eventual progress toward appropriate behavior.

TEACHING DILEMMA: TEACHER CAN'T DETERMINE CULPRIT

I was substituting in a middle school and felt a wad of gum pelt my shirt as I took attendance. As it turns out, the gum didn't do any damage, but I was insulted and didn't want to look like an easy target by letting the deed slide unpunished.

I could determine the general direction from which the projectile came, but couldn't pin the deed definitively on any particular student. I suspected a group of boys in the back, especially one who was looking away with such determination; I figured he must have done it. But without proof I couldn't do anything. Could I?

SUGGESTED SOLUTION

First, don't take it personally. Your students are probably not targeting you as a person; they're targeting their substitute teacher—who happens to be you at the moment.

Don't make accusations without solid proof. With this kind of misbehavior, the odds are that the culprit was male, but are those boys smirking in the back of the room smiling because they're guilty, because they enjoyed watching the crime, because they're nervous about being accused, or because they're so disconnected from class that they didn't even see the gum fly and are enjoying some entirely unrelated private joke? False accusations not only cause resentment among the accused, but they're also one of the quickest ways to stir up trouble with parents. They can also mark you as an easy-to-fool simpleton.

Try to determine the culprit yourself. Preserve any physical evidence to see if you can match it to any student. For example, if you can track the gum back to a particular student, that's a good starting point for your inquiry. Move among your suspects, looking and listening for evidence, or for someone in the class to give you a subtle clue.

If you feel it's an important enough issue to stop the class to resolve it (for example, if it's the start of the class on Monday and you are scheduled to lead that class for the rest of the week), try moving your suspected troublemakers to the front of the room. If there are several suspects, this will inevitably involve shifting around a large portion of the room. Avoiding such an "unfair" inconvenience may be enough incentive for a student to tell you who did it. This might sound like, "You can't move all of us! James did it."

Offer a warning against future misbehavior and then watch surreptitiously (e.g., in the reflection of a window or computer monitor) for additional misdeeds. If you catch your suspect causing further trouble, you can crack down with the stiffest available penalty. Invoke the "severity clause" because you already offered the class a general warning.

Even if you don't discover the culprit, document your suspicions of particular students. Mere suspicions are not useful as formal evidence, but could help you spot patterns in case you deal with this group of students again in the future.

If that fails, ask a trusted student after class if he saw anything. Certain students' unwritten code against *snitching* might leave you empty-handed, but frequently the students who cause you grief are not loved by their classmates, who may give you information if you promise not to cite them by name. While you can't pursue disciplinary action based on second-hand knowledge from an anonymous informant, knowing who to watch is half the battle.

HOW NOT TO SOLVE A MYSTERY

Be careful to avoid traps like the one this substitute teacher laid for himself. After seeing a piece of paper fly across the room, he singled out a student he suspected of wrongdoing and started a public confrontation.

Teacher:	Pick that up.
Student:	Huh?
Teacher:	Pick that up!
Student:	I didn't throw it.
Teacher:	I didn't ask that. I told you to pick it up.
Student:	No, man. I didn't throw it.
Teacher:	You can pick it up or you can leave.
Student:	Fine. I'll leave, then.
Teacher:	Get back here!

A better alternative? Pick up the paper yourself and be vigilant from that point on. If there's a lot of trash on the floor in a particular spot, quietly tell the student you suspect, "Look, I know you didn't do this, but we can't leave things like this. Can you give me a hand by picking this up, please? You'd really be helping me out. Then some day, when you need a favor, I'll remember this."

4. If a Few Students Gang Up on You, Turn the Tables.

Occasionally, problems will persist with a small knot of students. You can solve this by turning your cooperative students momentarily against the resisters in their midst.

You don't have to punish the class; just inconvenience them. For example, one of the most powerful ways to invoke peer pressure on your side is simply to make everyone else wait for noncooperative students. In elementary school, this might sound something like, "No one can leave until everybody's cleaned up. But it looks like Brandon and Chris haven't finished putting their books away. We're waiting." Or perhaps, "It looks like Christina's group left her with a lot of things to clean up. Would somebody from that group like to help finish that job? You understand that if it doesn't get cleaned up, nobody leaves."

The same approach (with appropriately adapted language) can work at the secondary level, as well. If students complain about being treated like "little kids," inform them that as soon as they start acting consistently like adults, you'll start treating them that way. This simple message works brilliantly with some groups.

What if parents of well-behaved students object to group sanctions that punish their children along with chronic wrongdoers? One secondary teacher explains:

> *There's a difference between punishment and loss of privilege. . . . I'd never keep an entire class in for detention because of one student's behavior. That's a group punishment . . . [but] going to the restroom during class time is a privilege. Eating in class is a privilege. Having a night without homework is a privilege. Free time is a privilege. To some degree, even having an interesting class can even be seen as a privilege.*
>
> —L. Thlick-Katchadourian, personal communication

Indeed. We've seen superb teachers inform entire classes that they were going to do nothing but read out of the textbook for days because a few students really screwed up when a substitute was in class, and their peers failed to keep the misbehavior in check. Or because the teacher—patient but not without limits—issued multiple warnings and finally got fed up with their attitude, as a group.

TEACHING DILEMMA: TEACHER ENCOUNTERS ORGANIZED RESISTANCE FROM ENTIRE CLASS

In my first few days as a teacher, I met organized resistance from an eighth-grade class. Their first prank was after they were all seated and the bell had rung; in unison, they counted to 3, and dropped their books on the floor. Later, they passed their books along their rows, until the person in the desk next to the windows pushed the entire pile of books out the window. At the end of the class period, they all sat up rigid, stood, and slammed their desks. Then, as if on command, all marched out of the room without permission. Since they all participated, I couldn't pick out one or two troublemakers.

SUGGESTED SOLUTION

This is perhaps the most complex problem presented here. We have encountered similar situations with teachers hired midyear to replace teachers the class had previously driven out. Students in that position feel invincible, multiplying the difficulty of the teacher's task.

Analyze the Situation

Before you can address the problem, you must realize that these students did not get this hostile and this organized overnight. Understanding and unraveling the problem is therefore bound to be a long-term, multistage process. Don't get frustrated if you don't see results in the first hour. To keep things in perspective, you might keep a journal in which at the end of each day you list the best thing that happened, the worst thing that happened, any pleasant surprises, and three efforts you made to improve the situation.

Documenting your progress will

- let you spot patterns in *their* behavior
- help you spot patterns in *your* behavior that may be contributing to the problem
- provide a positive outlet for your frustration
- produce a record of events that you can analyze in a quiet moment and/or use to seek specific assistance from colleagues or administrators

When analyzing the situation, seek first to understand what students are trying to achieve throught this behavior. Fun? Honest students would probably tell you outright, "Yes, at your expense." For them, the game "torment the teacher" is something of a thrill ride—the advanced version of "torture the bugs on the sidewalk" and "harass the new kid." Why? Is their goal to humiliate you? Perhaps, but since they can't possibly know *you* in the first week of school, try not to take such attacks personally.

Maybe school as they've experienced it thus far is boring to them. If so, you'll have to spend time and energy devising lessons that will take advantage of, rather than ignore, their creative energies. Maybe you've replaced a beloved or even legendary teacher. In that case, give them time to adjust. They'll come to appreciate you as well. Or maybe their previous teacher humiliated them, and they've become hardened by that experience. In that case also, time will teach them to trust you.

Several Strategies to Help Correct This Behavior

First, pay attention to when the misbehavior tends to start. Is it at a particular time each day? Usually, students try to take advantage of moments when your back is turned or when they think you're distracted.

Also, watch carefully to see who starts the misbehavior— someone must be plotting the activity and is likely sending out a signal. Change the seats of the students you identify, and call home to offer your concerns. Better yet, take the time to visit those parents at home, and invite them to come to your class to see how their children are performing.

In some cases, the parents will talk to their children and the misbehavior will cease. Other parents might take you up on your offer and actually come to school with their children. With another adult in the room, the students will probably cease their subversion. If not, at least you'll have witnesses to the events, and possibly suggestions for improvement. If the parents don't believe you or don't cooperate, ask a mentor teacher or administrator to sit in on one of your classes. Or try the videotaping strategy discussed earlier in this chapter.

You can also request to transfer some of the students out of your class. Often, one or a few students will poison the entire atmosphere, and their removal to another setting will change the dynamic of the room. Talk to other teachers, counselors, and administrators if you can't determine who should be removed.

No matter how bad things may seem to get, keeping a sense of humor can preserve your sanity. It can also throw off-balance your would-be tormenters. Learn from martial arts experts who use their opponents' energy against them. In a fierce wind, a reed will bend and spring back. An icicle, in contrast, will shatter. Which would you rather be?

If your students seek a particular reaction from you, give them the opposite. If they want you to explode with anger, you can either play into their hands by providing the fireworks they came to see, or you can "take your sail out of their wind" by calmly and definitively applying the discipline hierarchy set forth in this chapter, and watch their misbehavior eventually extinguish itself from lack of fuel.

If ignoring their behavior proves ineffective or impossible, surprise them. Applaud their organization. Show that you're impressed by the skills they've demonstrated. Single out for special attention those students you think had a leadership role in the activity and suggest a career (perhaps theater, political organizing, or event planning) in which such skills would be of great value.

Also start thinking of opportunities in the class for positive use of their leadership skills. For example, why not offer students the option of taking a couple of class days to help you plan a future dinner, perhaps to showcase for parents what students are doing and how much they've accomplished?

This, conveniently, would serve several functions. It would

- channel students' energies away from negative behavior
- generate an esprit de corps proving that you are not their enemy but in fact their leader
- give students the powerful experience of using their influence to create good works rather than mischief
- encourage them to become academically productive every day until the event

In our experience, students who seek to create chaos generally do not believe that anarchy would create the best of all possible worlds; they just prefer anarchy to bad government. Once you give them a taste of *good* government—that is, one in which they have a stake and a voice—they are unlikely to return to their former adversarial stance.

A SAMPLE DISCIPLINE HIERARCHY

A *discipline hierarchy* is the escalating series of consequences teachers invoke when students break the class rules. Here (in a form suitable for reprinting, enlarging, and framing on your classroom wall) is a five-level discipline hierarchy we have found almost universally effective (see Table 5.2). We urge you to post, refer frequently to, and faithfully follow yours. Doing so will help create a predictable classroom environment and shield you from the common parental protest, "But you didn't warn my child about that."

Because everyone deserves a chance to correct misbehavior before being sanctioned, the first two levels of this discipline hierarchy are mild. We think of them as Strike 1 and Strike 2—and in fact this is a useful way to describe them to students. You can deliver these every day because even the most cooperative students sometimes need to be nudged back on track.

Table 5.2. Discipline Hierarchy

	In 1 day	In 1 week	In 1 week	Predetermined Sanction
Level 1	Strike 1 (1st offense on any given day)	Strike 1 (1st offense on any given day)	Strike 1 (1st offense on any given day)	Notice
Level 2	Strike 2 (2nd offense the same day)	Strike 2 (2nd offense the same day)	Strike 2 (2nd offense the same day)	Verbal Warning
Level 3	Strike 3 (3rd offense in one day for the **first** time that week)			Relocation to a new seat within the classroom and teacher-student conference
Level 4		Strike 3 (3rd offense in one day for the **second** time that week)		Call home and/or removal from the classroom for the day
Level 5			Strike 3 (3rd offense in one day for the **third** time that week)	Notification of the administration

Any student who misbehaves a third time in the same day, however, should receive a *third strike*—Level 3 sanctions. If a student's behavior calls for Level 3 sanctions for a *second* day in the same week, the third strike should be a higher-level sanction—still called Strike 3, but this time more severe.

Keep in mind there will be times when you throw the order of these sanctions out the window. For egregious misconduct, feel free to invoke what Lee and Marlene Canter call a *severity clause* and jump straight to a higher-level sanction. Just be sure to inform students in advance that this is a possibility. If a student wants to engage you in any kind of verbal war, for example, jump immediately to "Level 4: Removal" and proceed from there.

Also, students themselves may occasionally prefer a higher-level sanction—as with a student who would rather relocate herself (with her classwork) from your classroom for the day to avoid getting stirred up by bothersome classmates, one of whom she knows she would probably end up clobbering before the end of the period. Check with your administration and/or colleagues before class to see whether this could be an option for you. However, beware of the student who does this too frequently, as she may be trying to game your system by projecting false emotion as a pretense for getting out of your class.

Creating Your Own Sanctions: A Cautionary Tale

Of course you may choose to substitute other sanctions for those in our chart, but we caution you to avoid a common trap—creating sanctions that penalize you along with your intended target. One university professor learned this the hard way from her parenting experience:

> One day my daughter wrote all over the wall, and I was so angry I threatened to pack up all her toys and send them away if she did it again. But she quickly figured out this wasn't a credible threat because packing up all her toys would be a lot of work and she knows I'm too lazy even to make my bed. That punishment would have punished me, which is why I never really did it.

Now her punishment is getting sent to bed early, and that's much more effective because she senses that my husband and I actually enjoy imposing that sanction."

—S. Marciano, personal communication

Level 1: Notice

Notice is Madeline Hunter's term to describe silent cues teachers use to correct student behavior without disrupting the flow of class. Notice can consist of a simple look or hand motion that conveys a directive like "Keep your eyes here," "Turn down your volume," "Keep your hands to yourself," and so forth. Or it can entail the teacher's physical movement to the offending student's vicinity. Frequently distracted and forgetful by nature, teens often do not realize they are engaged in misbehavior until it is pointed out to them. Notice is often all that's required to fix behavior problems that are really just bad habits rather than intentional disruptions.

If students given nonverbal notice remain off task, try what Lee and Marlene Canter call *proximity praise*—drawing a distracted student's attention to nearby peers who are behaving well. For example, if George is seated between Francisco and Harriet, you might remark aloud how you appreciate the latter two being on-task. This tactic's impact is twofold: First, it reinforces Francisco's and Harriet's productive behavior through public recognition. Second, it highlights for George what he is failing to do without even mentioning his name, let alone lobbing accusations or otherwise stirring up negative feelings (Canter & Canter, 1992, p. 166).

If the abovementioned techniques fail, try the intense and inscrutable gaze we call "The Stare." This technique derives its power from its mystery; like footsteps in a horror movie, it is frightening mostly because it represents the unknown. Students sense it, but have no way to assess precisely how dangerous it is and so tend to assume the worst.

To invoke The Stare: Let your eyes glaze over, fix your lips into something short of a snarl and then, saying nothing, walk slowly toward the offending student. Inside, you might be thinking about how you want your hair cut that afternoon, or what you're going to have for dinner ("Hmm . . . salad or pizza?"). But your students won't know that. All they'll see is an approaching stone face that is *not* happy.

How effective is The Stare? One veteran junior high teacher testifies, "I just look at them. I don't say anything. I don't have to say anything. I don't smile; I just stare. Pretty soon they get uncomfortable, and then they just melt. They can't take it" (J. Stanford, personal communication). Another teacher reports a similar effect. "A lot of times, I won't have to say a word. I just stand there with my mother's look, and they quiet down. They're like, 'Shh! Shh! Or she's gonna get mad'" (C. Davis, personal communication). We observed another teacher using The Stare, and the target student's response was humorous, but distinctly uncomfortable. "Why's he looking at me like that? He's gonna burn a hole in my forehead."

If notice, proximity praise, and The Stare fail, move to Level 2.

Level 2: Verbal Warning

As mentioned previously, sometimes students who make spectacles of themselves are not testing you as much as testing their own attention-getting skills. Their goal is to distract you and the class. In such cases, a quick public warning can quash the misbehavior. If you can stop the behavior without allowing the class to grind to a halt, you win twice. If you can defuse any accumulated tension with a funny but not denigrating comment along the way, even better.

Alternatively, summon the offending student to your desk and make a notation in your discipline file as you tell the student, "I've given you several signals that you've chosen to ignore. This is your formal warning. The next time your behavior distracts anyone, your seat will change. Understood?" Some teachers mark a student's name on the board when they've given a verbal warning; this keeps everyone honest and aware of the score.

One verbal warning is enough. If you give students multiple warnings about behavior problems, you're giving them unnecessary opportunities to disrupt others' learning. In addition, such indulgence risks conveying, not understanding and compassion, but, weakness and naiveté. If student misbehavior persists after you issue a verbal warning, proceed to Level 3 sanctions.

Don't Be a Screamer

Some teachers issue verbal warnings in the form of a scream. This we do not advise. Occasional loudness has its advantages, but the law of diminishing returns is never more applicable than to a screaming teacher in a classroom. What's effective the first minute can become innocuous within the hour and start to backfire soon after that. If you're always screaming to get your way, people—particularly teenagers, many of whom have themselves perfected that tactic—will quickly learn to tune you out, the way people living or working in loud environments tune out car alarms, sirens, trains, and so forth.

If your larynx is one of your most powerful weapons (you know who you are), you might raise your voice—but not your temper—to cut through classroom noise from time to time. Be aware, however, that every time you yell over students you are missing an opportunity to put responsibility for being quiet and attentive on them, where it belongs.

More effective ways to silence a noisy class include bells, buzzers, gavels, flashing lights, predetermined visual cues, or simply a silent pose in front of the class that students recognize means business.

Level 3: Relocation and Teacher-Student Conference

Relocate the offending student within the classroom and demand that she or he fill out a behavior citation form (see Figure 5.1). Once relocated, the student should remain in the new seat for the remainder of the week. If the student's behavior improves, you might return the student to a seat she prefers the following week—assuming the improved behavior continues.

At some point that same day, find 2 minutes to discuss the completed behavior citation with the student. If you don't have time at that moment, track the student down later that day (perhaps during lunch or your prep period or just after school) for a brief conversation. This is critical, as talking through the incident can not only help the student understand the nuances of the behavior, but also demonstrate that you play fair by giving the student an opportunity to explain her side of the story.

And don't forget to discuss the student's ideas about the problem. For example, it's possible that you've seated the student in front of her worst enemy, or too far back to hear, or perhaps the student needs more frequent reminders to stay on task. Often, students know what's wrong and can help fix their own problems, but no one asks them what they think.

After your 2-minute conference, be sure the student signs the form (not because it carries any legal weight, but because signing things tends to impress students with a sense of adult responsibility). Then try veteran teacher George Watson's suggestion: Seal the behavior citation in an envelope addressed to the student's parents and put it in a salient place—anywhere the student can see it regularly but not tamper with it—and inform the student that, upon the next infraction, the incriminating document will be sent home and you will call to be sure it got there. Then sit back and watch the student check her own behavior to prevent this (Watson, 1998, p. 5).

If that student's same problem behavior continues at any point, follow through on your promise and send the letter home, with a copy to the school administration or counselor. If the student improves for an extended period, keep the letter in place but consider making a surprise call home to the parents—to offer a compliment on the student's improvement. The student will likely return to school grateful and amazed, and you can inform the student that although you still have the past infractions on record, as long as the positive behavior continues you will let past trouble remain "in the past." All but the most hardcore troublemakers will be happy to cooperate after this.

Level 4: Call Home and/or Removal for the Day

If a student insists on misbehaving in the same week he has been relocated to a different seat in the classroom, pick up your telephone and dial the parent or guardian. If doing this on the spot is not feasible—either because you don't have a phone or you can't take time at that moment or you simply prefer to call in private— be sure the offending student has a behavior citation to fill out and classwork to do, then remove him from your classroom for the rest of the period. Instruct the student to return to you at some specific later time, then call home.

BEHAVIOR CITATION

Student _____   Teacher _____

Date _____   Time _____   Location _____

You have received this citation because your behavior has disrupted the class.

You may rejoin the rest of the class tomorrow if you complete the following to your teacher's satisfaction:

This is what I did to earn this citation:

This is why I did it:

This is how the teacher or class could help me monitor my behavior to prevent this problem in the future:

If I do not correct this behavior, this is what I will tell my guardians when the school contacts them:

Figure 5.1.   Behavior citation form.

No parent wants to hear that his kid is screwing up. And no child wants his parents called. So from my 30 years as a teacher and administrator, I can tell you that one of teachers' most powerful weapons in managing classroom behavior is the telephone."

—R. Cornner, personal communication

If you have a phone in your room and a moment to use it, calling home with the student and class in the room is often the best option—particularly early in the year—because it sets a great example. You don't have to make an announcement or a show of it; just pick up the phone and dial; students will know from the look on your face exactly what's going on and word will get around.

If when you pick up the phone the student asks what you're doing, you can simply explain, "I don't want your parents to be shocked by a low grade on your report card, so I want to give you the chance to explain to your mother why you're not willing to do the classwork." Ninety-nine times out of a hundred, the student will scramble to begin the work before you even finish dialing.

Remember that your goal is not to humiliate the student in front of peers, but to demonstrate to everyone just how serious you are about enforcing your rules. Therefore, in the unlikely event that the student is among the incorrigible 1% who does not correct his behavior immediately and you find yourself speaking to the parent you called, we do *not* recommend discussing the student's problems in detail while the rest of the class is listening. Just tell the parent there is a problem with the student's behavior and set up a mutually agreeable time later that day to discuss the issue.

In some cases, the parent might ask to speak to the student right then. Although this may seem like a great opportunity to let someone else do your disciplinary work, politely but firmly deny any such request. First, the experience could humiliate the student and cause long-term resentment. Second, the student could use the occasion to create a bigger scene in the class. Third, making the student wait to learn what the parent will say will force the student to reflect in the interim on the consequences of his poor behavior. Fourth, you'll want to be the first to speak to the parent about the issue. If the student gets to tell his version of events first, countering the student's spin on the story will become an uphill battle and your version may be viewed with suspicion.

If you face a dubious parent, you might try the tactic we overheard one student relating to his classmates: A previous teacher, exasperated by the young man's classroom antics, surreptitiously telephoned his mother at her work "and let her listen to me acting the fool in the classroom. Man, when I got home . . . Bam! Boff! Bam!" Curiously, the student regaling his peers with this tale was neither embarrassed nor angry about the episode; rather, he was in awe of the teacher who had so cleverly arrested his misbehavior.

For the unusually recalcitrant student, consider inviting the parents to join their child at school for a day, or visiting the student's home as described earlier.

Your school should have guidelines for temporarily removing a student. Some schools prefer that students be sent to an administrative office, but others allow or even prefer troublesome students to be relocated to a quiet corner of a neighboring teacher's classroom. Collaborate in advance with a nearby colleague about serving as each other's emergency pressure release valves for such rare situations.

Ideally, any time-out space should be a setting where the student doesn't know anyone. Drop a mischievous sophomore into a roomful of studious seniors who aren't in the least amused by his immature antics, and watch his will to misbehave evaporate. If you're lucky, he might even grow up a little from the experience.

Level 5: Notification of the Administration

We recommend sending students to the office as a last resort. First, learning is what they're in school for and the most troublesome students are typically those most in need of academic attention. Second, the less you burden the administration with your classroom management problems, the better you'll look to them. And third, once students realize you're so competent on your own that you don't even need the school administration to intercede on your behalf, they'll find some other poor teacher to torture.

6

CLASSROOM MANAGEMENT II: CHRONIC AND SEVERE TROUBLE

Many people avoid conflict at all costs, sometimes because they associate it with violence, emotional trauma, or simply discomfort. However, experienced teachers and other managers understand that conflict per se is not inherently a bad or dangerous thing. It's often simply an inevitable outgrowth of scarcity—of money, natural resources, time, space, attention, affection, or any other resource.

On the other hand, the outcome of conflict can be distinctly healthy or unhealthy. In the classroom, as in life, conflict can be managed in a productive way that improves mutual understanding and collaboration, or in a damaging way that generates mistrust and enmity, or occasionally not ended at all but drawn out indefinitely. Of course, conflict among teens is often exacerbated by the hormonal highs, insecurity, theatricality, territoriality, and various other quirks inherent to adolescents.

How should you cope with disruptive conflict in the classroom? First, act to prevent it. In chapter 3, "Preparing for the First Week of School" and chapter 5, "Classroom Management," we offer numerous suggestions to create a classroom environment that helps to avoid or, failing that, to manage potentially explosive situations. This chapter discusses additional ways to handle conflicts that do arise.

CONFLICT RESOLUTION: HEALTHY VERSUS UNHEALTHY STRATEGIES

Unfortunately, adolescents left to their own devices commonly resort to *unhealthy* methods of conflict resolution, including some of the tactics shown in Figure 6.1. Though these strategies usually appear to "solve" the conflict, they often merely repress symptoms of discord and allow the underlying conflict to fester and possibly grow.

The most challenging situation in the classroom is when emotions overwhelm all rational attempts to control them, and tempers flare in yelling or even violence. Why does this happen so frequently among certain young people? Often it's because they have little experience with alternative models of conflict resolution, and because quick and dirty solutions promise an easy way out of challenging situations.

Many young minds are easily seduced by elegant or dramatic but ultimately specious arguments. For example, suicide: In purely rational terms it makes little sense as a problem-solving tool—its chief logical flaw being that in most cases it is *a permanent solution to a temporary problem*—yet many youth find it tremendously appealing at some level.

Violence toward others holds similar allure for unsophisticated thinkers; it promises a simple exit from complex problems, while offering a potent adrenaline rush and feeling of control. To many, threatening or attacking someone appears to be a relatively quick and easy way to end an argument. Yet, like suicide, this violates basic rules of logic—in most cases by providing *a temporary solution to an ongoing problem*. As evident through much of history, this kind of thinking can engender lingering resentment that fuels a desire for retribution, sometimes for generations.

Healthy conflict resolution typically employs some form of controlled, rational discussion to reach a settlement. Emotions are kept in check by mutual agreement, cultural standards, and/or organizational structures designed for that purpose. Examples of healthy conflict resolution mechanisms include elections, courtrooms, business or political negotiations, and peer mediation programs. We will explore some healthy conflict resolution options in this chapter.

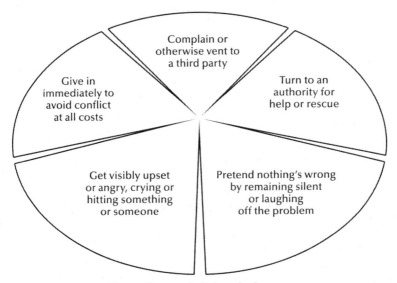

Figure 6.1.   Unhealthy conflict resolution methods.

WHAT TO DO WHEN CONFLICT ARISES

If your best conflict-prevention efforts fail, you will face a dual challenge: first, coping with conflict in the moment that it arises, and second, helping students to shift over time from unhealthy to healthy modes of resolving conflict. Here, we provide practical tools to meet both these needs.

Quick Solution: Mediate the Conflict Yourself

If a disruptive conflict breaks out in class and students are unable to manage it on their own, immediately apply the discipline hierarchy presented in chapter 5, "Classroom Management I." As soon as you regain control, resume regular class activity. Later, debrief the conflict privately with the students involved. This can not only help students understand exactly what happened and why, but also keep similar conflicts from recurring in the future. Here we explain how to use the "Getting to the Bottom of this Conflict" form to manage this process (see Figure 6.2). Download a full-sized blank version of this form from our website (www.classroomadvisor.com).

Student _____ Teacher _____

Date _____ Time _____ Location _____

1. This is what this conflict was about:

2. This is what the other student(s) involved in the conflict did:

3. This is what I imagine they were thinking and feeling when they did it:

4. This is what I did:

5. This is what I was thinking and feeling when I did it:

6. This is what I could do differently next time:

7. This is what I hope would happen if I chose this alternate behavior:

8. This is what I would like to ask the other student(s) to do differently next time:

9. This is what I agree to do to resolve this problem:

10. This is what I agree to do to prevent future conflicts like this:

Optional. This is what the teacher and/or the class can do to help monitor and prevent similar conflicts:

Figure 6.2. Getting to the bottom of this conflict.

The first step in this process is to hold a brief, individual conference with each student involved in the conflict. Ask the student to complete the first eight questions on the form, then review and discuss his responses. Answer any questions and coach him to understand both how his behavior may have contributed negatively to the situation and what he might have done differently that could have generated a different outcome.

Then bring the parties together in a calm space to debrief the conflict. Position yourself physically between the parties in case anything goes awry. Post and review the Peace Education Foundation's "Rules for Fighting Fair" and frame the discussion as a collaborative session in which instead of fighting each other, everyone will need to join hands to solve the problem.

Next, talk through the completed questions one by one, with students taking turns presenting their answers. To keep the discussion

RULES FOR FIGHTING FAIR

1. Identify the problem.
2. Focus on the problem.
3. Attack the problem, not the person.
4. Listen with an open mind.
5. Treat each person's feelings with respect.
6. Take responsibilty for your actions.

FOULS

blaming	name-calling	not listening
pushing	making threat	bringing up the past
sneering	getting even	put-downs
bossing	making excuses	not taking responsibility

Source: Peace Education Foundation, 1996.

on track and on schedule, you may need to lay out basic debate-style ground rules—for example, a 1-minute time limit for each party to answer a given question, plus 30 seconds for the other party to seek clarification and/or offer a civilized rebuttal.

If everyone agrees on Questions 1, 2, and 4 (what the conflict was about and what actions each party took), focus on Questions 3 and 5 (what each party was thinking). Question 3 (what the student imagines the others were thinking) is particularly important to encourage the kind of empathetic perspective-taking that can help humanize everyone involved and prevent future conflicts. Be sure to explore *why* each person interpreted the other's thoughts and emotions the way he did. Often, this process will surface misinterpretations that fueled the conflict.

Then focus on Questions 6 and 8 (what each person could do differently, and would want the other person to do differently). Agree on future behavior changes that are acceptable to all (students will list these under Question 10).

Finally, discuss what actions, if any, need to be taken to resolve the current conflict (Question 9) and get each person to commit in writing to what he will do differently (Question 10). A final, optional step is for students to discuss any structural or behavioral changes in the classroom that could help prevent future conflicts.

Option 2: Conflict Resolution Frameworks to Help Students Manage Their Own Disputes

Although conflicts will often necessitate your intervention, interceding in *every* dispute is actually counterproductive. This habit will not only bog you down but also deny your students the opportunity to build their own conflict mediation skills. Given that the larger purpose of teaching is to help students survive without the teacher, students should learn to work through minor problems on their own. Luckily, with a little guidance from you, they can.

The bad news: As with the other routines discussed in chapter 3, "Preparing for the First Week of School," teaching students to solve their own conflicts takes a lot longer than stepping in and imposing a unilateral solution. The process will require a great deal of your energy and personal supervision, particularly in the startup phase. And students will often flail at first, producing some mind-bogglingly bad ideas (e.g., "Let's get giant boxing gloves so Jared and David can pound on each other in the center courtyard! We can charge admission to pay for cleanup") before settling upon actual workable solutions.

The good news: Creating a conflict resolution framework will demand a sizeable investment of time and effort up front, but maintaining the system will consume much less of your energy than establishing it. Once it's launched, students will do most of the heavy lifting—useful, since they're the ones who really need the practice. The big payoff: this approach encourages self-reliance by helping each student develop an internal locus of control—the necessary foundation for enduring self-discipline and social collaboration.

Conflict Resolution Framework A: Class Meetings

In their series of Positive Discipline books (originally designed for elementary schools, but surprisingly adaptable to older students as well, depending on the setting), Jane Nelsen, Lynn Lott, and H. Stephen Glenn (2000) propose several strategies to engage students in the day-to-day management of their own classroom behavior. Drawing heavily on the work of Alfred Adler and Rudolf Dreikurs, Nelsen et al. start with the belief that all students can behave well and solve their own minor conflicts if given encouragement, modeling from fellow students, and the chance to practice.

Central to their approach are regular "class meetings"—not unlike "family meetings" in some homes—encouraging ongoing communication and collaboration among all students in the class. Such plenary gatherings are carefully structured to build positive relationships and surface conflicts before they degenerate into fights, solving them in an open and mutually respectful way.

As with any peer tribunal, this forces students to contemplate and address their own conflicts. In the process, it helps students sharpen their emotional awareness as well as critical thinking, communication, and negotiation skills. And, not incidentally, it teaches responsibility (for oneself and others) to everyone involved.

Unlike many courts or tribunals, however, the Nelsen model focuses on prevention rather than retribution; it seeks to replace alienating punishments imposed from above with workable solutions generated by students themselves. In lieu of sanctions often delivered by authority figures—including detention, extra work, yelling, beating, grounding, humiliation, and so forth—Nelsen's method harnesses students' collective creativity and perspective to generate positive behavioral alternatives for troubled students.

> We cannot sufficiently stress the importance of student participation in the problem-solving process. By taking part in the process, teachers and students create cooperation, collaboration, positive motivation, and healthy self-esteem. . . . If you want your students to learn cooperation, are you teaching them to give and take instead of defining cooperation as, "Do what I want you to do"? (Nelsen et al., 2000, pp. 10, 19)

Although the class time required to implement the Positive Discipline framework would likely make it a tough sell in conventional high schools with thousands of students, for middle school or any classroom with high levels of emotional dissonance, it could prove an ideal solution. The success stories—including leaps in student self-control and cooperation, and reductions in teachers' stress levels—are spectacular. Our website (www.majorandmajor.com) offers links to useful resources for establishing and running class meetings.

Conflict Resolution Framework B: Suggestion and Grievance Box

For those unwilling or unable to implement regular class meetings, try inviting (or requiring) students to put complaints about others' behavior, your teaching techniques, and so forth in a locked class suggestion and grievance box. The beauty of this tool from a classroom management perspective is that, instead of wasting time intervening in a thousand minor squabbles, you can simply tell quarreling students to "put the problem in the box" for later discussion.

Most students will be too lazy to actually write down their petty gripes, leaving only real problems to solve.

If you are applying the class meeting model described above, these complaints would go onto the regular class meeting agenda. Alternately, you could choose to read through the box and address that week's big issues at a predetermined time—say, the last 15 minutes of class one day a week. Frequently, students will have resolved the problems themselves before you even get a chance to discuss them.

Conflict Resolution Framework C: Formal Peer Conflict Mediation

Another highly effective way to harness students' own energies to solve behavioral problems is peer conflict mediation. Peer mediation takes many forms, from formal schoolwide programs with specialized, trained student mediators to smaller in-class ad hoc panels. One of the most popular and effective frameworks, used in more than 20,000 schools worldwide, is promoted by the nonprofit Peace Education Foundation (PEF; www.peaceeducation .com).

Solidly researched and thoroughly field-tested, the PEF curriculum—of which peer mediation is a key component—offers alternative problem-solving skills students can apply in and beyond the classroom. It focuses on these social skills, often neglected in the classroom:

- General social competence: ability to empathize and communicate with others
- Problem-solving skills: ability to imagine feasible alternatives to violent conflict
- Autonomy: ability and will to think and act independently
- Sense of purpose: ability to envision, plan for, and work toward future success (Diekmann, 1999–2004)

Student role-play: conflict styles. In addition to detailed conflict resolution curricula for every grade level, the Peace Education

Foundation offers numerous supplementary resources, including Judith Bachay's superb book *Creating Peace, Building Community.*

Designed for middle school but applicable to many grades, Bachay's book offers simple but powerful activities to help students build social skills and a sense of community and social responsibility, as well as practice anger management, peer refusal, and conflict management techniques.

One of Bachay's many activities highlights how different personalities approach conflict. Each style is associated with an animal to help students remember the behavior.

- **Shark.** "Take the offensive. Blame, accuse, or put down others. Intimidate. Relationships don't matter. 'It's my way or no way.' Goal: to win at all cost."
- **Fox.** "Try to cut a deal. Manipulate others. Use a lot of fast talk. Make an offer that often sounds a lot better than it really is. 'Meet me half way.' Goal: to find a quick fix and be done with the conflict."
- **Ostrich.** "Keep your feelings and opinions to yourself. Look away, fidget, or leave during a conflict. Pretend that things don't bother you. 'There's nothing I can do.' Goal: to avoid conflict at all cost."
- **Sheep.** "Agree with everything and everyone. Show concern for other people's feelings and concerns at the expense of your own. Speak submissively. 'Anything you want to do is okay with me.' Goal: to maintain relationships at any cost."
- **Owl.** "Listen attentively to everyone. Treat all parties with respect. Identify issues and come up with options. 'We can make it work.' Goal: to benefit all parties involved" (Bachay, 1996, S-32).

We recommend asking students to assume the various attitudes described above and role-play different conflict situations. These scenarios can be culled from your own experience, gathered from your colleagues, or recommended by students themselves.

You may be surprised at how involved students get in this activity—and how much they enjoy recognizing themselves, their peers, their family members, and sometimes even their teachers onstage. Feel free to leave these descriptions posted throughout the year so you can refer back to them as necessary and remind students what behaviors they're demonstrating.

CLASSROOM FELONIES: BULLYING, VIOLENCE, AND ILLEGAL BEHAVIOR

Bullying

Verbal harassment, physical intimidation, and other types of bullying can harm both individual self-esteem and class morale. And bullies who fail to correct their misanthropic behavior can eventually carry it into the greater public sphere, landing in jail (or worse) for it.

How damaging can bullying be among young people? A 2003 study of nearly 5,000 Dutch children revealed that bullied youth are much more likely than other children to feel depressed or suicidal. The study examined feelings of depression and thoughts of suicide among students subject to *direct bullying* (being hit, kicked, threatened, teased, etc.) as well as *indirect bullying* (being deliberately ignored or excluded). We have summarized the study's central findings in Figure 6.3.

Note that when subject to *direct* bullying, girls reported more feelings of depression and thoughts of suicide than did boys. *Indirect* bullying, however, caused boys greater distress. In any case, the surprisingly serious impact of indirect bullying on student well-being led the study's primary author, Marcel van der Wal, to observe that "teachers do not always consider social exclusion to be a form of bullying, or they consider this form of bullying to be less harmful . . . [but they ought] to pay more attention to indirect forms of bullying" (Carroll, 2003, p. 1).

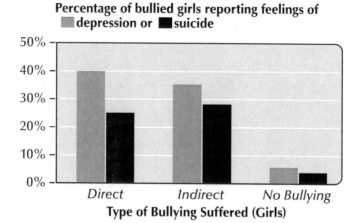

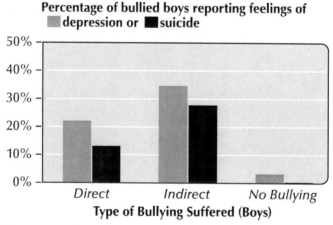

Figure 6.3.   Effects of bullying.

Inside the Mind of a Bully

What causes bullying? According to the research of psychologist Daniel Goleman and others, angry children, and particularly those who become bullies, often share three characteristics:

1. Bullies tend to be "highly sensitive to injustices and being treated unfairly . . . [often viewing] themselves as victims and

[able to cite numerous] instances when, say, teachers blamed them for doing something when in fact they were innocent."

2. Bullies commonly misinterpret social cues, often perceiving "slights where none were intended [and] imagining their peers to be more hostile toward them than they actually are. This leads them to misperceive neutral acts as threatening ones . . . and to attack in return."

3. Bullies are unschooled in emotional management. When "in the heat of anger, they can only think of one way to react: by lashing out" (Goleman, 1997, p. 235).

Another key finding of Van der Wal's study was that the *objects* of bullying were not the only casualties of the behavior—compared to average boys, 3 times as many boys who *perpetrated* bullying also felt suicidal (Carroll, 2003, p. 1). Although this is surprising to some, this coincides with conventional wisdom identifying low self-esteem and feelings of social inadequacy as common traits of many bullies. Often, bullying and other obnoxious behavior is the outward manifestation of deep negative feelings about oneself and the surrounding world—including confusion, anger, frustration, envy, insecurity, and so forth.

The bright spot in this news is that feelings of depression among bullies may also reflect cognitive dissonance over behavior they know to be wrong but don't know how to resist. In other words, at some level many bullies likely feel sorry not only for themselves, but also for the act of bullying. We have known many bullies who, when asked in a calm setting about their behavior, were quite ashamed and interested in learning about alternatives. Goleman also observes that many bullies would prefer to control their behavior but don't know how. This marks a substantial opportunity to intervene before bullying leads to more severe antisocial behavior.

Violence

Is violent behavior instinctive or, like prejudice, learned over a protracted period? Though the precise combination of nature and

NO-TAUNTING PLEDGE

In the wake of various U.S. school shootings in the 1990s, students started to sign and pass around "No-Taunting Pledges" like this one, useful as both a conversation catalyst and a reminder of behaviors to avoid.

No-Taunting Pledge

I WILL pledge to be part of the solution.
I WILL eliminate taunting from my own behavior.
I WILL encourage others to do the same.
I WILL do my part to make my community a safe place by being more sensitive to others.
I WILL set the example of a caring individual.
I WILL eliminate profanity towards others from my language.
I WILL not let my words or actions hurt others, and if others won't become part of the solution, I WILL. (McCrimmon, 1999)

nurture that incites young people to violence probably differs for each child, three factors hold relatively constant across various school populations:

1. Teachers have much more influence over the *nurture* part of the equation than the *nature* part.
2. Children see and hear everywhere that violence is an acceptable solution to conflict. This message, in subtle and overt forms, pervades not only the greater political and media culture but also the discourse and demonstrated values of many students' peer networks and even their families.
3. To help reduce violence, teachers must teach and model consistently for students one basic principle: While conflict is inevitable, violent conflict is not.

We hold no illusion that children so immersed in violence—and particularly those from violent families—can somehow unlearn these tendencies overnight. But here are some steps you can take immediately to help prevent violent behavior in your classroom.

Demand Respect—for Everyone, Always

Chapter 1, "Cultivating a Classroom Culture," discussed the importance of mutual respect in the classroom, as well as awareness and prevention of student-on-student harassment. Although much harassment occurs outside the confines of the classroom itself, most teachers could do more to convey unmistakably to students that respect means no put-downs, period.

Structure Your Space to Minimize Physical Conflict

As discussed in chapter 3, "Preparing for the First Week of School," help prevent conflicts by designing your classroom's physical layout in a way that anticipates student needs—for their own space, for necessary movement, and for visual reinforcement of the order you expect from them.

Help Students Unlearn Violent Habits

Though most peer harassment fortunately does not provoke a physical reaction, violence will likely arise at some point in your teaching career because, as mentioned previously, many students lack models for alternative behaviors and therefore view violence as a quick and reliable way to attack problems. Additionally, the adrenaline rush accompanying anger makes it seductive for many adolescents. One way to address this deficit is by teaching the conflict resolution strategies discussed earlier.

Also critical is helping students better comprehend their emotions. Most adults take for granted their familiarity with and sense of control over their own drives and passions. Adolescence, on the other hand, is largely defined by the absence of such awareness.

Asking a typical 14-year-old to explain his moody temperament is not unlike asking him to map the far side of the moon.

For example, teens frequently use belligerence—ordinarily signifying anger—to conceal other emotions, like guilt, insecurity, and fear. This is usually not premeditated or even conscious but rather an instinctual default pose to avoid the appearance of vulnerability. (Students know as well as puffer fish that in the Adolescent Kingdom, if you look vulnerable, you're finished.)

Anger-prone students can often control themselves if they can learn to

- recognize the flow of angry thoughts before the trickle becomes a torrent
- distract themselves (physical removal from the source of distress works well)
- redirect their thinking and emotion onto a different path (try calming activities)

Teaching students to recognize various emotions—and particularly the components and early signs—can help them understand their own emotional makeup, and learn that even if they can't control their feelings, they can control their behavior.

Trigger: Words or actions that cause anger

External Situation: Common scenarios students should know to avoid because they often lead to anger (note that the presence of peers can exacerbate many problem situations)

Physical Effect: Signals that should tell students that angry feelings are rising—these commonly include an adrenaline rush, clenched muscles, quickened breath, and/or blurry vision

Internal Thought: Mental responses that inflame anger, as in, "You can't do that to me and get away with it"

Escalating Action: Outward actions that turn anger into overt conflict—e.g., yelling a name or profanity, making threats, hitting or kicking, or destroying property

De-escalating Action: Outward actions that dissipate anger—for example, asking the perpetrator to stop, counting to 10, reciting a mantra (e.g., "If she gets me angry, who's in control of me?"), hitting a soft object instead of the person, walking away

Consequences (if escalated): Big Trouble

Consequences (if de-escalated): Big Trouble averted

Adapted from Bechay, 1997, p. S-25.

Since actually de-escalating from the edge of violence is easier said than done, try role-playing several scenarios with your at-risk students. Students can probably produce plenty of ideas for authentic conflict situations; just ask them to spend 5 minutes writing on the topic "What makes you mad?" or "Describe a situation that made someone else mad." We recommend analyzing these with students as follows:

- *When* (trigger) *and* (external situation) *happen, I sometimes feel* (physical effect) *or think* (internal thought).
- *This is the critical point when I can decide to escalate or de-escalate the conflict.*
- *If I do* (escalating action), *I will cause more trouble.*
- *If instead I do* (de-escalating action), *I will solve the problem better because* . . . (students fill in the blank).

Note that this exercise asks students to fill in the final blank. To internalize the message, students must ponder and explain for themselves how everyone benefits from alternatives to violent conflict.

How to Cope When Violence Occurs

If a fight erupts on your watch, failing to intervene would constitute negligence. Intervention does not have to mean diving into the melee, however. In fact, physical intervention is a particularly bad idea if

- you are physically smaller than the combatants
- you are neither athletic nor particularly nimble
- you are heavily dependent on eyeglasses to see
- you are wearing loose clothing, slick or high-heeled shoes, dangling jewelry, or a necktie

"Reach, Throw, Row, Go" is a risk-assessment device lifeguards commonly use to determine how to resolve dangerous situations without endangering themselves unnecessarily. When facing a potential drowning, they prioritize the possible solutions in the order shown in Figure 6.4.

Although most school districts have specific policies on intervention in physical fights, before determining how to intercede in any fight we advise dispatching a student to get outside assistance, and then applying the modified lifeguard's rule shown in Figure 6.5.

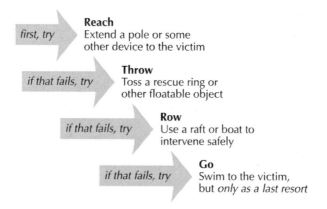

Figure 6.4.   The lifeguard's rule.

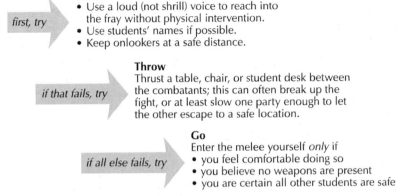

Figure 6.5. Modified lifeguard's rule.

If you choose to intervene physically, be sure not to restrain only one combatant; otherwise, other students might capitalize on this sudden shift in power to attack. Also be sure not to exert too much force against any student, as this could cause unwelcome legal troubles after the fact. Education law specialist Mitchell L. Yell explains that, in the United States at least,

> Teachers accused of assault and battery are typically given considerable leeway by the courts, . . . [which] are generally reluctant to interfere with a teacher's authority to discipline students. . . . Courts have found teachers guilty of assault and battery, however, when a teacher's discipline has been cruel, brutal, excessive, or administered with malice, anger, or intent to injure. (Yell, n.d.)

As soon as possible after any physical altercation, refer the matter to an administrator. Depending on the severity of the offense, a suspension, schedule change, or possibly expulsion could be in order. A minimal acceptable follow-up response to any sort of physical violence, even if it ends quickly and without injury, is a temporary time-out from class (usually Level 4 on the discipline hierarchy).

TEACHING DILEMMA: FIGHT ERUPTS IN CLASS

Some time ago, a couple of boys in my class just started fighting out of nowhere. Before that point they'd hung out a lot together and seemed to be friends, but one day their voices just started rising and before anyone knew what was happening they were slugging it out in the corner. I wasn't sure what to do so I stood up and yelled at them, then called security. They didn't stop, and couple of girls started snickering at my reaction. I think they figured that because I'm male I should have jumped in and put a stop to it, but I'm not much of a fighter and don't know what good that would have done.

SUGGESTED SOLUTION

First, in most cases fistfights do not actually spring up "out of nowhere." There were likely warning signs of imminent violence that this teacher did not notice. Many conflicts simmer for days or weeks before exploding into violence; this incubation period can give alert teachers ample time to try to defuse the problem. To anticipate conflicts, pay enough attention to student-student relationships that you notice shifts in their rapport. Also tap into the school gossip train; if you express interest in hearing about students' lives, you can usually find a chatty student in the know who's eager to share the latest news with you.

Second, if two students had time to stand around and snicker it doesn't sound like this fight got too out of control. In many cases, however—for example, if the conflict threatens to ignite the room spontaneously like a bar fight in a bad Western movie—one of your top priorities should be to remove all observers from the area. Be aware that the presence of onlookers not only potentially endangers them, but also typically raises the stakes for the combatants, making them less willing to back down for fear of looking weak and losing face in front of their peers.

Third, contacting security is certainly a valid course of action. Never feel obligated to intervene physically in a fight just because you think students expect you to do so. If you're concerned about your image (as to some degree you should be), consider the message you'll send if you step in and get clobbered; this could earn you a reputation not only as a lousy fighter, but also as someone with poor judgment. This is not to say that if a student is being brutally battered, you should not intercede. Consider the lifeguard's rule when determining whether and how to intervene physically in a fight.

Illegal Behavior

Familiarize yourself with your district's policies regarding action to take when you suspect or witness students engaged in illegal behavior like theft, vandalism, or possession of weapons or controlled substances. Most districts have standard reporting requirements and procedures to follow in these circumstances. Whatever your district's policies, we recommend erring on the side of caution and informing your administration in writing of *all reasonable suspicions* of student misconduct. Draft a memo, date it, and keep a copy.

If you report your fears and they turn out to be unfounded, what's the worst that could happen? You could feel momentarily foolish, and perhaps get labeled a nervous exaggerator. One teacher we know took such a risk when he reported to administrators his belief that students may have had a gun on campus. Because no gun was found (though this did not prove that no gun existed), his action earned brief ridicule and the temporary animosity of a handful of students. It also alerted students generally that this was a teacher who took his job very seriously.

In contrast, imagine the worst-case scenario if he had failed to act on his intuition but there *had* been a gun. This lapse would have been unforgivable. Students could have been harmed and depending on the situation, the teacher might have been sued and/or fired.

TEACHING DILEMMA: TEACHER DISCOVERS MONEY IS MISSING

In my first year of teaching, I left my wallet in my desk for a few minutes while I went out to the hall to check on a commotion. When I came back, I saw a student I didn't know come out of my room. In checking my desk, I saw that a $20 bill was gone.

SUGGESTED SOLUTION

Don't leave money in an easily accessible place. Lock it up. Better yet, don't leave money in the classroom at all. If this is impossible, imagine you're in a bank in Rome or Bangkok or Sao Paulo. Would you stroll out the door and then casually stuff a wad of bills in your back pocket? If so, good luck making it through the week.

If for some reason you *must* have valuables at school, don't make their existence or their location obvious. Hide them at a time when no one else is around—for example, in a locked drawer or cabinet after the classroom is empty—and move them to a safer location (perhaps to the main office or ideally off school property altogether) as quickly as possible.

You can solve other similar problems before they arise by eliminating what lawyers call *attractive nuisances*. In the same way that parents install safety latches on medicine cabinets and hotels fence off swimming pools, you should lock up any valuable items you have (including your grade book) whenever you leave the room.

On a related note, *never* leave food, drink, medicine, gum, or anything similar in a place where students can reach it. This applies particularly to middle school and junior high teachers. Leave your coffee cup alone with students even for a moment and you might return to find an unpleasant surprise waiting inside.

TEACHING DILEMMA: STUDENT CLAIMS PERSONAL ITEM STOLEN DURING CLASS

One time I was substituting in another teacher's room and, with 3 minutes remaining in the period, a student claimed her purse had been stolen by someone in the class.

SUGGESTED SOLUTION

Once you have determined with reasonable certainty that (a) the student is serious, (b) the item was actually stolen and not merely borrowed or misplaced, and (c) the item was stolen in your class, we urge the following actions:

1. Ask the class if anyone has seen the item in question. Frequently, a prankster will have simply hidden the item and will reveal it once you make clear the seriousness of the issue.
2. If sufficient time remains in class, offer to turn your back (or perhaps ask all students to close their eyes) for a minute and promise to forgive the perpetrator should the missing item magically reappear on your desk. In case the missing item does not reappear, use that moment to contact your administration to ascertain their willingness to participate in Steps 3–5 below. If the item *does* reappear, follow through on your promise of forgiveness.

Proceed to the following steps only if you have the support of your administration. If they do not approve of this course of action, they may be able to offer an alternate plan.

3. If no one produces the item, announce the suspected theft and inform the class that if the issue is not resolved immediately, security will be called to search everyone in the class. This normally causes a few students to berate whomever they believe the thief to be, giving you a possible sense of the likely offenders. It can also trigger in others a scrambling—and occasionally fruitful—search for the item.

4. If the item still fails to appear, order all students to remain seated and call security immediately. If the class period ends before security arrives, ask students to remain seated and assure them that no one will be marked tardy to his or her next class. Inform any student who becomes belligerent or threatens to leave without your permission that insubordination is also an offense.

5. When security arrives, ask that they take your students outside the classroom and search them there so your next class can enter and begin working as soon as possible.

FACTS ABOUT TROUBLEMAKERS

1. *No student wants to fail.*

   As obvious as this sounds, many teachers treat angry, defiant students as if they are asking only for trouble. Defiant poses notwithstanding, what they are usually really asking for is attention, and sometimes help. With the exception of a handful of severely emotionally disturbed youth, every student we have spoken with would love to succeed. Sometimes they need a little guidance.

2. *Students with behavior problems are generally low academic performers.*

Perhaps the most common cause of student misbehavior is the simple inability to do the work. Because reading is intertwined so closely with every academic subject, poor reading ability leads to frustration and embarrassment, which often manifests itself as depression and/or disruption of the class. Tutoring can transform demons into angels.

3. *Students with behavior problems often receive little support at home.*

Habitual classroom offenders often lack stable and nurturing homes. To students from families that are overworked, impoverished, or burdened by drugs, crime, or violence, success in school can seem quite distant from other more significant and pressing realities. Additionally, for such students, models of healthy problem-solving can be few and far between. Before judging these students, ask yourself what life circumstances they deal with outside your classroom.

4. *Everyone has a conscience.*

In our experience, even youth who seem bent on violating every regulation ever written value norms and traditions of some sort. For example, urban gang members we've taught are some of the most rule-abiding students we've met. They may not always live by the regulations promulgated by government or school, but they follow closely the laws of the street—sometimes out of fear, but often out of respect for community. And just watch how most students react if someone insults their mother. Tapping into their sense of honor can help you communicate effectively, and eventually nudge them in the right direction.

CHRONIC MISBEHAVIOR: WHAT LIES BENEATH?

Child psychologist Rudolf Dreikurs identified four common root causes of misbehavior among youth:

1. a desire for attention
2. a desire for power
3. a desire for revenge
4. a feeling of inadequacy

In Dreikurs' view, children are frequently unaware of their true motivations. Part of the teacher's job, then, is to help uncover these. Here we examine the problems each hidden drive generates in the classroom context and suggest solutions (Major, 1990, pp. 70–75).

Attention Seekers

Everyone needs attention from others; this in itself is not a problem. However, attention seekers attempt to monopolize the instructor's energies or gain students' attention at inappropriate times, and display obnoxious behavior when rebuffed. Dreikurs attributed the vast majority of classroom misbehavior to this motivation.

Attention-seekers come in several forms, including *class clowns, helicopters*, and *brownnosers. Class clowns* sacrifice the order of the class for a wave of laughter from their peers. Sometimes they inject a welcome bit of levity into class; other times their antics are simply disruptive. *Helicopters* hover around the teacher and other adult figures, continually soliciting approval or assistance. They may pretend not to understand assignments, or they may be perfectionists who crave continual affirmation; either way, their behavior siphons attention from genuinely needy classmates. *Brownnosers* offer their teachers compliments, assistance, and other unsolicited support that, although occasionally helpful, can quickly usurp other students' opportunities for participation and makes the teacher look like she is playing favorites.

Power Seekers

No one likes to be without power, and many students in this category are merely seeking influence over their own destinies. Beyond this, however, students who thirst for power threaten to upset the delicate balance of the classroom. Many power seekers are intellectually or physically gifted youth who need guidance learning how to earn socially acceptable recognition for their talents. Many also share an unconscious belief that life is a zero-sum game; they assume that anyone else's victory will automatically cost them something, an erroneous presumption that leads to confrontation with classmates and teachers.

Power seekers commonly appear in the shape of *bullies, alphas,* and *bomb throwers. Bullies* use their physical bulk or aggressiveness to bulldoze their peers, and often their parents and teachers as well. Teens we call *alphas,* after their counterparts in the animal kingdom, enjoy a natural magnetism that gives them influence among their peers, frequently at the expense of established authorities. *Bomb throwers,* not unlike class clowns, rely on mockery and cleverness to distract and destabilize the class, and gain notoriety and the influence that comes with it.

Revenge Seekers

Students who feel neglected, abused, or otherwise wronged, denied power, and frustrated with regular channels of communication sometimes release their anger through subversive acts. Many harbor fantasies of vengeful behavior, but those who actually act on these impulses tend to be socially isolated and perceived as misfits and misanthropes. Their failure to fit in commonly feeds their embitterment, which given their lack of friends often surfaces in antisocial behavior. This, in turn, deepens their isolation and perpetuates a vicious cycle.

Revenge seekers include *gossips, vandals,* and *saboteurs. Revenge-seeking gossips* (not to be confused with less venomous, garden-variety gossips) spread lies about classmates and often teachers to inflict maximum damage on others' comfort and reputations. *Vandals* damage property, sometimes targeting sentimental or irreplaceable items, to cause pain, grief, or inconvenience. *Saboteurs* aim to subvert existing processes—particularly class routines and academic work—by disruptive or obstructive behavior.

Revenge-seeking behavior can be difficult to detect because (a) it is usually covert and (b) often the target of a revenge attempt is *not* the person who committed the offense, but a safer substitute. This can result in a student who is angry at a figure too powerful to be challenged (a parent, for example) lashing out in other settings—for example, at school or on the street.

Escape Seekers

Feeling frustrated with a difficult task is normal. We would love to meet the person who never wanted to give up any effort—perhaps deciding after multiple failures that pole vaulting or poetry writing or chemical engineering was simply not her thing. Escape seekers, however, tend to feel frustrated constantly. They are often the students who have tasted so much failure and humiliation that, in their minds, anything is preferable to more of the same. They would rather not try at all than try and risk reinforcing—in their own minds as well as those of their peers—their image as losers.

Wallflowers, class slugs, and *chronic daydreamers* are common types of escape seekers. *Wallflowers* have mastered the art of stealth in the classroom. They waft in and out of the room, keep quiet, often avoid eye contact, and otherwise lie low from bell to bell. *Class slugs* do anything to avoid work, from feigning illness to refusing to perform assignments because they're "too hard," "too easy," "too boring," and so forth. *Chronic daydreamers* continually imagine themselves elsewhere, sometimes spinning elaborate, fantastic tales to convince themselves and others why the work at hand doesn't matter, or that somehow in the future their circumstances will magically improve.

Note that these four categories are not absolute. All have somewhat amorphous borders and bleed into each other—for example, bullying behavior to conceal perceived inadequacy, or vandalism that seeks not to cause pain but to draw attention to a perceived injustice. Also, many students do not fit neatly into one type, but may misbehave in various ways, for various reasons, at various times.

Therefore we caution against using these classifications to pigeonhole students; rather, their best use is for categorizing behavior, which changes over time. Young people are always growing and this implies continual evolution in both thought and action. Were this untrue, the world would have little need for teachers.

CHRONIC MISBEHAVIOR: STRATEGIES TO COPE

Dreikurs and others recommend several possible tactics to address these misbehaviors. (This section includes insights originally noted by Rudolf Dreikurs, chronicled in Major, 1990, pp. 70–75; and Nelsen et al., 2000, p. 85.)

The Attention Seeker

Case 1: Sheila's speech is so loaded with profanity that her own mother wonders whether she knows anything but four-letter words. In class she speaks out of turn continually, making loud comments that are sometimes genuinely funny but often merely distracting and occasionally insulting to students and the teacher. Her teacher warns her several times a day about her clowning around, but hesitates to react too strongly for fear of hurting her feelings or crushing her unique personality.

Case 2: Marcus refuses to stay seated and constantly distracts those around him. He regularly pokes and prods his classmates, friend and enemy alike, until they scream at him. In addition, he asks for help with his work twice as much as every other student in class. His classmates deride him as a "butt-kisser" and "teacher's pet" for the attention he demands (and receives) from the teacher.

To manage attention-seeking behavior, in the moment: Try to avoid getting sucked into delivering attention at the moment the student demands it. Ignore or respond as unemotionally as possible to inappropriate comments. If a student persists in demanding attention, redirect his energy by assigning a specific task that does not require much of your time. Then, if necessary, promise and deliver special attention at a better time. If ignoring the behavior is not feasible, the sidebar "Dreikurs' Theories in Practice" offers one possible response.

For the long term: Talk with the student to discover precisely which of the student's needs are generating his misbehavior. Usually the student won't have a clue what this means, so Dreikurs suggests asking a series of simple, explicit questions to determine the precise problem. Does the student want you or the class to

- notice her more?
- do more or do something special for her?
- fully occupy yourself with filling her needs?

Note that these cravings are not unique to the classroom. Your friends and family may put the same demands on you. The difference is that in the classroom you are professionally responsible for meeting the needs of numerous youth, not just one. This you must make unmistakably clear.

To balance these competing demands, establish signals you can send when you're beginning to feel annoyed to help the offending student recognize when demands are excessive. Or try assigning this student special tasks to help you, especially tasks that involve interacting with others, so the student can earn the recognition he or she craves from multiple sources. The attention-seeking student is also often a good candidate for being a peer mentor (Major, 1990, pp. 70–75; Nelsen et al., 2000, p. 85).

ONE WAY TO HANDLE CLASS CLOWNS

If a student wants to be the class clown I say, "Okay. Get up in front of the class and perform. I'm going to sit down. Since you want to perform in class, I'm going to give you the stage. Go ahead, perform. Get up there and do your act." Then they don't want to do it. When you give them the stage, they don't want it. They just want to steal it. (C. Davis, personal communication)

In the unlikely event that a student takes you up on this offer and delivers a great performance, we recommend gracefully offering applause and then asking the student to have a seat and engage in jokes at a more appropriate time. You may find a student talent contest or periodic "performance hour"—for example, at lunch—a useful outlet for such energy.

TEACHING DILEMMA: STUDENT VIOLATES RULES OF DECORUM

On my first day of teaching—literally the first hour of the first day—I entered my classroom and found a senior boy standing on my desk. The class immediately started laughing and yelling. I didn't know anyone in the room and had no idea what to do.

SUGGESTED SOLUTION

Ordinarily, something like this could only happen if you arrive late to class. Your classroom should normally be locked until you arrive at school, well before any of your students show up. On occasion, however, students befriend custodians and security guards to secure illicit access privileges, so challenges like this—or more serious problems like vandalism or theft—are not unthinkable.

This particular incident is so unusual it will probably *not* happen to you, but we have included it here as a reminder that many students defy social norms in bizarre and unexpected ways. Except for rare cases of psychological disorder, the student who flouts convention generally does so deliberately. He does not necessarily intend to cause harm (note that the behavior in this case was nondestructive) but often seeks merely to test his power and differentiate himself from his peers as "the defiant kid," "the clever kid," or perhaps just "the weird kid."

If you find yourself in a similar situation, stay calm—particularly if other students are present. Don't give the student the dramatic reaction he seeks; instead, ask firmly that he cease his offensive behavior. If he does not comply, intensify your response. This may involve moving close and speaking sternly. It may involve reaching for the phone to call the office. Or, if you are a returning teacher with an established reputation, it may involve making a joke to de-escalate the situation, thereby letting the student save face while he climbs out of the hole he dug. In any case, your goal should be to return order to the group while clearly defining the classroom as your territory and yourself as the undisputed master of that domain.

When the student eventually does comply with your demand, isolate him from the other students, behave calmly to let the class know you're not ruffled (even if you are), and quickly move on to your plan for the day. Later, take note of the behavior in your discipline file and if you haven't sent the offending student to the office, tell him privately that you want him to remain after class to discuss the issue. See the discussion of the behavior citation form in chapter 5, "Classroom Management I," for specific advice on this procedure.

If in addition to offending your sense of propriety the student has caused physical damage, we *do not* suggest forcing him to fix it (e.g., by cleaning the desk he was standing on) in front of the class, as this would only escalate the situation. A student this audacious will probably not back down and meekly submit to performing such a "demeaning" chore in front of his peers, and the last thing you want to trigger is a public power struggle. Although you'd probably win, before the end of the day every student in school would hear about the new teacher who got sucked into overreacting to a cheap stunt, and your colleagues and administrators might start questioning your judgment—not an ideal first impression.

Instead, hold the student after class to clean up his mess. You don't have to make a public spectacle out of it; just ask him to stay after class, explain your needs—repeatedly if necessary—and don't let him go until the trouble he caused is fixed.

TEACHING DILEMMA: IMMATURE STUDENT DISRUPTS CLASS CONTINUALLY

My first year [as a teacher], Sam turned my ninth-grade class into a nightmare. He was 14 but acted much younger. He disrupted class continually, threw things, made obscene noises, vandalized others' property, and consistently failed to follow directions. Needless to say, he completed little schoolwork.

Sending him to other classrooms for the period had little effect; when he returned to class, he exhibited the same problem behavior. He could not be permanently transferred to other classes because our tiny school only offered one section of each class. And I was reluctant to contact Sam's parents because his classmates told me his father beat him severely whenever this happened.

SUGGESTED SOLUTION

One teacher offers this response to the problem:

> Well, if the child knows his dad's going to beat him, why does he come to my class acting like that? I called one student's mom and the next day another student came to me, "Ms. S., you called Gina's mom? Gina got a whupping. I heard it. I live in the same apartment building." I said, "Gina needs to come here and act right, then." I have given that girl every opportunity." (A. Smithee, personal communication)

This approach, although gratifying to the "tough love" impulses in all of us, fails to address the danger that such a student might return to school physically (and probably emotionally) scarred, and even less ready to learn than before.

If the various strategies described by the teacher in this dilemma fail, we would recommend working with an administrator and Sam's counselor to prepare a group conference with Sam, his parents, and perhaps his other teachers to create an individual improvement plan, whereby everyone acknowledges that

- Sam's current behavior is unacceptable
- Sam is capable of behaving better (people in the meeting would undoubtedly have evidence of this)
- Sam needs to adhere to a plan for improvement that applies both at home and at school
- Sam's improvement plan should lay out general principles of better behavior (e.g., to listen better in class) supported by specific examples so there's no confusion about what's acceptable (e.g., don't interrupt others, raise your hand before speaking, never yell, etc.)
- Sam's improvement plan may need to take the form of a daily card that he brings to all his teachers to sign at the end of each period, to verify that his behavior has improved
- Sam should receive reinforcement for positive and negative behavior (i.e., consequences both for when he sticks to his improvement plan and for when he violates it) in a way that's consistent both at home and at school
- Since the beatings Sam receives at home clearly aren't solving the problem, reinforcement at home might need to change to improve Sam's behavior (you may need to suggest alternatives; many parents simply discipline their children the same way they were disciplined growing up, and are open to more effective approaches if presented in a respectful way)

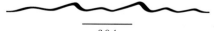

The Power Seeker

Case 1: Andrew uses his large size to intimidate other males in the class and flirts with almost all the females, most of whom have no interest in returning his affections and tell him so. He regularly insults his classmates, calling them names, destroying their property, and otherwise trying to provoke fights.

Case 2: Natalie argues vociferously and relentlessly in class, often with the teacher. She never likes to be told she's wrong, and frequently works herself into a frenzy in response to incidents most students would treat as minor. She quarrels regularly with her classmates, and often claims to be acting in self-defense of her "territory" or her "right" to do things her way or to be left alone.

To manage power-seeking behavior, in the moment: Don't get lured into an argument. Fighting the student's aggressiveness with your own anger will only escalate the situation. Don't ignore the misbehavior either, however. Instead, give the student warnings as set forth in your discipline hierarchy and circumscribe the student's options by offering limited choices designed to redirect her negative impulses in a positive direction.

If this proves ineffective, remove the power-hungry student from contact with peers and/or ask the student to help you with some quiet task—for example reading, clerical work, or tutoring a fellow student in a quiet corner for the period. If this also fails, remove the student from the room temporarily and deal with the problem after class.

For the long term: Again, follow Dreikurs' suggestion and try to determine as specifically as possible the student's underlying motivation. Does the student want you or the class to

- let her be in charge?
- appreciate her superiority in some area and show deference?
- allow the student to do what she wants, when she wants, with impunity?

Investigate training this student as a peer tutor or peer conflict mediator, discussed earlier in this chapter. Alternately, tap this student's power needs by helping her find a school activity matching his skills and interests and showing her how to take a leadership role. These approaches can not only channel the troubled student's energy to a socially beneficial end, but also help the student recognize and learn to correct destructive behavior patterns (Major, 1990, pp. 70–75; Nelsen et al., 2000, p. 85).

The Revenge Seeker

Case 1: Crystal sits in the back of the classroom and rarely interacts with anyone. Her taste in reading material leans distinctly toward the macabre: Drug overdoses and torture devices captivate her, and her class journal reveals an obsession with death that transcends the normal adolescent fascination with anything that might shock or irritate nearby adults. Although content to read quietly when left alone, Crystal greets any request to engage in classwork with a dark look and feral snarl.

Case 2: David is on every teacher's watchlist because he was expelled from a previous school for making violent threats against school officials. He claims it was all a misunderstanding, but his poor peer relations tell a different story. Though he is bright and tries to fit in, his physical appearance, unusual hygiene habits, and perennially negative attitude make him an outcast who is often the butt of classmates' jokes. David injects weapons into every class project and presentation, and daydreams about joining the military because there "it's legal to kill people."

To manage revenge-seeking behavior, in the moment: Because revenge-motivated misbehavior is so often covert, its perpetrators frequently cannot be identified with certainty. If you suspect one of these students to have committed a particular act of destruction, think twice. Be sure you're not assuming "Crystal [or David] must have done it" because they fit a particular profile. And however strong your evidence, avoid the temptation to launch a barrage of accusations and blame. Deliver appropriate consequences for the behavior, but in doing so try to focus on fixing the underlying problem to avoid its recurrence rather than on taking sides and punishing the wrongdoer.

For the long term: Determine as best you can what the student is really seeking. Does the student want to

- get even with or hurt you or the class?
- make you or the class feel guilt over his situation?
- show you or the class how it feels to be in his shoes?

In response to those who presume that only very young children act out over hurt feelings, we point to the rash of middle- and high-school shootings in the United States in the 1990s. Though youth who wreak terrible violence on their schools are a small minority, they generally share a common thread: They feel the above desires with alarming frequency. And they are not alone. Many more students share these feelings but act out in less dramatic ways.

To address this problem, strive to integrate *all* students into your classroom community. Those who feel like misfits often lack even one good friend, yet we have found that—however they may behave—few teens are truly asocial. Many use abrasiveness to mask fear and insecurity. It's as if at some level the student thinks, "They're probably not going to like me, but I'll preempt that. I'll be so obnoxious (or withdrawn, or strange) that it'll be obvious that I don't want or need anyone to like me. Then they definitely won't like me, but I'll be in control, not them."

Several tactics can help break this cycle of alienation. When organizing student groups for class projects, take care to include in the outcast's group classmates potentially able to connect to that student in some way. Outside class, you might try introducing the student to peers he may not know but who might make good friends.

Also, since many of the aforementioned school shooters were bright but socially inept and full of resentment for their more popular peers, involvement in school activities offers troubled students multiple benefits. First, they'll meet people who share their interests, some of whom may befriend them. Second, they'll lose their incentive to attack the school community as they gain ownership of some piece of it, however small. Third, they'll have a chance to enjoy relatively high-profile successes, which will increase their positive feelings about themselves and the school.

In addition, listen to your revenge seekers' grievances. Do they relate to you? If so and you made some mistake, make a sincere effort to make amends. If the grievances are unrelated to you but simply reflect unfortunate external circumstances, you can still commiserate and help the student get back on track. If another student is involved, try to get the two together to discuss the problem. Once the disputants have discussed the issue, consider cementing their progress by asking them to collaborate on some kind of joint project (Major, 1990, pp. 70–75; Nelsen et al., 2000, p. 85).

The Escape Seeker

Case 1: Tim is a wanna-be ladies' man who excels at fixing cars and computers, but rarely turns in any coursework, complaining that it's too easy or meaningless. Using bravado to mask his low academic skills, his life plan appears to be to charm his way through school until he reaches the age of legal emancipation and then charm his way through life, despite being virtually illiterate.

Case 2: Lorena sits silently through class, refusing to participate and failing to respond to her teacher's best attempts to engage her. She comes to school impeccably dressed and consistently minds her manners, never making a scene or lashing out, but never wants to talk about herself. For her teachers to try to discern her problem is like a physician trying to diagnose a mute patient.

To manage escape-seeking behavior, in the moment: Don't pity the student or lower your standards—for example, by doing the assignment for the student as he looks on; this can tempt the student to take advantage. On the other hand, don't try to force an obdurate resister to comply with your wishes, particularly in front of his classmates. This will only frustrate you and alienate the student in question. Instead, focus on the student's strengths and build from there. If necessary, adapt the present assignment and adjust its due date to accommodate its delayed completion. Make clear to the student that your expectations remain high but the student will receive whatever help she needs to succeed.

For the long term: Again, strive to determine the student's underlying motivation. Is the student avoiding work because she

- is afraid to fail and doesn't want anyone to see her misstep?
- feels she is giving maximum effort, which is unrecognized and unappreciated?
- is distracted by outside influences or her own heavy thoughts?

A particular challenge with this type of student is that many have perfected the art of becoming invisible. Their protective coloration, developed mainly to hide themselves from their peers, is often all too successful with teachers also. Among the many balls teachers must juggle continuously is the need to watch for these invisible students.

Keep in mind that many escape-seekers suffer from depression, illness, family trouble, emotional distress, chronic fatigue, or drug addiction. Many students exhibit this behavior under extreme personal stress. Sometimes they're in serious family trouble—perhaps with parents or guardians who fight constantly, or were recently separated. Sometimes they've survived the death of someone close. Sometimes they've recently broken up with a significant other, or run away from home, or learned they're facing pregnancy. The point is, numerous causes can underlie this behavior. Don't assume you understand what they're going through. Investigate.

If the student can't or won't help you determine the problem, consult the student's other teachers, counselor, parents, the school administration, and any written records you have. Does the student have a history of failure in school? Is there a history of depression, drug abuse, or family problems?

To assist the escape-seeking student, integrate into the class some activities or topics you know the student would enjoy. Whatever the student does in his spare time should give you a clue to his passions.

Tim seems to like mechanical things, and both he and Lorena probably take great care with grooming and fashion. These are places to start. If you need more insights, find out which class is the student's favorite and ask that teacher for ideas.

Defeatism arising from repeated failure cannot be vanquished until the student can approach the classwork with confidence. This will not happen, of course, until the student actually has the skills to succeed, which is where you come in. Perhaps the student needs to learn to focus better when reading, or to budget time. Or maybe the student needs help constructing an argument, or writing a coherent paragraph, or using a particular math formula.

Jane Nelsen et al. recommend breaking tasks into small steps and setting short-term goals so the student can see the light at the end of the tunnel. As many times as necessary, show the student—or have a skilled classmate show her—how to perform tasks, but never do the work for the student. And, if necessary, find activities (even non-educational activities) the student especially enjoys and intersperse these with other work to motivate the student to complete all of it (Nelsen et al., 2000, p. 85).

Once you have provided enticing opportunities to learn, prod the student into action. Encourage the student consistently. Note aloud every step in the right direction. Offer genuine praise for the effort expended, and emphasize that *effort creates ability*. Help the student envision completing the task at hand, how that will feel, what rewards it will generate, and what additional successes might follow.

Don't hesitate during this process to reveal a personal hurdle you had to work hard to overcome. Frequently, students seek escape because they feel isolated and unique in their failures. Low performers need to understand they're not alone, and you might be surprised how much they respect your success. Hearing that authority figures also struggle can impact them enormously.

Finally, don't withhold extra attention from a student who needs it for fear of being somehow unjust to the rest of the class. Consistency is important, but remember that treating everyone *fairly* does not mean treating everyone *the same*.

One teacher describes a student for whom education was not a family value. Every day, he came to school without supplies.

I bought him a backpack. And he brings that backpack to my class every day. And now he does the work, and participates in class. The other students complain sometimes. "That's your pet. You like him better." I say, "I like all you guys." "Yeah, but you give him extra." I say, "He needs extra." They all know that's true. (C. Davis, personal communication)

DREIKURS' THEORIES IN PRACTICE

Teacher Duen Hsi Yen reports substituting in a high school class in which a student approached the front of the room without permission and started writing gibberish on the overhead projector. Seeing this, Yen expounded briefly on Freud's theory of unconscious motivation, then engaged the student in the following exchange:

Teacher: Do you know why you're up here?

Student: I'm writing poetry.

Teacher: I don't think that is the real reason. I want to play 20 questions with you to try to guess the real reason, and class, I want you to help me by watching her reactions.

Student: Great!

Teacher: Could it be that you want more attention?

Student: No.

Class: We think she wants more attention!

Teacher: I don't think I guessed it quite yet judging by your reaction. . . . Could it be that you want more power?

Student: No.

> At this point the student's expression and body language told the teacher he was getting warm.
>
> Teacher: Could it be that you want to show the class that you are more powerful than the teacher?
>
> Student: Look! I *am* more powerful than the teacher!
>
> After the cathartic flourish that ended this mini-drama, the student returned to her seat and, Yen reports, "participated in the ensuing discussions with more respect for me and the class" (Duen Hsi, 2000).

ADVICE FROM A NOTORIOUS TROUBLEMAKER

After years of raucous misconduct, Darius landed at a Los Angeles alternative school, where he continued tormenting his teachers and spent countless hours in the discipline office. In Table 6.1, the 16-year-old shares what strategies have worked with him—and what strategies haven't (D. Jackson, personal communication).

"WHAT IF I SCREW UP?"

Expect to make some mistakes; this is only human. Of course, we hope that the more experience you gain (and the more you internalize the advice in this book), the fewer errors you will make. However, great leaders distinguish themselves not by avoiding all missteps, but by the way they handle those they *do* make.

Being upfront about your fallibility will increase students' respect for you more than you can imagine. As discussed in chapter 1, "Cultivating a Classroom Culture," one thing you should always be is honest. Don't know an answer? Say so. Make a mistake you regret? Say so. And apologize, if necessary. Those things can be forgiven. But bullying and dishonesty cannot. If students sense you don't respect them or they feel they can't trust you, they won't respect you. If they don't

Table 6.1. Advice From a 16-Year-Old Troublemaker

How not to approach him	Teachers [who] come at me the wrong way or try to embarrass me in front of the whole class . . . make me act more negatively than normal. They try to correct my behavior in front of everybody rather than pull me to the side. Or they threaten me; they say they're going to suspend me or call my mom before they've even let me finish what I have to say. When you do that, I have to get real loud in order for you to listen to me. Now I'm going to disrupt the whole class because you didn't listen to me. Why can't you say, "I need to speak with you after class," or send me to the office and sort it out later?
How one effective administrator coped with him	Mr. C. always respected me. He doesn't have his mind made up before you walk in. He'll listen to your story and if you did something wrong, he'll ask you what you think a fair punishment would be. If you come up with a pretty fair punishment he'll let that go. If you realize you were wrong, he'll tell you to write the person an apology or go speak with them. A few times, after I thought about it and realized I was wrong, I didn't have a problem [apologizing].
How one teacher provided an outlet for his energy	Ms. G.'s [art] class gave me an outlet, rather than me having to sit in a class if I'm hyper or in a bad mood. When I'm hyper, I know that gets in the way a lot. I'll disrupt the classroom, and then it gets all the other kids to talk and that's not right. So Ms. G.'s class is . . . like a time out space.
How teachers can help him learn	Math is not fun. It's difficult. Mr. W. helps me to the best of his ability. He always lets me try to do it my way. If I'm about to do a problem and he knows it's wrong, he will still let me do it my way. That's good because after I've done it my way and I see my answer's wrong, then he'll show me how to do it right. And then I'm ready to listen.
What he's learned about human nature	You control the way people act towards you. If you're talking to a cop, you control whether or not you're going to get a ticket. If you start using profanity, the person's not going to like it. Personally, I wouldn't like it. If you come at him like a normal person and explain, things could go your way.
How he manipulates weak teachers	Some teachers feel that if they don't give in to me, I'm going to start acting like an ass. And I know I can go ask Mr. H. and if he tells me no, then I can start acting up and he's going to give it to me either way it goes. It's wrong, because I'm using my behavior to my advantage [by] disrupting the class and stopping everybody in the classroom from learning. That's a negative behavior. That's wrong of me. But I still do it if I'm having a bad day.

respect you, you will fail. Period. They will make your every move a struggle, and you might begin to wish you'd never become a teacher.

What if you keep an entire class after school because someone emptied a pencil sharpener in the corner of the room? Maybe no one in that class did it. If you hadn't looked in that corner since the beginning of the day, any student in any class could have done it. What if, after counting your textbooks at period's end, you discover someone has failed to return a book and announce that no one can leave until you get that book back? Could you have miscounted? Could someone who left the room in the middle of the period have taken the book, perhaps inadvertently? Could you have forgotten to count your books at the end of the previous period? Vigilance, as stressed earlier, will help prevent many such awkward situations.

What if, after a disastrous class, you ponder what went wrong and realize you made a serious error—overreacted, say, or otherwise showed lack of good judgment? Is it too late to apologize on the following day? Not at all. In fact, sometimes this is better, because time will have passed for everyone to contemplate and put in perspective what happened. Frequently, a new day puts everyone in the mood to make a fresh start.

If you find yourself needing to apologize, we suggest three guidelines: Make the apology sincere, make it 20 seconds or less, and move on. One sample, heard from the mouth of a substitute teacher in a tough high school: "I had forgotten you have silent reading scheduled right after your break. It was foolish of me to ask you to put your reading materials away last period, because now I'm going to ask you to get them out again. I apologize." Simple, concise, no big deal. Another example: "That wasn't you making that noise? I'm sorry. I thought it was you. Do you accept my apology?" Done. Move on.

For more serious errors, such as verbally attacking a student, you might try something like: "That was completely out of line. I want to apologize to you, Veronica, and to the class for an unacceptable abuse of power. No teacher should speak to a student like that. I'm very sorry."

You can probably imagine how few teachers are so forthcoming with students about their own mistakes, but the impact of such honesty can be profound. Many teenagers rarely see an adult apologize to anyone, let alone to them. A sincere expression of contrition can not only convey respect for students, but also model the kind of maturity and emotional security adolescents need to develop. And, almost without exception, teachers willing to address their own shortcomings are the teachers whom students most respect.

TEACHER REGRETS IMPULSIVE THREAT

A cautionary tale: No matter how close students push you to the edge of sanity, beware of making threats because you'll be forced to follow through or risk losing credibility with your students, and with it your control of the class. Here, one teacher recounts a rash move he quickly wished he could undo.

We're in the inner city here, so hats have always been non gratis on campus, but this was a time when we were specifically having a gang war and the blues and the reds were really going at it off campus. So hats, of course, were verboten. The warnings were everywhere: "No hats on campus, no hats on campus." And this kid kept wearing his hat. And I had given him a warning. I said, "If I see that hat again, I'm going to take it and chop it up." Well, he brought it the next day, and sure enough I took it. I took it to my paper cutter and just chopped it to little pieces. In front of the whole class. It got real quiet, because this was his personal property.

I mulled this over and after a couple of days I bought the kid a new hat. I told him my behavior had been inappropriate, to take his personal property and destroy it. I apologized publicly. And then I told him I didn't want to see the hat again or else I'd chop that one up. He didn't bring a hat after that, but I wouldn't do that again. Next time I would confiscate the hat and have a parent pick it up after school. (C. Hipkins, personal communication)

TEACHING DILEMMA: TEACHER MAKES OUTRAGEOUS THREAT TO QUASH STUDENT MISBEHAVIOR

In one of my most challenging classes, the boy who instigated most of the trouble had his own little following. I had tried every type of discipline, to no avail. I also asked the principal for help, but got no useful assistance there either. Finally I got so frustrated I threatened to put animal manure on their noses if they didn't behave. Looking back, I'm not sure what I was thinking or why I said that, but they still didn't behave so for the sake of the other students I felt obligated to follow through. So I did.

SUGGESTED SOLUTION

Though this incident occurred in an elementary school, we have included it here because the moral resonates: Beware of making threats, because you will be forced to follow through. This teacher trapped herself in a Catch-22: If she failed to make good on her injudicious ultimatum, she would risk losing her credibility among students and with it her power in the classroom; on the other hand, if she *did* make good on her threat, she risked an unknown backlash. In the end, the incident drew attention not only from parents and administrators but also from the local media, and she was removed from her teaching position.

Take three lessons from this unfortunate event:

1. Think before you speak.
2. Never make a threat unless you are able and willing to follow through on it.
3. In the worst-case scenario, back down and apologize rather than fulfilling a foolish vow; a temporary credibility setback beats charging ahead to your own gallows.

If you practice the recommendations in this book and still find yourself mired in an impossible discipline situation, don't break out the manure bag; reach out for help first, as discussed earlier. Pick up the phone and call the troublesome student's parents. Visit them at home. Invite them to sit in on your class to see just how their child behaves. If they show up and the child improves, you'll know that he is capable of behaving properly, but chooses not to do so in your presence. The student may be so embarrassed by his parents' presence that he improves generally after this.

Alternately, as mentioned earlier, consider videotaping your troublesome class and ask a trusted colleague to watch the tape with you, to figure out what you're doing wrong and to suggest possible solutions. This is well worth the inconvenience, both for the insights you'll gain and because the mere act of recording students' behavior often improves it. The tape may also prove useful in proving to parents and administrators that you have a problem requiring their intervention.

As a last resort, ask an administrator to transfer the key troublemaker to another teacher. You may have to bargain with a fellow teacher to do this, since in all likelihood no one else probably wants the student either. If you have a high concentration of rowdy students in your class for a certain period, however, you can make a strong case that the school should better balance the personalities in each teacher's classes. If all else fails, your teacher's union can probably supply additional suggestions specific to your situation.

7

COMMUNICATING WITH PARENTS, ADMINISTRATORS, AND OTHERS

BUILD BONDS WITH PARENTS

In chapter 2, "Who Are Your Students?" we discussed the value of getting to know your students as *whole people* rather than merely as students. To that recommendation, we now add one of the best ways both to understand your students and to prevent their misbehavior—get to know their parents. (Some students may not live with biological parents, but with other relatives, foster parents, etc. For simplicity's sake, we use only the term *parent* here, but intend it to include guardians of all types.)

Earlier we suggested possible ways to make contact with parents. Note that you don't have to take a lot of time to make a useful connection. Sometimes even a five-minute conversation can help you:

1. Make a personal connection.
2. Share your hopes and concerns about the student.
3. Leave a lasting impression, such as, "Wow! That teacher went to the trouble to reach out to me. She must really care."

In addition to this type of outreach, it's possible to meet parents at school.

Does your school have a back-to-school orientation session? Be there. Even if it normally only involves administrators and parents, invite yourself. Do parents show up *en masse* at school sporting events? Be there. Are there student concerts? Plays? Fund-raisers? Be there.

If you're lucky you might reach half your parents through such outreach—but which half? Consider which students involved themselves in extracurricular activities when you were in school. Were they the kids who spent their free time smoking dope with their friends while glued to video games until 3 A.M.? Were they the students who had to rush home every day to care for younger siblings, or work part-time to help pay the rent? Probably not. The implication: Attending school events is necessary but not sufficient for connecting with all parents. The parents you tend to meet this way are rarely the parents you most *need* to meet.

Alternately, you can lure reluctant parents to school. Try holding an open house. If an ordinary open house attracts only 20% of your students' parents, offering students extra credit for bringing their parents might increase your attendance rate by half, bringing you up to 30% of the total students in your classes. To further improve this figure, use the tactic community organizers figured out long ago: "Offer food and they will come." To excite students about it, make it a genuine event. Create a gala dinner with student performances, awards, speeches, and student work on display.

"Oh sure," you might be thinking. "How in the world will I have time for all this?" We've seen it happen. Why not collaborate with other school staff? And don't forget our cardinal rule of productivity: "Never do anything the students could do." The dinner doesn't have to be catered; make it a potluck. This will let students share their cultural heritage and take work off your own hands in one stroke. Also, encourage students to take the lead in planning, decorating, creating and distributing invitations, setting up and tearing down the room, and so forth. You'll have to relinquish some creative control and the arrangements will probably be less than perfect. But the more involved your students get, the greater their stake will be, the less work you'll have, and the better parental attendance will be.

Be aware that sometimes parents don't respond to invitations for school functions because they're overworked or don't have much control over their schedules. This is particularly true in less wealthy communities, in which parents often work two jobs and families tend to rely heavily on public transportation. And frequently, these same parents don't really believe it's important for them to attend. They figure school is for kids, not adults, and rationalize that in any case they wouldn't be missed.

One teacher describes her solution to this attitude:

> To get parents to our awards banquet, we practically send out wedding invitations. Then we send each student home with another copy. Then, a week before [the event] we have someone in the office call home to follow up. . . . It's a lot of work, but since we started it the number of parents attending has doubled. (B. Burket, personal communication)

Does all this seem too complicated? You may well be thinking right now, "I didn't intend to take on all this extra work. Being locked in that room with all those teenagers seems like enough to earn my paycheck. Why should I add unnecessarily to my workload?" But think of what's at stake—you have the chance to build positive relationships with students that will

- Help students engage more fully in their education (which is why you're there in the first place, right?)
- Cut the frequency of behavior problems in half for the rest of the year
- Spill over into subsequent years if you're a secondary teacher who will have some of the same students repeatedly, or younger siblings of your current students
- Make you look great in the eyes of the administration and the school board

GOLDEN GROUP EXCEEDS ITS FOUNDERS' EXPECTATIONS

In one underfunded urban high school, two committed teachers creatively leveraged a common resource to make a major difference in students' lives. At Libby High School, Title I (a U.S. government program that supports students needing help in reading and mathematics) went well beyond assisting students with reading and mathematics; the program coordinators used the funding as a cornerstone to build a comprehensive support network designed to offer students help building not only academic skills, but also self-esteem and hope for their future.

Before they began, the coordinators determined that most students who fared poorly in school did so because of lack of support. They were not stupid, merely underdeveloped. Their lack of confidence both caused and flowed from their low math and language skills, so both sides of the issue had to be addressed before either could be fixed.

The Libby Title I coordinators also set out consciously to counter the stigma commonly attached to students who need extra help in school. They named their Title I program "The Golden Group" and used elaborate ceremonies and generous portions of feel-good paraphernalia to reinforce among the students themselves the idea that being involved with the Golden Group was indeed special education—in a very positive sense.

To build student confidence, they celebrated small successes. A passing grade on a term paper or project was cause for heartfelt congratulations within the Golden Group. This reinforced each student's positive feelings about school, while stimulating others to rise to the same level of performance.

In a happy irony, the Golden Group was so successful that other students at the school soon began to express envy at the camaraderie and extra attention received by Golden Group participants. One teacher unaffiliated with the Golden Group revealed, "I had a girl who's always been at the top of her class complaining because the Golden Group was doing all this great stuff and she wasn't invited. That blew me away. Here are a bunch of kids who would have been laughed at before; now they're objects of envy. I told this student to be grateful for what she has, and luckily she hasn't brought it up again." (A. Smithee, personal communication)

10 TIPS FOR COMMUNICATING WITH PARENTS

In an ideal world, every conversation with parents would be positive, and your glowing reports about their children's superlative performance and angelic behavior would leave everyone beaming and warm inside. Sometimes, however, parent conferences take a darker turn. We encourage you to hope for the best and prepare for the worst.

In any meeting with parents—and particularly any conversation triggered by a serious problem with a student—we recommend that you

1. Arrange to have the student present
2. Prepare a short written agenda
3. Document everything
4. Always be patient and professional
5. Start with the positive
6. Present the problem clearly
7. Avoid edubabble
8. Solicit the parents' ideas
9. Create a plan for improvement with a timetable for completion, and get it in writing
10. Never get into an argument with a parent

1. Arrange to have the student present.

Frequently, misbehaving students have strong incentives to twist reality when discussing classroom problems with their parents. Having the student present in a parent-teacher conference eliminates this possibility. Of course there may still be times in a conference when you need to send the student from the room.

2. Prepare a short written agenda.

An agenda will demonstrate professionalism and keep you from being thrown off-track. Prepare it in duplicate—one for yourself and one for the parents. Use your copy to jot down notes during the meeting; this will not only help you remember what happened, but also impress upon the parents that you mean business. After the meeting, make a copy of your marked-up version for the school office.

You can always diverge from the agenda if you want, but if tempers turn sour you will be glad to have a written plan to focus on. It can also serve as a natural device to wrap up the meeting—"Well, it looks like we've reached the end of the agenda"—if you find yourself trapped with an endless talker.

3. Document everything.

Selective memories of what was discussed and agreed upon in your conference can come back to haunt you later. Prevent this problem by documenting everything. Write down any complaints, suggestions, or observations the parents offer—and quote them when you can—or ask them to put these in writing. Be sure to ask the parent to sign a summary of any agreement you make.

4. Always be patient and professional.

If you're frustrated with a student after an hour each day, imagine his parents' task—coping with him for the 75+ waking hours he's not in school each week. Often parents act hostile because they're at their wits' end, yet are too proud to ask for help because doing so implies they might have done an imperfect job of childrearing. If parents get personal or try to lay blame for the problem on you or on the school, don't respond in kind. Instead, focus on the real issue: the student.

Also take care never to use terms that might convey that you think the student is a "bad kid." We find it useful to approach parents (and indeed to approach teaching) with the attitude that there are no bad kids, only bad deeds and bad situations.

5. Start with the positive.

No parents like to hear bad news about their children, so if you have bad news, it's helpful to convey that the student does good things occasionally, too. Starting with good news will immediately establish your even-handedness, reinforcing in the parents' minds your commitment to their child's best interest. In fact, we recommend speaking to parents as if their children were in the room, whether they actually are or not.

This approach may also ease the reception the child gets when Mom or Dad returns home, which will work in your favor when the child returns to your class. After all, you'll have to survive the remainder of the term—if not the year—with this student.

6. Present the problem clearly.

Lay out the issue at hand in a planned and coherent way, for example:

- Explain your class expectations and precisely how the student is not meeting these.
- Unveil proof you have accumulated. Depending on the problem, helpful documentation might include samples of the student's work, written testimony from other teachers, copies of the student's attendance and discipline history, signed behavior contracts, and notes from your behavior file.
- Describe precisely how you have already tried to solve the problem.

7. Avoid edubabble.

Acronyms and industry-specific terms like *IEP, TLW, ESLR, Title I, 504 Plan, normative test,* and so on quickly become part of teachers' professional vocabulary. Although useful in context, this esoteric language can also be used by school officials to scare parents off and protect their own turf. Jargon thus becomes a tool to, as one researcher puts it, "underscore the message that 'I'm a professional. Give me your kid and leave me alone'" (Helfand, 2001, p. A18). Unfortunately, this intimidation tactic works on many parents, leaving them not only un-

COMMUNICATING WITH PARENTS, ADMINISTRATORS, AND OTHERS

enlightened about their children's progress in school, but also less likely to ask for—or offer—assistance in the future.

8. Solicit the parents' ideas.

Invite the parents to consider the problem. What do they think is causing the problem? What, if anything, have they already done to try to solve the problem?

If they demur, persist gently with questioning until you get at least some contribution from them. This will increase their sense of participation and ownership in the process, and the likelihood of an effective outcome.

9. Create a plan for improvement with a timetable for completion, and get it in writing.

Work with the parent to brainstorm possible solutions (ideally, you will already have mapped out several courses of action). Make sure that your suggested plan for improvement leaves most of the responsibility with the parent and the student, and that it includes a timetable for completion.

For example, the plan for a student who fails to complete homework might require the parent to call your school's homework hotline or check your class website every day, and/or sign a daily assignment card you create for the student. In addition, you might ask the student to carry a daily progress report to each class, on which each teacher can note the student's progress every day. Your administrative and counseling offices should have additional ideas.

Our website (www.classroomadvisor.com) offers useful resources on this topic, including links to several real-world class websites and tips on how to create your own.

10. Never get into an argument with a parent.

Unfortunately, a few parents act so much like children that you'll stop wondering why their children misbehave so frequently and start wondering why they behave properly at all. Parents may insult you, bait you, and even threaten you, but under few circumstances is it productive to fight back; you'd only be giving them more ammunition.

Patience in such stressful moments can not only help parents cool down emotionally, but also demonstrate the calm and professional way you deal with their children. This will often give you a long-term edge once the parent goes home and reflects on what transpired.

If a parent conference heats up until it threatens to spin out of control, imagine you just got into a traffic accident. Be courteous, do not say too much, and don't apologize unless you have made an obvious error that you are certain you can remedy immediately. If you feel uncomfortable, ask for an adjournment and call in an administrator.

WHAT IF PARENTS ARE PART OF THE PROBLEM?

As mentioned elsewhere, the majority of chronic "problem students" we have encountered live in dysfunctional home environments. In addition to parents who are physically or emotionally abusive, or who work during most of the hours their children are at home, we have seen parents who provide their children with drugs, parents who are themselves hardcore gang members, and parents who suffer from mental instability or debilitating physical problems.

To no one's surprise, such parents are typically of little help in correcting their children's off-target behavior; indeed, they're sometimes part of the problem, demonstrating little common sense and even less maturity. They may even treat you like the enemy—insulting or threatening you—particularly if, having exhausted their supply of solutions and their patience, they're desperately seeking a scapegoat for their childrearing shortcomings.

In these cases, the school must take the lead and establish a plan of action for improving the child's performance, behavior, attitude, and so forth. If this seems inappropriate or counterintuitive to you—particularly if you're 25 years old without children of your own—consider that school professionals (yourself included) deal with hundreds of adolescents daily, building an arsenal of time- and battle-tested behavior-management tactics, while most parents deal at most with only a handful of children—their own.

Of course, we urge you to include all parents—especially the troublesome ones—as much as possible in your efforts, because if they don't buy into your plans, any changes you attempt probably won't stick. And if their intentions are good they can be a productive part of the solution from the beginning. Sometimes ineffective parents sense something profoundly out of balance but have no idea how to improve their parenting skills. Like many of your students, they need someone to show them how to do the job right.

Here we present several teachers' real-life tales of challenges with parents, and suggested solutions.

TEACHING DILEMMA: PARENT FAILS TO GET CHILD TO COMPLETE HOMEWORK

One of my students' parents came to parent-teacher night complaining that her daughter wouldn't do her homework because all she did at home was stay in her room watching TV and talking on the phone. When the mother would ask her daughter what homework she had to do, the daughter would say there wasn't any. I suggested that the mother take the TV and telephone out of her daughter's room, but she told me that seemed too severe.

SUGGESTED SOLUTION

Yes, parents like this really exist. We recommend leading the parent through a series of Socratic questions emulating your own thought process on the matter, to encourage a more thorough understanding of the problem and adoption of a more productive response. The questions you pose might sound something like the ones in Table 7.1. Note that these questions, taken individually, are objective and inoffensive. Yet combined,

Table 7.1. Questions for Parents

Teacher Question	Comment
Can you help me understand this problem better? What activities does your child pursue in an average evening? How much time is spent on each?	If the parent doesn't know the answer, this is a major problem. According to media accounts, the parents of one of the 1999 Columbine High School killers claimed they didn't know their child was making bombs in their garage.
In what order would you prioritize these activities, to balance your child's personal and academic development?	Often the parent will not have thought this through fully, or will default to whatever priorities the child (who clearly has a strong stake in the matter) wants.
What do you believe your child's personal, familial, academic, and/or vocational responsibilities should be?	Reserve judgment here, but highlight the potential long-term ramifications of these and respectfully suggest any appropriate modifications.
When you ask your child to complete these various duties, what response do you normally receive?	Probe further to pinpoint any manipulative tactics used (pouting, tantrums, silence, etc.) and determine why the parent has been satisfied with the child's response.
Is this response acceptable to you, given the revelation in this conference that your daughter has been denying or conveniently forgetting the existence of her homework?	This is a critical point. If the parent is content for the child to lie or feign chronic forgetfulness, explore the reason. If the parent doubts you, present your evidence.
Has the child's behavior changed to your satisfaction? If not, what seems to be the obstacle? Does she not understand the homework? Are there distractions? Does she not eat or sleep enough?	This question applies if this is not the first discussion you've had with the parent over this issue, or if the parent has expressed frustration over the child's recalcitrant behavior in other contexts.
What do you believe your level of responsibility in this situation (as the adult and the parent) to be?	This can be a touchy topic; proceed with caution, and ask an administrator or counselor for assistance if necessary.
How would you suggest we resolve this problem? How are you willing to contribute to holding your daughter accountable? What do you believe appropriate incentives for success and sanctions for failure should be?	This question puts the onus for the student's behavior on the student and the parent, where it belongs. Be sure to veto any parental suggestions unacceptable to you (or to school policy).

they lead inevitably to the conclusion that the child is exercising too much control over the situation, and the parent needs to take more responsibility.

TEACHING DILEMMA: PARENTS DISBELIEVE AND THREATEN TEACHER

In my first year teaching, I read two students' term papers and they had phrasing that was practically identical. I didn't know whether one copied from the other or whether they both copied it from a third source, but I didn't care. As far as I'm concerned, letting someone copy your paper is as dishonest as doing the copying.

But one of these students' parents didn't see it that way. They didn't even want to hear what I was telling them or look at the proof I had. The father's attitude was, "My son would never cheat on an assignment. We've always pushed him to work hard in school. Are you aware of how serious an accusation academic dishonesty is? You could get him kicked off the track team. How long have you been teaching, anyway? As an attorney, I want to caution you against slandering my son." I couldn't even finish presenting my case before he stormed off to the principal's office.

SUGGESTED SOLUTION

In an ideal world, these parents would have had a rational conversation with the teacher first and then taken the problem to a higher level if necessary. That approach would have saved the administration's valuable time, demonstrated respect for the teacher's professional judgment, and spared their child the embarrassment of a broad audience for his troubles.

Some people, however, are accustomed to getting their way in every circumstance, regardless of the facts. They are the type of customers who create a living nightmare for every waiter, store clerk, and cab driver they encounter—the sort of passengers whose response to poor airline service would be to ignore the flight attendant and immediately summon the pilot. Take solace in the fact that you are not the only public servant to face them.

Also know that you can build a defense against this danger. If you've maintained scrupulous academic records and documentation of behavior problems as we urge in chapter 3, "Preparing for the First Week of School," and chapter 5, "Classroom Management I," you should have no trouble producing incontrovertible evidence of your students' malfeasance.

And most importantly, no matter how belligerent or insulting the parents become, resist the temptation to respond in kind. Losing your equanimity would reflect badly on you in the eyes of your peers, your students, and your supervisors— as it should, since it's unnecessary and unprofessional.

TEACHING DILEMMA: STUDENTS BAND TOGETHER IN ATTEMPT TO GET TEACHER FIRED

Last year I had a class that was so unruly I had to crack down on them pretty hard. Five students didn't like that, so they got together and went home to their parents with stories that I treated them unfairly, telling them I was basically a racist. Several parents then called the school and demanded to speak to my principal. "My daughter says this teacher is a racist. Why does he only fail students of such-and-such a skin color?" Then the next day the students all came in taunting me, like "We're going to get you fired."

SUGGESTED SOLUTION

Although this is a serious charge, remember that you are not alone. We once watched a teacher change a student's seat because that student had ignored the teacher's repeated requests to stop talking. Angry that the teacher had targeted her instead of the classmate with whom she had been chatting, the girl muttered, "You're racist." Mercifully, a third classmate—of the same ethnicity as the other two students—jumped in to point out, "That doesn't make any sense, girl. How are you going to call him racist when you're both black?"

Unfortunately, as this dilemma demonstrates, level-headedness like this third student displayed does not always prevail. Ignorance and malice can sometimes snowball into a career-threatening spectacle if not detected and arrested early.

First, remember that you are effectively onstage at all times. And realize that in teaching, as in politics, avoiding the appearance of impropriety is often as important as avoiding actual misdeeds. Don't make any comments—especially jokes—that could be interpreted as racially insensitive. Monitor yourself to stay conscious of the way you're treating students, and that you're not giving particular groups extra attention (positive or negative) without very good reason. And solicit ideas from other teachers about any special teaching or assessment techniques that they've used to help students of all backgrounds to succeed.

Second, if you allow students to choose their own seats, they will often cluster by ethnicity or common language; breaking up these cliques can help equalize the level of teacher contact and quality of education they receive. For example, if students of a particular ethnic group who are also friends cluster in a back corner, they may not only distract each other, but also receive less attention than their classmates. Such students could learn less and underperform their peers.

This situation also underscores the value of getting to know parents one-on-one. Do you have a history with them? Do you have other students or parents (preferably of the same ethnicity as the students in question) who can vouch for your commitment to their children and your general fairness? Can you find a parent willing to write you a letter of thanks for what you've done for their children? If you have good relationships with your colleagues and administrators, they should be able to vouch for you as well.

Lastly, we urge you to join your local teacher's union. Most associations will not only advise you how to counter such an attack but also offer insurance that will pay attorney's or other legal fees you incur contesting such charges, should the situation escalate to that level.

TEACHING DILEMMA: PARENT DENIES CHILD'S POOR PERFORMANCE

I had one student whose mother was in total denial about who her child was. After report cards came out the mother called to ask me, "Why did you give my daughter a D?" I said, "I didn't give her a D. She earned a D." "Well, she did her work." "No, she did not. She doesn't do the work in class. I've called you about this issue repeatedly, but nothing ever changes. When I told you I was generous giving her a D, it was not an overstatement."

Not only that, the child had her mother wrapped around her finger. The child would be sitting in her seat and all of a sudden I'd look over and she'd be standing up doing all this suggestive dancing. So we had a conference—the child, her mother, and I—and I told the girl, "Get up and show your mother how you dance in class." And you know what the mother's response was? "Well, if you're doing that, don't do it anymore." She wouldn't even look at her daughter.

SUGGESTED SOLUTION

This type of parent is the reason we urge you to keep thorough documentation—of behavior, of attendance, and of academic performance. And if a child is performing poorly in your class, send home notice sooner rather than later and demand that it be returned to you, signed by the parent.

This will give you insurance in case the parent tries to approach an administrator later with a complaint like, "Well, I never knew he was in danger of failing. If the teacher had told me, I would have done something about it." Absurd as this complaint may sound, some parents do abdicate responsibility until disaster strikes, at which point they look for someone to blame. Don't make yourself an easy target. Talk to parents early and often.

TEACHING DILEMMA: PARENTS ACCUSE ABSENT TEACHER OF DENIGRATING THEIR CHILD

One day several colleagues and I were pulled out of class for an important meeting. While I was gone, a fight broke out in my classroom between two of the worst-behaved students in class, and later my principal asked me to prepare written documentation of the event. This is what I wrote (I have changed the students' names):

"Though I was not in the room at the time of this incident, Ms. P. (the substitute teacher) related the following to me. At least two students corroborated each detail listed here. According to these witnesses, Kevin grabbed a personal note Melanie was writing, ran to a corner of the room, and started to read it aloud. Melanie chased after him, at which point Kevin passed the note to Brian, who continued reading Melanie's personal writing to the class.

"Melanie cornered Brian, who refused to give her the note. At this point, Ms. P. was on the telephone to security and so did not witness exactly what transpired, but according to students sitting close by Melanie 'threatened' Brian, and when he still did not give her the paper she 'went crazy,' stabbing him near the eye with the pen she was carrying.

"Brian punched Melanie in response, knocking her down. Melanie then chased Brian around the room, with both students dripping blood as they ran. I returned to the class to find a broken fan and small bloodstains on the carpet and on various student desks."

Brian was removed from school after the incident because it was his third major offense and he was legally old enough to be transferred to the district's adult school. Several days later, an administrator who sat in on Melanie's disciplinary hearing told me my description of events had caused quite a stir. Apparently Melanie's parents argued that the description was "biased" against their daughter, and the disciplinary committee agreed she should be allowed to stay in school.

I was shocked. Melanie was far more abrasive, disruptive, and disliked than Brian in school. And if the eyewitness testimony was accurate, shouldn't Melanie have been disciplined with equal severity because she attacked Brian first? And why was I being blamed? I wasn't even in the room during the altercation, and if I had been there, things would not have gotten out of hand.

SUGGESTED SOLUTION

A little familiarity with proper administrative procedure would have saved this teacher a lot of trouble. The school administrator should never have asked someone not present during the dispute to document the incident. The substitute teacher was the only person who could have performed this task correctly, and anything the teacher wrote would be hearsay at best.

Since the teacher agreed to write the report, however, several minor changes would have improved it. First, although including student eyewitness testimony in his report may have enhanced its authenticity, the teacher should have used the most neutral terms possible. Under no circumstances should a value-laden word like "crazy" have been included, even though that was clearly part of a witness's quotation.

Second, this teacher remarks that Melanie was a polarizing figure at the school, but fails to realize that if she was disliked by many, this would likely have colored the language they used to describe the incident and perhaps even their perception of who was provoking whom. In Melanie's disciplinary hearing, her parents may have seized on the students' general animosity toward their daughter to paint her as a victim.

Third, this teacher should have known that, because of the seriousness of the event, Melanie's parents would eventually see the report he wrote. The moral: In any public service occupation, never put in writing anything you wouldn't want to see splashed across the front page of the papers.

Good Cop, Bad Cop

One of the most effective approaches to get collaboration from recalcitrant students as well as unaware or unresponsive parents is the time-honored *good cop, bad cop* routine, in which two authority figures collude to elicit cooperation from a target. The *bad cop* is typically a serious, hard-nosed presence who presents evidence against the accused and argues for a harsh penalty. The *good cop*, meanwhile, appears more sympathetic and reasonable, enticing the target to cooperate. Let's examine how the technique can work in the school setting.

Case 1

Sam's teacher, Ms. Henry, heard Sam use profanity toward her. Sam, Ms. Henry, and the principal have a conference to discuss the problem. Here, the principal plays the bad cop and the teacher plays the good cop.

Principal:	Ms. Henry writes on your referral form that "when I told the class to finish the work over the weekend, I heard Sam tell his friends what a b—-h I was."
Student:	It wasn't like that.

Principal:	Are you saying Ms. Henry is lying?
Student:	No. I *did* say that, but not to her—
Teacher:	It was noisy. I imagine Sam thought I couldn't hear.
Principal:	That's no excuse. We're talking about blatant disrespect. What would happen if we didn't respond to this, Sam? What would all the other students think?
Student:	I don't know. . . .
Teacher:	The good news is he's never done this before, at least in my class. I don't know that he would do it again if this situation came up again.
Principal:	Maybe, but looking at his record, I'd say he's had a lot of chances. This seems pretty serious, don't you think?
Teacher:	Well, those *are* the rules. And the rules have to be respected. It's your choice. Unless Sam has a better idea?
Student:	Huh?
Principal:	Hmm. . . . What do you think would be a fair solution to this problem, Sam?
Student:	Um, I could apologize.
Principal:	For what?
Student:	For saying Ms. Henry was a b—-h.
Principal:	Well, here she is. What are you waiting for?
Student:	I'm sorry. I didn't mean anything by it.
Teacher:	I understand. We all get angry sometimes. I'd appreciate it if you could keep those thoughts to yourself in the future, though. Or if you're going to call me names at least wait until you're outside my classroom.
Principal:	So how are we going to make sure this doesn't happen again? Sam? Do you have any ideas? We'll need to get an agreement in writing.

Case 2

The school's vice principal has requested a conference with a disruptive student, Sheree, Sheree's parent, and Mr. Jackson, a teacher who has complained numerous times about her behavior. Here, the vice principal (VP) plays the bad cop and Mr. Jackson (Teacher) plays the good cop.

Student:	I didn't do that.
Parent:	She said she didn't do it.
VP:	Well, that's what Mr. Jackson wrote here. (*to student*) Are you suggesting Mr. Jackson made this up?
Student:	I don't know. I don't know why I'm always getting in trouble.
Parent:	She comes home and says this teacher—Mr. Jackson—is always picking on her.
VP:	Really? Well, for a teacher to fabricate a charge against a student would be a serious offense. Mr. Jackson has been teaching here for 3 years, and I would be surprised if he'd risk his credential and his future in the teaching profession by knowingly lying about a student's behavior. But let's look at your daughter's record. In the last 2 months alone, I have similar complaints from two other teachers. Here, on the 24th of last month, Ms. Parrish sent Sheree out of class for "insubordination"—it appears Ms. Parrish wouldn't let your daughter go get a drink when she wanted, so she refused to do her classwork.
Parent:	(*to student*) You never told me that, Sheree.
VP:	And again on the 15th of December, Mr. Bajorek wrote her up for sneaking out of class 5 minutes early. Then of course, there's her trouble with the security guards over her attitude when they brought her to the office for inappropriate attire. They wrote, "student was confrontational, using profanity. . . ." Would you like to hear the quote?
Parent:	(*to student*) How come you never told me any of this?
Student:	You're going to believe them over me?
Teacher:	Now in her defense, I ought to point out that Sheree has never caused this kind of trouble in *my* class before.

VP:	But didn't you write her up earlier this year for trying to use her cell phone in class?
Teacher:	Well, yes, but we worked that out. . . .
Parent:	(*to student*) You were using your cell phone in the middle of class?
Student:	It was Jarod. He needed a ride.
Parent:	I don't care who it was. You don't use your phone in the middle of class.
VP:	So you see, when you add this to the rest of the pile of incidents, I think it paints a pretty convincing picture. Don't you agree?
Teacher:	We'd like to help Sheree improve her performance. If either of you has any ideas for how to help track and improve her behavior, I'd love to hear them.
VP:	If not, I have some good ideas that have worked with other students.

Case 3

A teacher, Mrs. Bryson, has requested a conference about a disruptive student, Brenda, with her parent and the vice principal. Here, Mrs. Bryson (Teacher) plays the bad cop and the vice principal (VP) plays the good cop. The student herself is not present until she is called in midway through the conference.

Parent:	I don't want my daughter in your class anymore, because you won't let her get on the computer.
Teacher:	This is my classroom. It is my place of work and I am responsible for what goes on here. And in my classroom she's going to follow my rules. I'm not going to change the rules because one parent doesn't like the way my classroom runs. It runs the same way for all students.
Parent:	(*to VP*) She doesn't like my daughter. That's the only reason she's saying all this stuff. Did you ever see anything happen like what she's accusing Brenda of?
VP:	Well, I haven't been in the classroom for this particular class, but I have been in Mrs. Bryson's classroom be-

fore and I've been very impressed. I also see in our records here that not long ago you wanted Brenda to have two periods with Mrs. Bryson because you suggested Mrs. Bryson was the only teacher on campus your daughter could get along with. Has that changed?

Parent: Yeah, in the beginning it was like that, but now for some reason she's turned on Brenda.

Teacher: No, it's not that I turned on Brenda. It's that Brenda wants to come to class and run her own program. And I'm not allowing it. I don't know what rules or consequences you have at your house, but I have strong ones and your daughter is no different from any other student. When she breaks the rules, there are consequences. I don't let the other students get away with it, and I'm not going to let Brenda get away with it. The problem seems to be that you want me to treat her differently. But I'm not going to do that.

Parent: Well, she doesn't act like that at home.

Teacher: Well, she seems to act like that pretty consistently at school. Why do you think I was the only teacher she could get along with?

Parent: Maybe she's going through a hard time—some growing pains.

VP: Mrs. Bryson wrote here that your daughter called her a b---h and a tramp.

Parent: She doesn't use that kind of language at home.

(VP calls student into the conference.)

VP: I believe you owe Mrs. B an apology.

Student: I didn't say anything!

VP: Yes you did. And you owe her an apology. Why would you call her that, anyway?

Student: I don't know.

VP: What did you call her?

Student: I called her a b---h.

VP: So?

Student: (*to teacher*) Sorry.

Teacher: Brenda, isn't it true you've stayed after class several times to talk about various things—to get my advice?

Student: Yeah.

Teacher: (*to parent*) So if I didn't like your daughter, as you said, why would I even take the time after class—my time, that I could spend any way I want—to talk to her? You see, I told you last time we all met—when it was just you and me and Brenda in the room—I told you these things were happening, and all you told her was, "Stop doing that." But let me tell you something. If you were her teacher and you came to me and told me she called you a b---h, you would not want to see my reaction. I wouldn't allow her to disrespect anybody like that. And the reason I'm going to insist she get suspended is that she said it in front of my other students. I'm not going to let the rest of my students get out of control because she's out of control. I'm going to remove the problem that's out of control, and that's Brenda.

Parent: You can't do that.

VP: This is not a matter of choice, or discrimination. We need to deliver on our promises. One of our promises is to maintain order. Another promise is to treat all students equitably. Imagine what our other students, parents, and teachers would think if Brenda came back to class tomorrow and we had delivered none of the consequences we promised? Our promises wouldn't mean very much.

Parent: I want her out of that class anyway.

VP: Let's talk about taking her out of Mrs. Bryson's class after she returns from her suspension. But in the meantime I'd like to ask you to think seriously about something. Since there have been these problems in nearly every class Brenda has been in, have you considered that maybe the problem is not the teachers? If you'd like to talk about this more, I'd be happy to discuss some options for helping Brenda work better with everyone.

INTERACTING WITH ADMINISTRATORS

Administrators will sometimes be there to support you 110%, and sometimes less. Ideally they should always be available to support those on the front lines—the teachers—but in reality their diverse responsibilities often conflict. If an administrator seems unresponsive to your needs, put yourself in her shoes. You are not the only stakeholder; she must constantly juggle demands from not only students and teachers, but also higher-level administrators, the school board, and the district's parents.

One teacher-turned-administrator advises new teachers who want to send all their problem students to the office:

> If you can handle it in the classroom, do that. I don't want to see a problem until I know the teacher has done everything possible to solve it. Administrators have enough to do in their own jobs. They don't want to do your job too. (R. Cornner personal communication)

So do everyone a favor. Practice the management steps we outline, and send troublemakers up the line as rarely as possible. An added bonus: Those teachers who rarely send students to the office are taken very seriously when they do.

But don't administrators have a lot of experience they could share with new teachers? Typically, yes. However, they lack abundant free time to assist you. Also be aware that part of their job is also to document the productivity—including the failings—of subordinates, just as you should be doing with your students. Be cautious, therefore, when approaching administrators about troubles you're having. Why set off bells that could be interpreted as "this one's incompetent" in your first week?

In many districts, administrators can fire teachers *without cause* anytime in the first few years of employment. Depending on the jurisdiction, tenure often kicks in soon after that, at which point removing a teacher (even an ineffectual one) becomes much more difficult. The result: Some administrators would rather eliminate a lagging employee than commit to improving that person's performance. Although this decision may seem foolish, especially considering the high recruitment and training costs for replacement personnel, the fear of an incompetent teacher getting tenure often overrides other concerns.

Does this mean no administrator can be trusted because they're all out to get you? Of course not. Just be aware that office politics plague every organization, and be smart about the company you keep. Unsure how to solve a problem? Before you burden an administrator, ask a colleague for advice. If you're not satisfied with that answer, ask another. Or consult your professional teachers association (union). Or ask whether your district has a mentor teacher program; that way a qualified colleague will get paid to help you and you won't feel like you're imposing.

NEVER FORGET THE SUPPORT STAFF

The secretaries, custodians, equipment technicians, and other indispensable support personnel at your school deserve your appreciation and respect. In any case, you don't want to get on their bad side. Trust us. An arrogant or neglectful attitude toward these crucial members of your team can create unnecessary tension for everyone, and eventually catch up to you in the form of mysteriously unreturned phone calls, forgotten messages, cancelled appointments, slow response to equipment repair requests, and the like. We are not suggesting that any member of your school staff would stoop to deliberate sabotage, but we have occasionally witnessed a certain karmic retribution effect we call "death by a thousand lost photocopies."

On the other hand, a friendly and gracious attitude on your part will improve the workplace for everyone and can pay off in unexpected ways. Teachers who are thoughtful and inclusive toward support staff, who make requests with humility and show sincere gratitude for services delivered, can find their load lightened when they need it most. Important meetings with administrators become a bit easier to schedule, critical inquiries get answered a little faster, and tricky tasks that only support staff can achieve get bumped up in priority. You may also find yourself with backup when you need it—like extra hands when deadlines loom, or someone to put in a good word for you in conversations you don't even know are happening.

Ultimately, whether in the classroom, in the school office, or in a conference with a parent, you have the capacity to make your own "luck." Treat others as you'd want to be treated, and they will tend to reciprocate. Delivering responsiveness, reliability, and courtesy will earn you the right to expect the same in return. And remember that positive energy is contagious. Given the large portion of your life you will spend working, why not make it the most enjoyable experience you can—for yourself, your colleagues, and your students? All this will enhance your impact and legacy in what we hope you'll agree is one of the most rewarding jobs on Earth.

REFERENCES

Abayasekara, D. (2005). *Let your body speak*. Retrieved November 26, 2005, from drdilip.com/body_language.htm

American Academy of Pediatrics. (n.d.). *Abuse*. www.aap.org/advocacy/childhealthmonth/abuse2.htm

Arnold Bennett on emotion. (n.d.). www2002.stoke.gov.uk/council/libraries/infolink/b-quote.htm

Bachay, J. (1996). *Creating peace, building community*. Miami, FL: Grace Contrino Abrams Peace Education Foundation.

Bloom, Benjamin S. (Ed.). (1956). *Taxonomy of educational objectives, handbook 1: Cognitive domain*. Boston: Addison-Wesley.

Brendtro, L. K. (2001). Worse than sticks and stones: Lessons from research on ridicule. *Reclaiming Children and Youth, 10*(1), 47–49. Retrieved October 25, 2007, from Research Library database.

Buffington, P. (2003). *Cheap psychological tricks for parents*. New York: Fine Communications.

California Department of Education. (n.d.). *California Education Code Section 233.5(a)*. Retrieved January 15, 2007, from www.cde.ca.gov/ls/yd/ce/ec233.asp

Canter, L., & Canter, M. (1992). *Assertive discipline: Postive behavior management for today's classroom*. Santa Monica, CA: Canter and Associates.

Carey, B. (2001, August 20). When a "good death" isn't for everyone. *Los Angeles Times*, pp. S1, S6.

Carroll, L. (2003). *Victims of bullying more often depressed, suicidal*. preventdisease.com/news/articles/victims_bullying_often_depressed.shtml

Columbine High School timeline. (n.d.). Denver.rockymountainnews.com/shooting/timeline.shtml

Cottringer, W. (2002). *The power of likability.* Retrieved January 9, 2005, from sq.4mg.com/Cottringer_article.htm

Descant, R., & Gregor, D. (2001). *Critical incident management.* Unpublished course handout, Families First.

Diekmann, C. H. (1999–2004). *Research-based effectiveness of the Peace Education Foundation model.* www.peaceeducation.com/whoarewe/whitepapers/faq.pdf

Dresser, N. (1996). *Multicultural manners: New rules of etiquette for a changing society.* New York: Wiley.

Duen Hsi, Y. (2000). *Could it be that . . .* Retrieved September 7, 2003, from www.noogenesis.com/malama/discouragement/Dreikurs/could_it_be_that.html

Environmental Defense. (n.d.). *About Environmental Defense.* Retrieved June 16, 2007, from www.environmentaldefense.org/page.cfm?tagID=381

FindLaw. (n.d.). *Abington School Dist. v. Schempp,* 374 U.S. 203 (1963). case law.lp.findlaw.com/scripts/getcase.pl?court=US&vol=374&invol=203

Gardner, H. (1993). *Multiple intelligences: The theory in practice.* New York: Basic Books.

Gibson, P. (1994). Gay male and lesbian youth suicide. In G. Remafedi (Ed.), *Death by denial: Studies of suicide in gay and lesbian teenagers.* Boston: Alyson.

Ginott, Haim G. (1972). *Teacher and child: A book for parents and teachers.* New York: Macmillan.

Goleman, D. (1997). *Emotional intelligence: Why it matters more than IQ.* New York: Bantam.

Goodlad, J. I. (1984). *A place called school.* New York: McGraw-Hill.

Gothic. (n.d.). www.geocities.com/SoHo/9094/gothic1.html

Gray, D. (1989, Fall). Putting minds to work. *American Educator,* 16–22.

Helfand, D. (2001, August 16). 'Edspeak' is in a class by itself. *Los Angeles Times,* pp. A1, A18.

Henkle v. Gregory. (n.d.). www.lambdalegal.org/our-work/in-court/cases/henkle-v-gregory.html

Howard Gardner's multiple intelligences theory. (n.d.). www.pbs.org/wnet/gperf/education/ed_mi?overview.html

Human Rights Watch. (2001). *Hatred in the hallways: Violence and discrimination against lesbian, gay, bisexual and transgender students in U.S. schools.* New York: Author.

Hunter, M. (1976). *Improved instruction.* El Segundo, CA: TIP.

Hunter, M. (1990). *Discipline that develops self-discipline.* El Segundo, CA: TIP.

Interview with Derek Henkle. (n.d.). Retrieved June 22, 2007, from www.pbs.org/wgbh/pages/frontline/shows/assault/interviews/henkle.html

Jameson, K. (1989). *The nibble theory and the kernel of power.* New York: Paulist Press.

Jensen, E. (1996). *Brain-based learning and teaching.* New York: Turning Point.

Jordan, Shirley E. (1996). *Multiple intelligences: Seven keys to opening closed minds.* NASSP Bulletin 80: 29–35.

Jung on apathy. (n.d.). www.nonstopenglish.com/reading/quotations/k_Apathy.asp

Kane, P. R. (Ed.). (1991). *The first year of teaching: Real world stories from America's teachers.* New York: Walker.

Kelley, W. M. (2003). *Rookie teaching for dummies.* New York: For Dummies.

King, J. (n.d.). *Test anxiety.* Retrieved November 11, 2006, from www.uoregon.edu/~counsel/test%20anxiety.htm

Kohl, H. R. (1969). *The open classroom.* New York: Random House.

Lavoie, R. D. (1989). *How difficult can this be? The F.A.T. City Workshop* [VHS, DVD]. New York and Washington, DC: Public Broadcasting Service.

Lavoie, R. D. (2002). *The teacher's role in developing social skills.* Retrieved January 9, 2005, from www.ricklavoie.com/teacherart.html

Listening skills. (n.d.). Retrieved June 15, 2007, from www.casaaleadership.ca/mainpages/resources/sourcebook/listening-skills.html

Magruder, J. (2005, November 28). Experts: Introverted youth have deep roots for behavior. *Gannett News Service.*

Maister, D. H., Green, C. H., & Galford, R. M. (2000). *The trusted advisor.* New York: Free Press.

Major, R. L. (1990). *Discipline: The most important subject we teach.* New York: University Press of America.

The marshmallow test. (n.d.). Retrieved December 10, 2006, from www.cde.state.co.us/ssw/pdf/SSWConf2005_Caselman_Tonia_Marshmallow.pdf

Maslow, Abraham H. (1987). *Motivation and personality* (3rd ed.). New York: HarperCollins.

Mayo Clinic. (n.d.). *Choose your response for greater stress relief.* www.mayoclinic.com/health/stress-relief/SR00037

McCrimmon, K. K. (1999, May 9). *Students pledge to end taunts.* Denver.rockymountainnews.com/shooting/0509will2.shtml

McIntosh, P. (1989, July/August). White privilege: Unpacking the invisible knapsack. *Peace and Freedom.* seamonkey.ed.asu.edu/~mcisaac/emc598ge/Unpacking.html

Medavoy, M., & Young, J. (2002). *You're only as good as your next one.* New York: Pocket Books.

Mischel, W., Shoda, Y., & Rodriguez, M. L. (1989). Delay of gratification in children. *Science, 244,* 933–938.

Myers, D. G. (1992). *Psychology.* New York: Worth.

National Association of School Psychologists. (n.d.). *Bullying fact sheet.* www.naspcenter.org/factsheets/bullying_fs.html

National Education Association. (n.d.). *NEA vision, mission, and values.* Retrieved June 16, 2007, from www.nea.org/aboutnea/images/visionmission values.pdf

Nelsen, J., Lott, L., & Glenn, H. S. (2000). *Positive discipline in the classroom.* Roseville, CA: Prima.

Nike. (n.d.). *About Nike: Mission statement.* Retrieved October 2, 2006, from www.nike.com/nikebiz/nikebiz.jhtml?page=4

Nolte, D. (n.d.). *Children learn what they live.* www.geocities.com/Enchanted Forest/Meadow/2320/learn.html

Non-verbal communication. (n.d.). www.school-portal.co.uk/GroupDownload File.asp?File=25373&GroupId=7820

Orlich, D. C., Harder, R. J., Callahan, R. C., & Gibson, H. W. (1994). *Teaching strategies: A guide to better instruction.* Lexington, MA: D. C. Heath.

Parsons, S. (2001). *Bully pulpit.* Retrived May 1, 2008, from www.runet.edu/rumag/backissues/2001_W/pages/espalage.html

Peace Education Foundation. (1996). *Rules for fighting fair.* members.aol.com/pforpeace/WorkItOut/rules.htm

Postman, N., & Weingartner, C. (1969). *Teaching as a subversive activity.* New York: Dell.

Refusal skills. (n.d.). www.etr.org/recap/practice/refusal.htm

Roosevelt, E. (1930). *Good citizenship: The purpose of education.* Retrieved April 10, 2002, from newdeal.feri.org/er/er19.htm

Row, H. (n.d.). *Coping: Martin Seligman.* Retrieved December 10, 2006, from www.fastcompany.com/online/20/seligman.html

Rubinstein, G. (1999). *Reluctant disciplinarian: Advice on classroom management from a softy who became (eventually) a successful teacher.* Fort Collins, CO: Cottonwood Press.